Cisco Network Design Solutions for Small-Medium Businesses

Peter Rybaczyk

Cisco Press

Cisco Press
800 East 96th Street
Indianapolis, Indiana 46240 USA

Cisco Network Design Solutions for Small-Medium Businesses

Peter Rybaczyk

Copyright © 2005 Cisco Systems, Inc.

The Cisco Press logo is a trademark of Cisco Systems, Inc.

Published by:
Cisco Press
800 East 96th Street
Indianapolis, Indiana 46240 USA

Printed in the United States of America 1 2 3 4 5 6 7 8 9 0

First Printing: August 2004

Library of Congress Cataloging-in-Publication Number: 2003104990

ISBN: 1-58705-143-5

Warning and Disclaimer

This book is designed to provide information about small-medium business network design. Every effort has been made to make this book as complete and as accurate as possible, but no warranty or fitness is implied.

The information is provided on an "as is" basis. The authors, Cisco Press, and Cisco Systems, Inc. shall have neither liability nor responsibility to any person or entity with respect to any loss or damages arising from the information contained in this book or from the use of the discs or programs that may accompany it.

The opinions expressed in this book belong to the author and are not necessarily those of Cisco Systems, Inc.

Trademark Acknowledgments

All terms mentioned in this book that are known to be trademarks or service marks have been appropriately capitalized. Cisco Press or Cisco Systems, Inc. cannot attest to the accuracy of this information. Use of a term in this book should not be regarded as affecting the validity of any trademark or service mark.

Corporate and Government Sales

Cisco Press offers excellent discounts on this book when ordered in quantity for bulk purchases or special sales.

For more information, please contact: **U.S. Corporate and Government Sales**   1-800-382-3419, corpsales@pearsontechgroup.com.

For sales outside the U.S. please contact: **International Sales**   international@pearsoned.com

Feedback Information

At Cisco Press, our goal is to create in-depth technical books of the highest quality and value. Each book is crafted with care and precision, undergoing rigorous development that involves the unique expertise of members from the professional technical community.

Readers' feedback is a natural continuation of this process. If you have any comments regarding how we could improve the quality of this book, or otherwise alter it to better suit your needs, you can contact us through e-mail at feedback@ciscopress.com. Please make sure to include the book title and ISBN in your message.

We greatly appreciate your assistance.

Publisher	John Wait
Editor-in-Chief	John Kane
Cisco Representative	Anthony Wolfenden
Cisco Press Program Manager	Nannette M. Noble
Executive Editor	Jim Schachterle
Production Manager	Patrick Kanouse
Development Editor	Tonya Cupp
Project Editor	Karen Gill
Copy Editor	Meredith Brittain
Technical Editors	Kevin R. DeCato, Edmund A. Kudey
Team Coordinator	Tammi Barnett
Cover Designer	Louisa Adair
Composition	Interactive Composition Corporation
Indexer	Larry Sweazy

CISCO SYSTEMS

Corporate Headquarters
Cisco Systems, Inc.
170 West Tasman Drive
San Jose, CA 95134-1706
USA
www.cisco.com
Tel: 408 526-4000
 800 553-NETS (6387)
Fax: 408 526-4100

European Headquarters
Cisco Systems International BV
Haarlerbergpark
Haarlerbergweg 13-19
1101 CH Amsterdam
The Netherlands
www-europe.cisco.com
Tel: 31 0 20 357 1000
Fax: 31 0 20 357 1100

Americas Headquarters
Cisco Systems, Inc.
170 West Tasman Drive
San Jose, CA 95134-1706
USA
www.cisco.com
Tel: 408 526-7660
Fax: 408 527-0883

Asia Pacific Headquarters
Cisco Systems, Inc.
Capital Tower
168 Robinson Road
#22-01 to #29-01
Singapore 068912
www.cisco.com
Tel: +65 6317 7777
Fax: +65 6317 7799

Cisco Systems has more than 200 offices in the following countries and regions. Addresses, phone numbers, and fax numbers are listed on the
Cisco.com Web site at www.cisco.com/go/offices.

Argentina • Australia • Austria • Belgium • Brazil • Bulgaria • Canada • Chile • China PRC • Colombia • Costa Rica • Croatia • Czech Republic
Denmark • Dubai, UAE • Finland • France • Germany • Greece • Hong Kong SAR • Hungary • India • Indonesia • Ireland • Israel • Italy
Japan • Korea • Luxembourg • Malaysia • Mexico • The Netherlands • New Zealand • Norway • Peru • Philippines • Poland • Portugal
Puerto Rico • Romania • Russia • Saudi Arabia • Scotland • Singapore • Slovakia • Slovenia • South Africa • Spain • Sweden
Switzerland • Taiwan • Thailand • Turkey • Ukraine • United Kingdom • United States • Venezuela • Vietnam • Zimbabwe

About the Author

Peter Rybaczyk has been engaged in multiple technology disciplines since 1979, including applications development, database administration, network design and administration, technical writing and editing, professional IT training, and IT consulting. In addition, during his career, Peter has owned several IT consulting businesses. Currently, his privately held firm, Convergent Netcom Services, is located in Tucson, Arizona. He has delivered more than 100 IT seminars to audiences in the United States, Canada, Europe, Asia, and Australia. He has consulted and worked with Fortune 500 companies and numerous small- to medium-sized businesses, covering multiple vertical markets, including wholesale and retail distribution, health care, law practice, insurance, finance, manufacturing, and telecommunications. In addition, he wrote *Cisco Router Troubleshooting Handbook* and *Novell's Internet Plumbing Handbook* and coauthored *PC Network Administration*. Peter holds a B.S. degree in physics and several industry certifications, including CNE, CCNA, and CCNP.

About the Technical Reviewers

Kevin R. DeCato is a solution marketing manager for small-medium businesses at Cisco Systems. With more than 15 years in the telecommunications industry, he is tasked with the development, positioning, and marketing of small-medium business data solutions for Cisco Systems on a worldwide basis. He has vast experience in advanced technologies such as security, IP communications, routing and switching, and wireless. He is also a regular contributor to *iQ* and *Packet* magazine articles. Prior to his work with Cisco, Kevin was employed at SBC as a technical support manager for central offices within California. He also worked as a scientist in the medical device industry for more than 10 years, including at Johnson and Johnson, where he was awarded several patents.

Edmund A. Kudey is the senior manager of solutions development for small-medium businesses at Cisco Systems. With more than 20 years in the telecommunications industry, he is in charge of the technical development, direction, and positioning of small-medium business solutions for Cisco Systems on a worldwide basis.

Dedications

This book is dedicated to Morya, Maria, Yeshe, and Jacques, for your abundant displays of love, patience, comfort, and joy.

Acknowledgments

The vast amount of behind-the-scenes work that goes into producing a book continues to amaze me. A multitude of thanks to all with whom I had the opportunity to work directly to make this one possible: Jim Schachterle, Drew and Tonya Cupp, Chris Cleveland, Karen Gill, Meredith Brittain, and Tammi Barnett. No less thanks to all members of the Cisco Press team and those who participated in the proposal review process.

Thank you to the technical editors, Kevin DeCato and Ed Kudey, for their insightful suggestions and saving me from my own fat fingers, misunderstandings, and misconceptions. Special thanks to Mark Doering of Cisco Systems for taking the time out of his demanding schedule to discuss Cisco security solutions and to provide lab equipment. Thank you to Steve M. Mott, vice president of information technology at DM Federal Credit Union in Tucson, Arizona, for granting me an interview regarding DM's IT infrastructure and approaches to solutions deployment. Thank you to all of my dozens of clients and hundreds of course attendees over the past few decades for providing me with the experience and insights necessary for this kind of writing.

I also would like to acknowledge my parents, Anna and Henryk Rybaczyk, for the foundations that they've laid for me. Thank you to my family members and the many, many friends who've encouraged and cheered me on through this joyous, albeit at times very arduous, writing process. Thank you Barbara, John, Elizabeth, Gieniek, Bogdan, Maureen and Dan, James and Tonya, Leszek and Kelly, Rachel, Lawrence, Clarissa, Sophia, Athena, Edward, Eileen, Andrew, Kathleen, Carolyn, Monroe, Michael, Alice, Duane, Susan, Vern, Alexander, Linda, Jack, Antonio, Almirinda, Barry, Kay, Clyde, Sheila, Liz, Laurie, Jim, Czarek, and Ania. If I missed anyone, forgive me. It's not personal or intentional.

My deepest love and gratitude to my dearest friend and wife, Maria, for the unconditional support that you've offered through the long days stretching into months of this project. This acknowledgment would be incomplete without my expression of profound gratitude to the Magnificent Himalayan, Morya El, who's inspired me since my teenage years. Thank you all!

Contents at a Glance

Table of Contents

Introduction

Cisco Network Design Solutions for Small-Medium Businesses focuses on the vital networking solutions for small-medium business (SMB) environments: IP Telephony, wireless, security, unified messaging, routing/switching infrastructure, customer contact platforms, and more. Deploying a networking solution is a process that has varying approaches. The one-minute, do-it-yourself, plug-and-play, or drive-through approaches are valid under certain limited conditions. A more robust approach is based on a blueprint resulting from a design process that precedes the deployment. The latter approach considers the available technologies, incorporates the business strategy, defines the user requirements, and subjects the final design to the SMB's budgetary process to create a matching solution that scales and performs in support of the business mission. This book describes and recommends the latter approach when deploying the networking solutions that are explored within its pages.

Goals and Objectives

The fundamental goal of this book is to provide you with the necessary tools to tap successfully into the vast SMB networking solutions market. Understanding the technical aspects of a solution is necessary but insufficient. To bring a solution to fruition rather than simply extolling its capabilities and technological prowess while it sits on a shelf, you need to understand business scenarios, focus on the most critical of an SMB's needs—those needs that, when fulfilled, significantly advance the business mission—and design a solution that is scalable and within the available budget. The specific objectives of this book are as follows:

- Master the steps of an effective networking solutions design process.
- Understand the generic and unique design consideration for IP Telephony, security, wireless, front/back office integration, and more.
- Expand a wired network or create a purely wireless one with the Cisco Aironet product family. Understand wireless protocols and wireless local-area network (WLAN) components.
- Design effective protection for an SMB's information infrastructure by selecting from an array of security solutions, such as virtual private networks (VPNs), intrusion detection systems, firewalls, and security features within routers and switches.
- Understand the value and structure of a security policy. Translate security techno-speak jargon into scenarios that are understandable to nontechnical SMB managers and executives.
- Design an IP Telephony solution for small SMBs using Cisco CallManager Express. Design an IP Telephony solution for SMBs of any size based on one of the deployment models of Cisco CallManager, as incorporated in the MCS 7800 series servers and the ICS 7750. Understand Voice over IP (VoIP) protocols and key components of IP Telephony solutions for the SMB and ISP/carrier environments.
- Understand the role of the Cisco customer contact platforms, Intelligent Contact Management (ICM) and IP Contact Center (IPCC), in customer relationship management (CRM) solutions deployment. Identify environments that are ripe for CRM deployment. Understand issues and tools required for front/back office integration.
- Enhance SMB internal and external communications as well as training capabilities via Unity and IP/TV from Cisco.

Who Should Read This Book?

This book is aimed at the vast array of networking professionals, designers, engineers, specialists, administrators, and technicians who design, install, and keep the SMB networks tuned and humming — whether as employees, independent consultants, or members of larger services organizations. Network-related titles and positions are dynamic; they evolve and overlap, and their definitions often vary among SMBs and networking solutions vendors. As long as the demands by the employers and clients upon the individuals who bear the network-related titles are being met effectively, the exact job titles are unimportant.

The demands for effective networking solutions continue to grow in complexity as computer networks reach into every aspect of business operations. They require an understanding of the networking environment that spans the spectrum: from the transmission media through applications, with routing/switching, security, IP Telephony, wireless, and unified communications in between. IT personnel who face the challenges of fresh deployments, major upgrades, or integrations in the aforementioned areas can greatly benefit from the solutions descriptions, the relevant design considerations, and the application of the design process as presented in this book.

SMB chief information officers (CIOs) and vice presidents of technology need not feel left out. You are an integral part of any network solution design process. This book has been written with you in mind as well.

How This Book Is Organized

This book is modular but not discontiguous. It is organized in two parts and ten core chapters. Chapters 1, 2, and 3 compose Part I, "Network Design Process and Solutions Overview for SMBs," which lays the foundation that is required for readers to plunge into the design of solutions presented in Part II, "SMB Networking Design Solutions." Skip Part I if you've already mastered the solution design process, understand the profiles of SMBs, and know everything regarding an effective networking infrastructure, including routing, switching, cable plant, and data storage requirements for an increasingly complex applications environment. Otherwise, read the first three chapters in sequence or in whatever order you feel is most helpful. Chapters 4 through 10 and the Epilogue compose Part II. Chapters 4 through 10 concentrate on the specific networking solutions, and the Epilogue contains my concluding thoughts on the future of SMB networking. Consider the essence of each chapter:

- **Chapter 1, "Effective Networking Solution Design Process"** — This chapter presents a generic approach that can be applied to designing networking solutions that are scalable, well-performing, and within an allocated budget. It further advocates that an effective solutions designer must strike the balance during the design process between the "shoot-from-the-hip" and "paralysis-through-endless-analysis" methodologies.

- **Chapter 2, "SMB Networking Environments and Solutions Design Considerations"** — This chapter dissects the SMB market in terms of its sectors, sizes, and missions from the perspective of designing networking solutions. It also presents design considerations and for/against arguments regarding deployment of solutions that relate to security, remote access, IP Telephony, wireless, collaboration with partners, customer care, and front/back office integration.

- **Chapter 3, "Network Infrustructure Requirements for Effective Solutions Implementation"** — This chapter concentrates on the components of the network infrustructure that are required for effective solutions implementation. It considers the contents of telecom closets, routing/switching equipment and protocols, data centers, storage solutions, the user desktop environment, upgrades planning, and applications.

- **Chapter 4, "Overview of the Network Security Issues"**—This chapter examines network security within the framework of information corruption, information disclosure, repudiation and lack of authentication and authorization, and denial of service. It discusses the impact of common security breaches that are encountered in SMB environments, the structure and value of a security policy, and the available antidotes to security threats.

- **Chapter 5, "Cisco Security Solutions"**—This chapter explores the design considerations and features of the Cisco security solutions (VPNs, firewalls, intrusion detection systems, and router security) in the context of the corresponding Cisco product lines: the VPN 3000 series concentrators, PIX firewalls, 4200 series IDS sensors, and router IOS.

- **Chapter 6, "The Wireless LAN Solution"**—This chapter delves into the design of the Cisco wireless Aironet solution following the examination of generic WLAN security considerations, components, performance issues, and protocols.

- **Chapter 7, "Customer Relationship Management Solutions"**—This chapter addresses the CRM deployment considerations, reviews the relationship between Cisco products and popular CRMs, and explores how the Cisco ICM Enterprise Edition and IPCC create robust platforms for CRM deployments.

- **Chapter 8, "IP Telephony Solutions"**—This chapter examines IP Telephony success factors and deployment considerations, concentrates on the design of the Cisco CallManager Express and CallManager-based IP Telephony solutions, and overviews IP Telephony components and capabilities for SMB and ISP/carrier environments.

- **Chapter 9, "Unified Communications Solutions"**—This chapter explores the meaning of unified communications and messaging and how the components of the Cisco IP communications suite—Cisco Unity and IP/TV—enhance internal communications and training capabilities.

- **Chapter 10, "Front and Back Office Integration Solutions"**—This chapter covers issues related to front/back office integration, including tools, challenges, for/against arguments, and the integrators.

- **Epilogue, "The Future of SMB Networking"**—The Epilogue offers my insights on the future challenges and bright aspects of SMB networking.

PART I

Network Design Process and Solutions Overview for SMBs

CHAPTER 1

Effective Networking Solution Design Process

Designing a networking solution for a business of any size is an engineering process that's full of creative choices. The choices you make as you negotiate the key steps of the design process ultimately determine the post-deployment success, failure, or mediocrity of your endeavor. They will affect the individual stakeholders and the business as a whole throughout the projected life cycle of the solution, and possibly beyond. Whereas this book focuses on designing specific networking solutions related to security, customer relationship management (CRM), IP Telephony, and other factors, this chapter concentrates on the generic elements of the design process and project management that are essential components of successful solution deployment.

The increasing breadth of available networking technologies and software applications continually stretches the capacity of network design professionals confronted with developing comprehensive solutions. A collaborative effort between experts in many areas of networking technologies is often required when developing a complete end-to-end solution, regardless of whether that solution is for a small-medium business (SMB) or otherwise. And with that collaboration comes the responsibility of ensuring that nothing falls through the cracks; areas of expertise must dovetail to precipitate a seamlessly functioning end result. It is like running a relay without dropping the baton or falling along the way.

Like it or not, a network solution design process is a project that requires a roadmap and a degree of effective project management. The first and most absolute requirement for network professionals when designing a networking solution is to understand all of the technical capabilities of that solution. However, there are other conditions that must be met to ensure a high probability of success, including understanding the nature of the individual business (mission, vision, business goals, and objectives), the entire business sector (potential competition), and, ultimately, the people within and outside the business (stakeholders)—especially those who are the most critical players during the design stage and those who will be most directly affected by the solution.

The fact that businesses are made up of unique people tends to make them unique, even if they offer similar products or services. The generic design process for networking solutions that is outlined in this chapter represents a framework that should always be tailored toward the uniqueness of each business. Without a roadmap, a business engaging in a solution deployment process will likely end up getting distracted by peripheral issues instead of concentrating on how the solution will fulfill its business goals. When completed, a networking solution ought to be hardly visible. Only its positive effects should be felt: a high and fast return on investment (ROI) coupled with greater customer satisfaction in addition to increased motivation and morale among the employees.

Many kinds of solutions are discussed in this book, but from a down-to-earth, practical point of view, their goals, in the final analysis, are surprisingly simple. They boil down to communication. Ask yourself this question following any solution implementation: Are the business communications faster, more reliable, and more secure than before? Or, to put it in end-user terms: Do customers, vendors, and employees have access to the desired and necessary information in a timely, reliable, and secure manner? If you can unequivocally answer "yes" to these questions, it is likely that the right solution combined with the right implementation approach has resulted in a success.

When your knowledge of the solution's technical capabilities is coupled with the understanding of the business's mission, vision, and competition, adherence to the following steps in the design stage should increase your chances of a successful deployment:

Step 1   Identifying stakeholder requirements

Step 2   Validating stakeholder requirements

Step 3   Creating and reviewing the draft design document

Step 4   Creating a final design document before implementation

Step 1: Identifying Stakeholder Requirements

Before proceeding with a discussion of how to identify stakeholder requirements, it's important to understand who the stakeholders are and why, in the process of designing a network solution, you should invest time in identifying their requirements. The term *stakeholder* is defined in different ways, but a certain commonality exists among the definitions. From a project management perspective, according to Wideman's Glossary of Comparative Project Management Terms (http://www.maxwideman.com/pmglossary), *stakeholders* are "people or organizations that have a vested interest in the environment, performance, and/or outcome of the project." From a business perspective, stakeholders can be defined as groups who are directly or indirectly affected by the operations of a business. A more down-to-earth definition equates stakeholders with people who have something riding on the outcome of a project.

However you choose to define the term, it ought to be clear that stakeholders are people who in some way will be affected by the activity of designing and implementing a networking solution. Given the degree of business reliance on computer networks and the solutions that they offer, you should begin with the initial assumption that in any business that you approach with a networking solution, all employees are stakeholders. And that's not all—customers, vendors, and investors also qualify as stakeholders.

Figure 1-1 represents the concept of stakeholders and their most fundamental concerns in the context of designing and implementing a networking solution. In Figure 1-1, representative groups of stakeholders surround a stake (a networking solution) being driven (designed) into the existing company's culture and networking infrastructure. A networking solution represents a change that will meet with a reaction, be it good or bad. The designer must use imagination and skill to decipher that reaction and to deal with it appropriately to complete the design process and to bring the solution to fruitful implementation.

Figure 1-1 *Sample Stakeholders for Networking Solution*

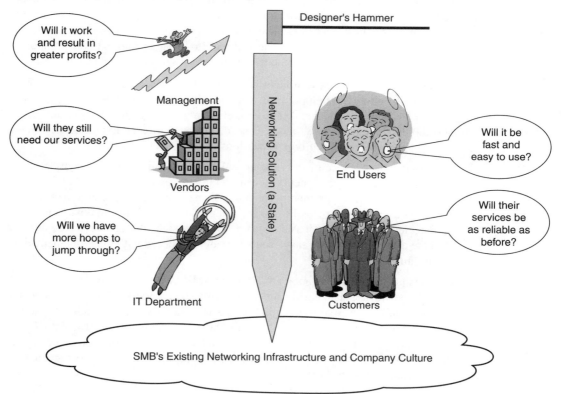

Obviously, not all stakeholders are going to have the same stake in the solution. Some stakeholders will be more crucial than others in helping to bring the solution to fruition even though they might not be directly affected by it. These are sometimes referred to as the *executive sponsors*. Some project management gurus swear by the fact that an information technology (IT) project (or solution) without an executive sponsor will fail. That might well be true, but it's also true that some projects with an executive sponsor fail as well.

NOTE   The key to avoiding failure and to maximizing the potential for success is to find the right kind of executive sponsorship and to ensure that if a solution entails a cultural change in the business, the executive sponsors are solidly behind the solution and are willing and able to rally everybody else in support of it.

Other stakeholders are more directly involved in the solution's use rather than bringing it to fruition. Before proceeding with the design, the needs and input of all the stakeholders must be brought out into the open for consideration; otherwise, the end result will likely be a partial success at best. So be practical in your approach. How do you consider the requirements of all of the stakeholders and still hope to bring a solution to the point of implementation instead of allowing it to remain in the design stage forever?

- Understand that the process of identifying the stakeholder requirements does not equate with getting direct input from every single stakeholder. Multiple techniques exist to facilitate practical stakeholder inclusion without getting bogged down. Stakeholders' input can be solicited as needed through direct one-on-one interviews, surveys, or representative group discussions.

- Approach the process of identifying the stakeholder requirements in stages. You identify the stakeholders. You get their initial input. You produce an initial document that identifies their requirements. You analyze and validate their requirements. You reach a consensus where conflicts exist. You produce a draft design document. You get it reviewed. You revise it as necessary. You get it signed off. Now you are finished with the design. The rest is easy! You are ready to proceed with the implementation and training.

The solutions presented in this book are aimed at SMBs with anywhere from 1 to 500 employees who, as stated earlier, are not the only stakeholders in the business. As the number of stakeholders increases, it might become necessary for a representative to provide input on behalf of a category of stakeholders. Or the organizational structure might dictate that a small management group makes decisions on behalf of all of the stakeholders, and you won't be able to do much about it. If this is what occurs, it should be documented early in the solution design stage.

WARNING   If a group of stakeholders that was not directly consulted during the design becomes dissatisfied with the solution following its implementation, a review of the design stage will probably reveal that the dissatisfaction does not stem from a lack of professionalism on your part or the lack of the solution's capability. In all likelihood, the dissatisfaction is due to the short-circuiting of the recommended design process, which involves the consideration of all stakeholders' requirements.

The following subsections describe the broad, representative categories of stakeholders (which you saw in Figure 1-1) that you should consider when designing a networking solution. At the time of actual design, you need to be more specific with categorizing the stakeholders as a function of the business size and sector. If an individual represents multiple stakeholder categories, you need to get input from that individual regarding each stakeholder perspective that he or she represents.

Questions deemed appropriate for each stakeholder category are presented in the following sections. Responses to those questions will serve as a basis for producing an initial document identifying the stakeholder requirements.

Management (Executive and Line of Business)

From the management point of view, the requirements for a solution often can be articulated in extremely simple terms. Will it work? Will it result in a greater profit and/or expansion for the organization? Will it result in a greater market share? Will it result in greater customer satisfaction? These questions can be asked in a few seconds, but answering them often requires painstaking research, in-depth understanding of all aspects of the anticipated solution, and, last but not least, presentation skills that convey a sense of confidence that the solution will accomplish its intended purpose.

The apparent simplicity of the management requirements should not be equated with the ease of a solution's design. It's also important at this stage to have a concept of what it means when a solution "works" from the perspective of management versus that of a networking professional. A perfectly working networking solution might be deemed unworkable by management because it does not dovetail with the current business objectives and operations. For example, the solution might be perceived as being too expensive, too risky, too disruptive to current operations, or simply deemed unworkable or useless due to lack of understanding of what it really offers. Or the right solution might be introduced at the wrong time, which is another formula for failure.

As a general rule, from the management point of view, implementing a networking solution represents a serious financial investment. Given the quickly changing field of networking technologies, the level of depreciation of networking components is usually rapid compared to real estate, vehicles, planes, or more traditional factory or office equipment. This means that if a wrong solution is designed and implemented, the equipment might have a minimal resale value following the implementation, which makes it even more important to design a solution that meets the business requirements from the start. In other words, the aim for network design professionals ought to be the right solution, at the right time, presented, designed, and implemented in the right way.

Here are some of the questions you should ask the management prior to the design of any networking solution:

- Are you satisfied with the currently implemented networking solutions in support of your business mission? If not, what are you missing?

- What are your greatest concerns regarding the current implementation?

- Are you aware of what networking solutions are available that can enhance profitability, increase market share, improve employee morale, and result in greater customer satisfaction? Would you be interested in finding out more about any solutions that you might not be familiar with?

- Are your employees satisfied and able to perform their jobs in support of your business mission, given the company's existing networking infrastructure and solutions?

- Are your customers satisfied with your products and/or services? How would you envision gaining a greater market share or increasing your customer satisfaction through the use of networking solutions?

- Are your vendors satisfied with the way you interact with them? Do you envision any networking solution that might enhance your interactions with your vendors?

- Do you personally have access to desired information in a timely and secure manner?

Hearing answers to these and any follow-up questions that might result should give you a sense of what's already in place and what networking solutions might be appropriate to recommend. You also should be able to get a sense of the degree of support or executive sponsorship that you can expect for the proposed solution.

A bit of advice might be in order here. It is one thing for a networking professional to understand and be intimately familiar with all aspects of a networking solution; it is another thing to be able to sell it to a customer or, better yet, sell it to the decision makers within a business. In some respects, a solution's design is your sales pitch. And as most consultants and network professionals operating in the trenches know, it's extremely hard to sell something to potential customers who are already satisfied with what they have. It's advantageous, then, to inspire your customer with a vision of what the proposed solution will do while at the same time not destroying a sense of pride or confidence that they might have in the current system.

IT Department

The IT function within an SMB is either in-house, outsourced, or a combination of the two. Many SMBs—including law offices, auto dealerships, health care facilities, or smaller financial institutions—are likely to have at least an internal nucleus of an IT department that interfaces with one or more outside consulting and IT services organizations to satisfy the varied IT needs of today's SMBs.

When designing a networking solution, it's critical to secure the support of and to develop a good working relationship with the IT staff if you hope to see the solution implemented successfully. Of course, that's assuming the solution is being proposed by an outside organization. But what if the internal IT department is proposing the solution? Alternatively, what if the management has decided upon a solution, but its design and implementation are being assigned to the IT department? It is possible that management will be interested in getting a second opinion and that you will be required to have your design evaluated by an outside consulting group.

Whenever the internal and external IT organizations must interface, they should approach the relationship with the right mindset, which is to work together toward achieving the common business goals for the organization. Otherwise, the focus might shift too quickly toward differing opinions about technical details, resulting in lengthy discussions that lead nowhere.

Some of the questions that need to be addressed with the IT department have to do with the nuts and bolts of the existing networking infrastructure. You can get quite specific here, because it's vital for the purposes of budgeting and resource allocation to determine exactly what will have to be done to implement the proposed solution. For example, assume that you are proposing an IP Telephony solution with all of its advantages over an existing PBX system. You are able to get the management excited about the prospects of implementing that solution, and the management tells you that it ought to be easy to do so because the organization already has a LAN that links all of the users together.

But what the management might not tell you is what the state of the LAN is. What if the LAN is still mostly based on hubs and only partially switched? What if there are serious bottlenecks during peak usage times? What if the cabling does not meet even the basic EIA/ TIA 568A or B standards for 100-Mbps transmission? What if there are topology violations that, even though they allow the existing system to function marginally, would result in more serious performance bottlenecks as a result of additional traffic and stress from IP Telephony traffic? What if the LAN has outages that are tolerable for data use but would hardly be tolerable for voice usage? These are some of the issues that a designer must consider when negotiating between different stakeholder groups. Their perception of the same items or conditions might vary greatly.

What you want to solicit from the IT department is a clear picture of the state of the current infrastructure—its scalability, availability, and performance. Here are specific questions you should ask the IT department, broken into categories:

- Network asset management.
    - What is the networking equipment (hubs, switches, routers) currently installed?
    - Is the equipment from a single or multiple vendors?
    - What is the remaining projected life cycle of the equipment? Is any of the equipment no longer supported by respective vendor(s)?
    - Is any of the equipment under warranty?
    - What are the equipment specs—that is, number of ports, supported bandwidth, supported media types, and level of interoperability with the new solution?

- Desktop.
  - What operating system (OS) is prevalent on the desktop? (It's wishful thinking to assume that only one would be present!)
  - Are any policies in place to standardize desktop OSes?
- Topology.
  - What is the existing network topology?
  - Is there a logical diagram of the network identifying the equipment and topology?
  - Is there a physical diagram of the network identifying the physical equipment locations?
- Network addressing.
  - What is the network-addressing scheme that's currently in use?
  - Are private or registered IP addresses being used?
  - Is the current addressing scheme sufficiently flexible to facilitate growth, or does it have to be redesigned?
- Internet and virtual private networks (VPNs).
  - How is the Internet accessed, and what is the aggregate capacity of the Internet link?
  - Does the organization have a single or multiple Internet service providers (ISPs)?
  - Are VPNs being deployed? If so, how and why?
- Security.
  - What level of security has been deployed on the network?
  - What specific security measures have been taken to protect the SMB from both the external and internal threats?
  - Does the business have a clearly articulated security policy?
- Network management.
  - Are there any long-term statistics that show network utilization?
  - What network management tools are in place?
- User support.
  - What is the volume of support calls from the end users? What is the nature of those support calls?
  - Are there patterns in the support calls that could be addressed through training, upgrading the infrastructure, or implementing a new solution?

You need to remember something else: Any respectable in-house IT department will have a few kludges in its bag of tricks to keep the network running, and they ought to be proud of that fact. After all, most network administrators and IT managers are overworked and underfunded. So if you are an outsider approaching a business with a networking solution, just make a basic assumption that you might encounter a few booby traps along the way to which the IT staff is emotionally attached.

Such booby traps can include topology violations (due to cabling that's substandard or exceeds the specs), servers that are on their last legs, or a diverse generations-spanning equipment environment (resulting from lack of planning and just adding new gear as a result of growth). There are numerous other ways that overworked, tired, and pressured IT staff push the networking envelope to get things done in a timely manner.

NOTE   When you encounter a kludge, always remain sensitive to the feelings of the IT staff and consider the state of technology and the financial and manpower resources available at the time of its implementation. I bring up the kludge issue because, however ingenious and useful a kludge might be, it is typically not scalable and will cause problems when new solutions are introduced into the overall networking equation. So handle kludges with velvet gloves, humor, tact, and diplomacy.

If you get through all of the preceding questions (and kludges!) and any resulting follow-ups, you should end up with a pretty good sense of what additional requirements, if any, must be fulfilled to proceed with the design and implementation of a new solution.

The mechanics of soliciting input to these questions might vary from one business to another. In some cases, you can interview the IT staff. Some businesses maintain hard-copy documentation that can supply most of the answers. Others have network management tools in place that can collect most of the requested information and make it available online or in an electronic format. Some businesses, which might have heard about documentation but have none, have networks that are dependent on the mercy and availability of the consultant who set it up and has since changed professions or left town. In such extreme cases, before you design a solution, you need to document what the customer currently has.

End Users

For the purpose of this discussion, consider that *end users* are those who interact directly with the customers or are involved in the design or production of a business product. From their perspective, the solution requirements most often can be reduced to system speed, availability, ease of use, and ability to complete a task or transaction in a single session without having to follow up later on.

For example, if an employee is speaking to a customer on the phone, it's more efficient for the transaction to be completed during the conversation rather than the employee having to spend additional time on it after hanging up. In general, if information can be accessed quickly and easily any time it's needed, you are likely to have satisfied end users.

Here are some questions to ask the end users when introducing a new networking solution:

- What do you like best about any of the currently implemented networking solutions? Why? What do you like least about them? Why?
- How do the currently implemented networking solutions allow you to serve your customers well or be productive?
- Which component of the current system do you interact with the most? Does that interaction involve large amounts of data transfer?
- Is your interaction in real time or does it involve batch processing?
- Are there specific databases that you access on a regular basis?
- Are there specific times of the day, the week, or the month that your interaction with the system is much greater than it is at other times?

It might not be possible to receive direct answers to all of those questions, and the answers that you receive will probably require further follow-up, either with the IT department or through your own independent investigation. For example, end users might be able to identify screens and programs that they use most frequently, but they might have little or no idea whether they operate in a client/server mode or a host terminal, which have drastically different bandwidth requirements.

Your objective should be to identify potential bottlenecks from the user perspective so that when a new solution is implemented, its positive impacts are clearly identifiable. In addition, you should get a sense of traffic levels and patterns with respect to time. Of course, you can supplement your information with a more objective analysis of bandwidth utilization and input from the IT department, but there is simply no substitute for direct feedback from the trenches.

Customers

Customer satisfaction stems from reliable and reasonably priced products and services, the ability to resolve issues quickly, and the perception of friendly and courteous customer service staff within a business. When a potential networking solution is going to necessitate changes in the way that customers interact with a business, it's important to understand how the customers view the current system, if they have any feedback regarding potential improvements, or if there is an aspect of the current system that they particularly like or dislike.

Because customers typically represent a wide range of businesses and individuals, it's highly unlikely that you will be able to get everyone's perspective. But in keeping with basic principles of customer relations, a business should know who are the best 20 percent of the customers. They are normally responsible for 80 percent of the revenue. (It's the famous 80/20 rule that applies in so many situations.)

If the business policy allows you to interact directly with the customers in the course of designing a networking solution, take advantage of that opportunity to identify the requirements of another important group of stakeholders. If not, work with the customer service personnel within the business to identify the customer requirements.

Some of the questions to be asked of customers include the following:

- Are you currently receiving goods and services from this business in a timely fashion that supports your own goals and objectives? If not, by how much would you want to shorten the delivery cycle? Are you willing to pay more if the delivery cycle is shortened to meet your requirements?

- When you have an unusual issue to resolve, are you able to resolve it in a timely and satisfactory manner?

- Is problem resolution a free service? If the service is free, would you be willing to pay for the service if it could be delivered in a faster and more satisfactory manner?

- What options do you have for interfacing with the business—for example, by phone, via e-mail, via a web interface, in person?

- Which form of interaction with the business do you use the most? Which form of interaction with the business is most cost effective for you?

- Do you have any special security requirements for your interactions with the business? Are those security requirements being met by the business?

What you are trying to do is figure out, from the customer perspective, if the solution that you are proposing is going to have an impact on the customer base. At the same time, try to determine if perhaps there is another or a complementary solution that ought to be considered. This means that you are taking an integrated, or spherical, approach to networking solution design and implementation rather than just simply performing an installation without fully understanding the impact on all the parties (stakeholders) involved.

Vendors

From the point of view of a vendor or a supplier of goods and services to an SMB the deployment of a new networking solution by an SMB customer raises fundamental questions relating to the vendor's own operations. Will the new system in any way affect the SMB's accounting functions in a way that would alter the payment schedule for the services offered? Or, perhaps even worse, will there still be the need to continue providing goods and/or services to the SMB as before?

A proposed networking solution might streamline vendor interactions, eliminate some vendors, and reduce the level of services required from others. Any projected changes or cost savings in the area of vendor interactions should be clearly communicated to the vendor during this stage of identifying the stakeholder requirements. For example, video conferencing and secure communications using a VPN might reduce the need for employee travel and minimize interactions with a travel agency. Network faxing might reduce the need for the number of external fax machines and the degree of service that they require. Digital document management and storage ought to result in less printing, less paper consumption, and less external storage requirements.

Direct feedback from vendors might not be necessary, but you should understand interactions with vendors. Those who are involved in purchasing, shipping/receiving, and accounts payable are perhaps the best resources for understanding vendor interactions.

Here are some of the questions you can use to identify the vendor requirements:

- Is the business able to meet its obligations to the vendors in a timely and mutually satisfactory manner? If not, why not?

- Suppose that the business is stretching out its payment cycle to vendors because the customers do not pay on time. Could improved customer service through a networking solution reduce the accounts receivable cycle, allowing the business to meet its obligations toward its vendors more promptly?

- What are the means available to vendors for the delivery of goods and services—for example, e-mail, fax, phone, via a web interface, or by physically using various shipping services?

- Is the business providing the vendors with all available options for the delivery of goods and services?

- Does the business suffer in any way from lack of timely delivery of goods and services?

- Are the vendors satisfied with their current interactions with the business? Is there anything that they would like to see changed?

- Do the vendors (just like the customers) have any special security requirements? Are those requirements being met by the business?

Identifying the vendor requirements, in addition to identifying the customer requirements, enhances the designer's understanding of how the business is being perceived from the outside. Such knowledge further increases the probability that you will design and implement a correct solution.

Output from the Requirements Identification Stage

After you identify the requirements of the different groups of stakeholders, you will have a collection of information that you will need to organize, sift through, and subject to the next stage of validation. There will be conflicts between the requirements of different groups of stakeholders. Eventually, they will have to resolved through negotiation, being subjected to budgetary constraints, or even through the technical considerations relating to the solution's capabilities.

To provide a degree of structure to the initial design document, organize the requirements in the context of broad issues relating to the design and implementation of any networking solution, including the following:

- Availability
- Scalability
- Performance
- Financial considerations

Availability

Network or solution *availability* relates to the impact that a network outage has on a business to carry out its normal operations. This consideration might overlap with the area of disaster planning and recovery, but every business should have some idea of the impact on its operations when certain components or the entire network become unavailable.

Suppose that you designed and implemented a new CRM solution, but the network on which it is implemented experiences frequent outages. The benefits of the new solution might be completely offset by the unreliable network infrastructure. Instead of stakeholders experiencing a benefit from the new solution, their perception might be that they are worse off than they were before.

Suppose a new VPN solution along with a new firewall is installed as part of a comprehensive security solution, but the firewall is subject to frequent outages that prevent users from getting on the Internet and telecommuters from accessing the inside network. The perception might develop that the new solution is not working, when in fact the security aspect of the solution might be working perfectly. However, proper steps have not been taken to ensure solution availability either through redundancy, power protection, or perhaps something as simple as increased physical security and proper placement of the equipment to prevent accidental shutdowns.

Scalability

A scalable solution works well on a micro as well as a macro scale. It facilitates business growth and, over a period of time, allows for incremental rather than forklift-style upgrades. Naturally, there are limits to scalability past which a drastic upgrade or a new solution might be required. This fact makes it even more important to bring to the fore and document the level of scalability during the design process.

A well-designed and scalable networking solution allows for an increase in the number of users, the level of usage, and even the type of usage without immediate post-deployment degradation or need for dramatic upgrades. Designing a nonscalable solution will not build a lot of goodwill between the business and the designer. It will likely result in the business losing its initial investment and being unable to take advantage of new opportunities. For the designer, it can result in a less than desirable reputation and loss of business opportunities.

Scalability needs to be considered from a technical as well as financial angle. Suppose it's possible to maintain scalability from a technical point of view, but only at a high cost. The management might not view that kind of scalability favorably.

Moreover, consider that scalability does not always translate into a continuous linear function. For example, consider the accounting profession's concept of *step costing*, where, at a certain point, a drastic expenditure is required to facilitate an ongoing gradual expansion. In the networking arena, a practical example of *step costing* with respect to scalability might be a situation in which all the slots on an existing modular router or switch get filled. To facilitate even a modest expansion, the business must purchase a new unit with a large number of slots, but only a minimal number of those slots will be used initially. That represents a drastic cost—a step cost bump—to facilitate a modest expansion.

Performance

You will be forgiven for going over budget and even for delays in implementation as long as what you design performs well. The corollary is also true: If a networking solution does not meet the performance criteria, it will matter little how much you saved or how fast you designed it. The entire effort will likely be considered a loss.

Numerous factors affect network performance. If a solution that you are designing integrates with the rest of the network, it is vital, as stated earlier, to understand the existing infrastructure and operating environment. One metaphor for network performance is that of a long water pipeline built with pipes of varying diameters. (Not that anyone would ever want to build a pipeline like that!) The pipe with the smallest diameter will slow the flow, and it almost doesn't matter how short the pipe is or where it is located.

Networking professionals should be familiar with the layered model of computing architectures as well as the concept of access, distribution, and core layers in networking topologies and traffic patterns. Any proposed solution must take these factors into account. The typical outcome of poor performance is frustration on the part of employees and customers, which, over a period of time, can result in reduced revenues and inability to maintain healthy growth. In general, technology is only wonderful when it works well. The same applies to any networking solution that you design.

Financial Considerations

Given the unreal situation of a business having an unlimited budget coupled with liberal design deadlines, chances are that a nearly perfect solution can be designed! Yes, occasionally, in this business, it's good for your health to dream! Dreaming aside, it is quite important that, at the fragile stage of producing the initial output from identifying stakeholder requirements, the design process is not subjected to the budget ax. The budget ax is unavoidable, but it comes later.

Not being overly concerned at this stage with the budget allows for wider and more creative solution options to be explored during the forthcoming validation stage. At the same time, the designer should have a sense of realism about the cost of the potential implementation of what has been brought up by the stakeholders when compared to the company's financial position.

This is also the stage at which you might want to research the total cost of ownership (TCO) of what's being stated as requirements. TCO extends past the immediate cost of a requirement or a solution feature and considers the life cycle, recurring, and maintenance costs. Make sure that there are no hidden costs of the solution lurking someplace that will rear their ugly heads at the most inappropriate time.

As you proceed with the solution design through the subsequent validation and then on to the draft design and review stage, you will need to acquire a sense of what the stated requirements are going to cost. When it's time to consider the budget in the draft design and review stage, you will be well equipped to juggle options as a result of the budgetary constraints.

Step 2: Validating Stakeholder Requirements

Following the identification of the stakeholder requirements and the creation of the initial document that combines them into a coherent—albeit conflicting—whole, it's time for the next stage of the design process, which is the validation of the requirements. The key elements of this stage are achieving consensus where potential conflicts exist and assigning priorities to all aspects of the proposed solution.

Achieving Consensus

No networking solution implementation occurs in a vacuum. If you are able to design an entire solution from the ground up without much concern for integration with existing systems, consider yourself fortunate because you can design the appropriate supporting components at the same time. It's more of an exception than a rule, but it happens. Generally, any proposed solution must integrate into an existing networking infrastructure and applications environment.

The process of identifying the stakeholder requirements leading to the creation of a design document is intended to flush out all of the relevant issues that need to be considered prior to implementation. For example, designing a CRM solution might bring up the issue of needing a greater level of network security. An SMB might have to decide whether or not the CRM solution implementation can proceed without upgrading security, or, if the SMB decides on security upgrades, then to what level, at what pace, and at what cost? This is where the designer's negotiation and mediation skills, as well as long-term vision, come in handy.

Assigning Priorities

Intuitively, it seems that everybody understands the concept of priorities, and there is sufficient lip service being paid to that principle in the business environments. However, when faced with multiple choices, assigning priorities and sticking to them usually requires a significant amount of willpower and can prove to be a daunting task.

If you are familiar with the Request For Comments (RFC) documents that specify numerous Internet protocols, you might already be aware of the terminology that's used in them. It's simple; the keywords used for identifying features of protocols that are to be implemented by vendors are MUST, MUST NOT, SHOULD, and MAY. These keywords also happen to be appropriate for assigning levels of priorities to aspects of complex networking solutions.

Do not confuse priority level with the order of execution of tasks that leads to solution implementation. When groups of tasks have been assigned the same level of priority, you still need to decide on the order of implementation.

MUST

The MUST keyword represents an absolute requirement. For example, if a CRM solution requires a certain type of server to support the application, then it's a MUST. The application simply will not work on anything else. If a certain bandwidth is required between servers because the CRM application is distributed, then it's also a must.

However, upgrading network security might not necessarily be in the same category as having a server with sufficient processing power or having sufficient bandwidth between servers. CRM will still work without a security solution, but the information that is collected through the application might be vulnerable to outside penetration or even an internal compromise.

MUST NOT

The MUST NOT keyword can be as important as MUST. If you are designing a security solution and identify that it's a MUST to have only one access point from the internal network to the Internet, it is equally important to state that there MUST NOT be any other access points—that is, end users placing modems into their workstations and bypassing the implemented security solution that offers protection from hackers and viruses.

SHOULD

The SHOULD keyword translates into something that is recommended. Whereas MUST and MUST NOT are quite clear cut, the SHOULD label is likely to entail a significant amount of debate. Generally, if something is recommended, it involves a certain amount of risk that must be taken under certain conditions if there is no follow-through on the recommendation.

For example, at an installation with a lot of sensitive data stored on its servers, having a firewall to protect the data from external security threats might be a MUST. But having an intrusion detection system (IDS) that checks for unusual traffic patterns on the internal network and potential penetrations through the firewall might fall into the category of SHOULD. If, however, there is no tolerance for any risk level related to security, an IDS becomes a MUST, just like the firewall.

MAY

The MAY keyword implies something that is optional. Assigning this label to an aspect of a solution can also be a challenge, because if it's really nonessential, why bother with it to begin with? But you will end up with some instance where MAY is appropriate if you go through the process of identifying the stakeholder requirements.

Have you ever listened to the news or read in a newspaper report about governments allowing their nonessential embassy staff to be evacuated from certain countries in times of crisis? Have you ever wondered what nonessential really means? One way to determine what is optional is to go through all of the aspects of the proposed solution and decide what is a MUST and what is a SHOULD. Everything that is left over will be MAY (that is, optional) by default.

Output from the Validation of Requirements Stage

Output from the validation of the requirements stage should be a set of functional requirements agreed upon among the diverse groups of stakeholders. It ought to present a basis for a common vision of what the solution is all about. It's a high-level blueprint; it's not a design document yet, but it's getting there. The MUST and selected SHOULD requirements can now be subjected to constraints of topology, performance, budget, and an implementation schedule.

Step 3: Creating and Reviewing the Draft Design Document

There is a real temptation on the part of businesses and perhaps even networking professionals to start the design process at this stage, skipping the previous stages. It seems so much easier to begin by identifying the solution to be implemented and to start talking about where to place it, how it will perform, and how much it will cost.

If you engage in a large number of projects over a long period of time, there will be a few where you will be able to get away with this approach. For multiple reasons, the pressure is always there to cut corners. However, skipping the identification and validation of requirements stages drastically increases your chances of designing a wrong solution at the wrong time and for the wrong reason. The good news: After you get burned once or twice, you will be less inclined to take the chance trying to succeed without doing your homework first.

If you are continuing with the recommended network solution design approach, it is at this stage that you will translate the stakeholder requirements into an actual design document that clearly addresses the following:

- Physical network topology
- Measurable performance requirements
- Viable budget
- Realistic completion timeline

Identifying the Physical Network Topology

Identifying the physical topology in which a network solution will function is a critical component of the design process. The topology considerations of the draft design document determine where the equipment or applications will be installed, what underlying LAN and/or WAN technology will be needed to support the solution, and whether or not the proposed solution is even viable. For example, when contemplating which wireless LAN solution to implement, much depends on topological considerations. Lower frequencies operate over longer distances, but they do so at lower rates and potentially with more interference. Understanding the topology of where a wireless local-area network (WLAN) is to be deployed is vital to a successful solution design and implementation.

If you are implementing a security solution, it is vital to understand the network topology so that a firewall or routers with security features can be placed in the correct locations. If an SMB is distributed geographically between multiple locations, you will not be able to do much about the topology between the locations, but the availability and the cost of WAN bandwidth between the locations might determine the specifics of a solution. For example, you might decide that each location should have its own access to the Internet with its own firewall and that the private network between the locations should not be burdened with the Internet traffic that otherwise might have to funnel through one central location. Or the availability and cost of WAN links for a private network might be such that a VPN solution utilizing the public Internet might be the best approach for linking the locations and providing Internet access at the same time.

Assume, for the sake of simplicity, that you have an SMB with four locations. A common WAN topology design is that of a *hub and spoke*, where one location becomes the hub that links to all the other locations. As a function of budget and requirements for redundancy, the next variant of the hub-and-spoke building block is a *partial mesh*, where the hub-and-spoke topology is maintained but, at the same time, there are links between some of the spoke locations. Extending this concept further, you can design a *full mesh* between all of the locations.

If there are multiple smaller hub-and-spoke topologies, the hubs can be linked in a full mesh, creating a core of the WAN, with the spokes connecting to each hub with no mesh, a partial mesh, or even a full mesh between them. That theme can be duplicated further as needed, creating a hierarchical topological WAN design that satisfies the bandwidth requirements, takes maximum advantage of the available technologies, and takes the requirement of network availability (redundancy) into account, all within the constraints of the specified performance requirements and budget.

LAN topologies also employ the concepts of hierarchy and layers, with a network switch being a typical building block. As you traverse the network from the access layer to the core through the distribution layer, the aggregate and port bandwidth tend to increase, and the devices become more capable and powerful. As is the case with WANs, redundancy that translates into network availability can be designed to the degree that satisfies that particular requirement within the budget constraint.

Determining Measurable Performance Requirements

Performance and budget are closely coupled and seemingly at odds, but the process of identifying the stakeholder requirements should allow you to make a balanced decision between the two. Something to consider when determining the performance requirements is whether they translate into a solution that is mainstream, a solution more on the trailing edge, or one that is on the cutting edge.

Typically, the cutting-edge solution represents the latest technology, and there is less data available to evaluate its effectiveness over a period of time. It is likely to provide the highest level of performance at a higher cost (as compared to mainstream or trailing-edge solutions), but it might not be as stable as the mainstream solution. If a company's policy is to present to its customers an image of being on the cutting edge of technology, the decision ought to be fairly straightforward in favor of performance at a higher cost, even if it means sacrificing a degree of stability.

Mainstream solutions tend to represent a balance between budget and performance and offer a degree of stability that is desirable for many businesses. It's pretty much a given that over a period of time, the mainstream solution will turn into a trailing-edge solution sooner than a cutting-edge solution will, but experience shows that many SMBs do not necessarily have a problem with this as long as the solution fulfills the requirements and is stable. Businesses are organic and go through their own growth cycles; as a result, they might opt for a solution that is congruent with the current stage of their evolution and an image that a business wants to present to its customers.

Designing a solution that lags behind the mainstream is basically not recommended unless, of course, that is specifically what the customer requires. This approach, however, is not without merit, especially in the arena of security. Most of the hacking and virus attacks are aimed at mainstream OSes and technologies. More obscure and less popular applications, OSes, and underlying LAN and WAN technologies might offer a degree of protection because they are not as well understood by those who try to disrupt your business activities.

As mentioned earlier, many factors affect performance. When specifying performance during this stage of the design process, keep in mind how performance is going to be measured at the time of solution implementation. The final design document needs to address the issue of performance measurement that is quantifiable in terms of response time, throughput, or number of transactions over a period of time.

WARNING   You should steer away from defining performance requirements in vague and intangible terms—for example, a requirement that "Users will really like the way the system responds." Instead, use precise, albeit flexible, language. For example, "Users will be able to complete this transaction or task in no more than X amount of time."

Although it might be a hard lesson to learn, in the business of designing and implementing networking solutions, it is better to underpromise and overdeliver than the other way around. This principle might be at odds with trying to sell a solution to a customer, but consider several simple facts. Networking has been around now for more than two decades (depending on one's perception of when it really took off in the business world). There is a degree of maturity and understanding in the business world regarding networking that was not there even a decade ago. The same information that is available to you is available to your customers on the Internet, which was often not the case a decade ago. Customers have become sophisticated in their approach to acquiring networking solutions.

Trying to dazzle a customer with unrealistic promises will sooner or later backfire. Thus, maintaining a balanced approach when it comes to solution performance, understanding well the customer requirements and the solution's capabilities, and erring a bit on the side of caution in favor of the customer being pleasantly surprised is the recommended approach to quantifying performance in the design document.

Formulating a Viable Budget

Ah, the budget! The squeezer, the dream buster, or the source of motivation, practicality, and ingenuity! However you relate to the budget process, you will have to deal with it when designing a solution. Whether you are buying or selling real estate, collecting stamps or coins, or paying for higher education, you generally have a sense of what something is worth as a function of numerous and often complex factors. It's no different with a networking solution.

The designer has a sense of the value of a solution, just as the business considering the solution has a sense of its value. The key is for the two parties to come to a numerically quantifiable consensus on that value. It's also important that in the process of formulating a viable budget, each party retains a sense of value for the proposed solution.

If you are a consulting business proposing a solution, and you offer the solution at a desperately low cost, chances are that corners will be cut and the customer's expectations will not be met. If you skip the training or the documentation aspects of the solution, you will potentially have a lot of frustrated users down the road. The management and the accountants might feel like they are getting a good deal, but in the long run, the reverse is likely to be true.

If the customer perceives that it is overpaying for the solution, this perception might lead to a set of expectations that are unrealistic and cannot be met even if you as the designer do everything right. So some haggling is involved during this stage, and you should not shun it. If it is conducted in an atmosphere of working toward a common vision for the solution, it will lead to a sense of fair value and realistic expectations, increasing the chances of successful implementation.

Budget negotiations are likely to be the trigger for a revision of the draft design. It is possible that, as a result of the budget negotiations, performance requirements will be reduced and functionality removed. That might translate into a lower-capacity, lesser-scalability, and lesser-availability solution. What you have in your favor at this point, however, is that priorities have already been assigned. If a solution task with a MUST priority is being removed as a result of budget negotiations, it is being done with everyone's full knowledge and understanding that funds are not available for that aspect of the solution at this time.

Creating a Realistic Completion Timeline

The focus of this publication is the solution design process rather than implementation scheduling. But when you design a solution, you should at least consider the implementation schedule and a realistic completion timeline.

Various tools assist with the development of a completion timeline and managing project tasks. For larger, more complex projects, you can develop project evaluation and review technique (PERT) and Gantt charts that show relationships between solution tasks and that can be used to derive a completion date. For simpler, smaller projects, all that you might need to come up with a completion date is a calendar and a good sense of how long it takes to accomplish a given task, which does take some practice and experience. A sign at a client's site still rings true: "Good judgment comes from experience and experience comes from making bad judgments."

Step 4: Creating a Final Design Document Before Implementation

If you've ever written a book, created a design document, or, for that matter, researched a subject and wrote a paper on it, you are well aware that it's an iterative process. It seems as if no matter how many times you go over your work, new issues surface, flaws and errors are uncovered, and refinements are required. At some point, it becomes a process of diminishing returns. There wouldn't be too many publications out there if the standard were absolute perfection. The same holds true for reviewing a draft design document. It might take one, two, or even three iterations, but there comes a time when you have an inner sense that it's ready to go. That's the time to get it signed off and to switch from the draft design stage to implementation. As mentioned earlier, budget considerations are also a trigger for draft design review and iteration.

The output from the creation and review of a draft design document stage is a final design document. You enter that stage with a set of functional requirements resulting from the identification of the stakeholder requirements process. You proceed by producing a draft design, and, after the necessary iterations triggered by budget considerations as well issues that come up during the prioritization and topology considerations, you leave this stage with a final design document that has been reviewed, agreed upon, and signed off (not unlike a bill proceeding through the legislative process!). Now, you are ready to proceed with the solution's implementation.

Networking Solution Implementation Considerations

The implementation of a networking solution is a distinctly different stage from its design, but it is a good idea to keep the implementation considerations in mind during the design stage. For example, if the implementation is going to require a significant amount of system downtime and disruption to normal business operations, you should consider that during the solution's design. You should incorporate appropriate recommendations in the design document regarding when would be the best time to proceed with such an implementation.

Figure 1-2 illustrates a designer's balancing act between the process of a solution's design and its implementation. When the desire to go through the design process is in balance with the desire to implement, it is deemed to be the optimal condition for ultimate success. Getting caught up in an endless design spiral or taking the rash approach of plunging into implementation without a design or only a cursory one carry corresponding risks of not getting anything done or producing something that simply does not meet the business requirement for a networking solution.

Figure 1-2   *Network Designer's Balance Bar*

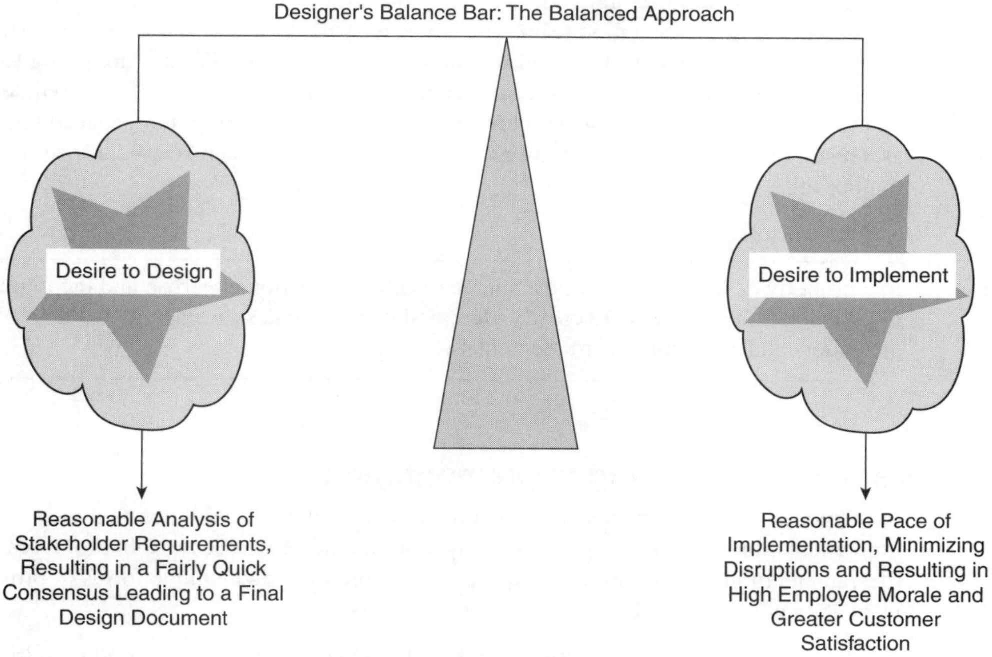

Designer's Balance Bar: The Balanced Approach

Desire to Design

Desire to Implement

Reasonable Analysis of
Stakeholder Requirements,
Resulting in a Fairly Quick
Consensus Leading to a Final
Design Document

Reasonable Pace of
Implementation, Minimizing
Disruptions and Resulting in
High Employee Morale and
Greater Customer
Satisfaction

At a minimum, generic implementation considerations include the following:

- Sources of implementation expertise
- Project management during implementation
- Performance testing
- Documentation
- Training

Sources of Implementation Expertise

Any networking solution is going to require either internal or external IT resources to implement. Use of internal resources can be a sore point with the IT departments at SMBs. The internal IT staff already tends to be overworked and often feels underappreciated and inundated with new projects, which is one of the reasons that the IT department was identified early in this chapter as one of the stakeholder categories. You need to ensure that the IT department's input is taken seriously and that the IT staff supports the project at every level, including who does the work after the design is completed.

The external implementation resources include the solution's vendor, partners, independent consultants, and contractors. The size and nature of the solution will determine the makeup of the implementation team. The key is to spell out as clearly as possible who is responsible for what aspect of the implementation. If internal IT staff are going to be involved in the implementation of a large, resource-intensive solution, it's a good idea to identify which of the tasks that are currently being performed might not get accomplished as a result of such a diversion of internal resources. This approach keeps surprises to a minimum!

NOTE   In a properly designed solution, the source of implementation expertise and the required implementation resources are clearly identified during the design stage to avoid a misunderstanding during the implementation stage.

Project Management During Implementation

Implementing a well-designed solution ought to be a lot easier than jumping into implementation without going through any kind of a design process. Both processes (design and implementation) are projects that require their own unique forms of project management.

During the design stage, you collect and analyze the requirements, negotiate with the stakeholders, consider all of the advantages and disadvantages of topology, define performance criteria, and, finally, submit the requirements to the budget ax to come up with a final design document, which you hope represents a consensus of all parties involved in the design process.

During the implementation stage, you ensure that what has been installed meets the performance criteria, is within the allocated budget, and is being delivered on schedule. You are potentially dealing with vendors who must deliver the solution in its entirety or components thereof according to an agreed-upon schedule. You have to plan for contingencies in case delivery deadlines are missed or performance criteria are not met.

You have to deal with the almost given fact that no matter how careful the design is, not everything is going to work out as planned during the implementation. There has to be a degree of flexibility and willingness to adjust the design even in this late stage. This is similar to how jobs proceed in the construction industry; there are architectural plans, and then there are "as-builts," which are plans that reflect what has been changed from the original.

It is certainly a judgment call whether or not the design team will also manage the implementation. Whoever takes on the job of project management during the implementation needs to understand the design well and be able to communicate well with vendors and stakeholders about how the implementation is proceeding and if there are any changes from the original design.

Performance Testing

Performance testing requires that performance criteria be clearly defined, as is recommended during the draft design and review stage. Here is the real question: What happens if the solution does not perform as specified?

If the solution does not perform according to criteria specified during the design, and the solution has not replaced a preexisting system that a business relies on, the decision boils down to whether to tolerate the lower level of performance and proceed with the implementation. Obviously, there are going to be financial implications for both the business and the solution provider that result from an unacceptable level of the solution's performance, but at least the current system is still in place. However, if a proposed solution irreversibly replaces a functioning system, the end result could be anything from an agreement to have a fix in a reasonable period of time, to lower or no pay to the solution provider, to possibly a lawsuit.

Ideally, the solution provider should understand the level of a solution's performance long before implementation. In fact, performance might be one of the solution's selling factors. So the idea of performance testing should be a verification mechanism where the outcome is reasonably certain. If possible, the solution's performance should be demonstrated in a test or prototype environment during the design stage and/or by running in parallel at the time of implementation.

Running *in parallel* means that the new solution is operating side by side with an existing one. That's sometimes easier said than done. And even if you take this approach, whether or not the solution performs as specified is generally revealed only when you go live with it and subject it to the stress levels of the actual operating environment.

If you choose to run in parallel, remember that it takes additional resources to maintain two systems side by side. But the effort might be worth it if you simulate the appropriate stress level on the new solution. Running in parallel often involves software-based solutions with a lot of transaction processing and potentially significant changes to the underlying databases. A situation in which you switch between CRM systems would certainly be a candidate for running in parallel, but so would an implementation of an IP Telephony solution that replaces a traditional PBX.

Documentation

The topic of documentation is controversial, with good cause. Detailed documentation tends to become obsolete as a result of ongoing changes and upgrades following a solution's implementation. To keep documentation up to date, someone has to maintain it on an ongoing basis, which is a task that often goes by the wayside. In addition, documentation that is too high level is often viewed as useless.

Documentation is necessary but, as is the case with training, it needs to be targeted at different groups of stakeholders. Examples follow:

- An executive summary with a few color diagrams might be all that is required to satisfy the documentation needs of the management.

- The end users might require a cross-referenced manual with screen shots, descriptions of procedures for dealing with different customer issues, explanations of tables and fields in a database, keyboard shortcuts for accomplishing common tasks, or instructions on how to use more complex networking equipment.

- The IT department might be completely satisfied with documentation that is in the form of online help or that can be derived in real time via network management tools.

- A business that is subject to external financial or security audits might need to provide documentation of its network that is satisfactory to the auditors. These documentation requirements would normally be understood by the business and would likely be stated during the stage of identifying the stakeholder requirements.

Regardless of the nature of a solution or the customer, a balanced, targeted documentation is an essential component of any solution implementation. It does not make the success of the solution contingent on contact with the provider; rather, it allows the business to take maximum advantage of the solution's potential.

Training

Often, little consideration is given to the training aspect of a networking solution implementation. To take maximum advantage of a solution, training is required at all levels of implementation. What a pity it is to see people use the absolute minimum set of a solution's features, just enough to get by, due to lack of sufficient training.

There are many ways in which the value of a solution can be minimized and even outright compromised because of lack of training. Take security, for example. Plenty of routers, firewalls, and IDSes simply are not properly configured or sufficiently fine-tuned to take full advantage of their features. There are even firewalls that permit all traffic to go through them. How about that for a false sense of security!

The key to successful training is to identify the appropriate target audiences for the different aspects of required training, make the training relevant to the solution at hand for each audience, and conduct it at the right time. Ideally, training ought to occur in several stages:

- **Prior to the implementation**—Training before implementation should concentrate on the solution's capabilities and the changes in existing procedures that the solution will introduce. If the solution involves a software application like a CRM, for example, it is useless to talk too much ahead of time about specific screens or keystrokes if the users are not able to use hands-on experimentation during the training. On the other hand, if the implementation procedure calls for having a test system prior to going live, that's the time to start getting all of the users used to the new solution.

- **During and/or immediately after the implementation**—Training during or immediately after implementation might fall into the category of user support at the earliest stages of going live with the solution. You want to make sure that whenever a new solution is implemented, users are not left to fend for themselves if problems occur. This type of training tends to be perhaps more informal and hands on than training that occurs prior to the implementation.

- **At a future time following the implementation**—Future training falls into the category of optimization. After a solution is put to use for a while, the designers and implementers should review its use and ensure that the solution's capabilities are being put to maximum use. If that is not the case, additional training is necessary. This training should incorporate user feedback as well as observations about the solution's use from the designers and implementers.

Most effective training incorporates a combination of training tools, including formal presentations, demonstrations, hands-on practice, question-and-answer sessions, as well as some type of assignments to be completed by the trainees. Self-study is also an important aspect of the overall training program. The implementation team should do everything possible to facilitate self-study by providing access to the new system in a simulated and/or live environment in which damage is not possible as a result of trainees' actions.

There are also creative ways in which an SMB can take advantage of information and resources during implementation that will complement the formal training process without placing additional strain on the budget. For example, make sure to take maximum advantage of the technical expertise of the vendor supplying the solution. There might be free white papers, free online training, or books that would complement the training being offered. Explore the training sources. Even if a solution provider does not usually offer training, it might be something that you could negotiate. Consider training a smaller group, who can in turn train others within the business.

Putting It All Together

Having gone through all of the steps of producing a design document, you are perhaps beginning to wonder what one would look like. No two will be identical, but Table 1-1 provides an outline of a typical design document that you could expect to see emerge from the design process.

Table 1-1 *Sample Design Document Components*

Design Document Component	Description
Networking Solution Design Objective	• A paragraph or two defining what the solution will accomplish for the business. • Incorporates the solution's capabilities and expectations from the stakeholders, mostly at the strategic business level.
Overview of the Current System	• Describes the current system to be integrated with the proposed solution in the framework of system availability, scalability, and performance. • A functional description of the current system, addressing areas of network asset management, topology, network addressing, security, Internet access, user support, and any other aspects of the system that come to the fore during the identification of the user requirements stage.
Functional Requirements and Priorities	• The heart of the design document. • Includes the distilled functional requirements that will be fulfilled by the solution. Requirements should be assigned priorities. • Can mirror the "Overview of the Current System" section in terms of how the proposed solution will impact system availability, scalability, and performance. • Clearly states the impact of the solution on all stakeholders. • Addresses areas relating to network asset management, topology, network addressing, security, Internet access, and user support.
Cost-Benefit Analysis	• Includes all of the relevant equipment and labor costs. • Details any relevant financial analysis relating to cost savings and/or TCO for the business resulting from the solution's implementation.
Implementation	• Addresses issues related to the solution's implementation. • As appropriate, includes sources of implementation expertise, project management, performance testing, documentation, and training.
Signatures and Dates	• A design document requires a degree of consensus, whether it's one individual making all of the decisions on behalf of the business or a representative from each stakeholder group. • Obtain the necessary signatures (they should be dated) signifying agreement to the proposed design.

Summary

This chapter introduced a generic approach to the effective design of networking solutions. The essence of the approach lies in recognizing the necessary steps that must be taken during the design process to ensure maximum potential for success during the implementation. The approach recommends the identification and validation of the stakeholder requirements, which result in a set of functional requirements from which a draft design document can be derived.

Skipping the design process or stages thereof and immediately jumping into the solution implementation is not recommended, even if the solution's designer is intimately familiar with the solution's capabilities. Review of interactive revisions of the draft document leads to the final signed-off design document, which serves as the basis for solution implementation. Remember the often-neglected issues of documentation and training during the solution's implementation stage.

CHAPTER 2

SMB Networking Environments and Solutions Design Considerations

The past two decades saw the commoditization of computer networking in the small-medium business (SMB) arena. In 1980, DEC, Intel, and Xerox (DIX) published a document known as the "Ethernet specification," the "Ethernet version 1," or the "Blue Book." In 1982, that document was updated to Ethernet Version 2. Espec-2 remains a valid and relevant standard even now, but it is much easier to set up a computer network today than it was back then.

Think for a moment about the networking hardware used in the early 1980s: 10 Mbps shared media, network interface cards (NICs) with external transceivers, vampire taps, thick coaxial cable, and repeaters to extend the network topology. In terms of networking operating system (NOS) software, think of minicomputers or mainframes; there were no viable network operating systems for PCs in 1982, although fledgling efforts were under way to develop them.

Add to those mental pictures (if you can still imagine them) PC platforms equipped with a whopping 640 KB or 1 MB RAM and CPU clock speeds of 4 MHz. You are now on the cutting edge of networking and PC computing of the early 1980s! And the aforementioned items were not available in office supply stores or online. Why? For the simple reason that in 1982, even though the precursor of the Internet (the ARPANET, developed by the Advanced Research Project Agency [ARPA] in 1969) was in existence, today's web-oriented Internet, which, using TCP/IP protocols, allows us to make online purchases with a click of a mouse, was not. In addition, the high cost and limited availability of networking and computing products in those days did not make them viable candidates for the shelves of office supply stores.

Fast-forward more than a couple of decades to today. Networking products like 10/100/1000 Mbps NICs, hubs, routers, switches, relevant cabling, firewalls, and plentiful high-performance PC hardware and software are commodity items. They are available at many types of brick-and-mortar outlets, from electronics stores to office supply stores to regular department stores. In addition, hundreds if not thousands of other networking products from numerous vendors (both hardware and software) are available at online stores and Internet auction sites. These products range from basic equipment that is applicable for home networking to complex multiservice devices and software applications that support the operations of even the largest of enterprises. Given the fierce competition in the networking field, many Internet sites specialize in providing price comparisons to allow potential buyers (from home users to SMBs and large enterprises alike) the option of purchasing a desired product at the lowest possible price.

One thing is certain: Wide availability of networking products has made them affordable (and indispensable, it is probably safe to say) to support the endeavors of every business category, including all sizes of SMBs. Many of the currently available networking products are also easy to use and to install, especially when they are deployed individually or in smaller networks. The network equipment vendors (including Cisco) are to be congratulated for making networking hardware and software easier to use.

At the same time that ease and simplicity have been prevailing for home users and small office/home office (SOHO) users, there has been a growing diversity and an increase in sophistication and capabilities of the networking gear, software, and business solutions meant for SMBs and large enterprises. Take IP Telephony, for example. All of the IP Telephony solutions operate over a data network (packet-switched) infrastructure and can nicely integrate with the circuit-switched legacy installations. Consider that telephony has been evolving for more than 100 years. Porting the existing telephony features, adding new ones, and providing for integration of IP Telephony with the existing telephony systems implies a degree of complexity and sophistication that is not exactly a "plug-and-play" operation yet. Progress is continuous, though, and even as this book is being written and released, Cisco and other IP Telephony vendors are crossing the technical chasms. IP Telephony solutions are discussed in more detail in Chapter 8, "IP Telephony Solutions."

When you combine the increasingly growing intelligence and capabilities of the networking equipment with the diversity of the SMB landscape, as discussed in the next section, it becomes advisable for anyone designing a network to adhere to a principle that seems to have withstood the test of time: Effective computer networks and networking solutions cannot be slapped together without going through a design process. If you do not follow this principle, the potential is too great for underutilizing the network capability and having an SMB operate in a reactive mode with the limitations and quirks of the poorly operating network driving business decisions rather than supporting them. Computer networks and networking solutions need to be designed and implemented to support the business and its mission instead of businesses barely making it or going under because of their networks.

One Name, a Multitude of Shapes and Sizes

Trying to fully categorize and analyze the SMB market might best be left to the market research firms, the Small Business Administration (SBA) in the United States, or the equivalent government institutions in other countries. Suffice it to say that it is hard to get out of bed in the morning and get through a day without numerous encounters with SMBs. Even though some businesses you encounter might seem to be large enterprises, from the perspective of designing a networking solution, those enterprises are composed of smaller units that effectively function as SMBs that are integrated with a high-capacity, high-performance core network architecture that a single SMB might not require. Effectively, on the edge of a network, even the largest of enterprises, regardless of its sector, size, or shape, can be thought of as an SMB. And even though networking solutions need to be tailored to support each SMB sector and size category, a commonality of the networking infrastructure and solution functions applies to the entire SMB landscape.

Business Sectors

SMB sectors span the alphabet, from automotive dealers through zipper repair shops and zoos, including everything in between: education, travel, health care, finance, legal, delivery, entertainment, food services, manufacturing, transportation, and real estate, just to name a few. These businesses serve the varied and ever-evolving needs of the societies that we live in, but at the same time they share three common fundamentals: They all offer a product or a service to a group of customers; they all have to remain competitive and fiscally responsible if they expect to survive and to prosper in the marketplace; and, generally, they all are working toward a certain goal. In for-profit organizations, the objective is most often profitability; for nonprofits, the goal is to offer a valuable service or a product that a society has deemed worthy of not being subject to taxation.

All SMBs, regardless of the sector in which they operate, rely on utilities that are now routinely taken for granted in a modern society: electricity, telephone service, running water, or physical mobility through a well-established transportation network. Computer networking has not been around for as long as electric service, telephones, or divided highways, but from my perspective, it is well on its way to becoming one of the common utilities. Consider electricity. Numerous appliances performing a seemingly unimaginable number of functions plug into standardized electric outlets to support the complex requirements of our lifestyles. Consider a well-designed computer network. Well, we are not quite there yet (being able to plug several different devices into the network and having them work instantly), but progress is heading in that direction.

A well-designed network should transparently support a wide range of business applications to advance the varied missions of SMBs and other enterprises, regardless of their size. Certain generic applications—such as payroll, billing, accounts receivable, or electronic mail—are common across all of the business sectors, although their specific features vary as a function of the size of the enterprise that they support. Other applications are unique to each sector, including specialized banking software, inventory control for retail outlets or wholesale distributors, automated production controls in manufacturing facilities, or custom programs that access patient databases in health care facilities. Often, the effective use of these unique applications ultimately offers an SMB a competitive edge and supports the fundamental business mission of delivering value to customers.

Consequently, when designing an SMB networking solution—subject to the design guidelines discussed in Chapter 1, "Effective Networking Solution Design Process"—it is important to keep in mind the ultimate goal that the solution will support, regardless of the business sectors that SMBs find themselves in. Supporting existing or future applications is, needless to say, extremely critical. A security solution is necessary to protect the effective functioning of the business applications and the attendant information that they generate. But remember that although a security solution might appear attractive in and of itself, to be effective and useful, it must integrate well with the existing applications. If this sounds like an implementation rather than a design issue, keep in mind that the line separating the two is often thin. That is true especially in the minds of stakeholders, who have a keen interest in the final outcome of a solution rather than in maintaining a technical separation between the two stages (design and implementation) relating to a solution's deployment.

When it comes to the design and implementation stages of a networking solution project, careful management of stakeholder expectations is critical when a proposed solution is a replacement for something already in existence. Consider IP Telephony, for example. If you are considering a brand-new telephony deployment, chances are that IP Telephony solution(s) will win compared to their circuit-switching siblings because IP Telephony solutions facilitate effective and inexpensive business communications.

However, because telephony has been around much longer than computer networking, IP Telephony solutions will more than likely replace or significantly upgrade the existing telephony infrastructure. The SMB might be willing to live with the limitations of its existing installation if a significant investment in it has already been made that would have to be scrapped to proceed with the new solution. Thus, deploying a brand-new solution is quite different from replacing an existing, functioning one. During the design stage, the issue of implementation needs to be considered in much more depth for significant upgrades or replacements than for a brand-new deployment. This principle applies across all business sectors and sizes.

Business Sizes

From the point of view of designing a computer network or a networking solution, the business size influences the quantity of equipment, the level of its performance, the layout or network topology, and the interconnections between the networking equipment. Business size should not necessarily affect the type of functions that a network offers.

At a minimum, basic functions for the network in any size business should include the following:

- Internal and external connectivity for resource, file, and database sharing
- Support for common and specialized applications
- Security

In environments with existing legacy networks, you always need to ensure interconnection with legacy equipment and support for legacy applications. The business size might well determine the following:

- Whether the typical three layers (access, distribution, and core) are going to remain distinct or be collapsed into one or two layers

- Whether a single integrated appliance will be able to accommodate the relevant business needs (LAN/WAN connectivity and security, for example) or whether discrete devices optimized to perform routing, switching, or security functions are required

Consider a small office with a dozen or so employees occupying a fraction of a large office building. Then consider an enterprise with thousands of employees occupying several office buildings. What is the difference between these two environments from a network solution design point of view? Think about modularity and scalability. In every product category—whether it is routers, switches, firewalls, or telephony solutions—Cisco offers a scalable spectrum of products to accommodate a spectrum of business sizes. At the lower end of the spectrum, the approach might be to use fixed configuration and/or integrated products. Refer to Chapter 5, "Cisco Security Solutions," for a discussion of the spectrum of security products and solutions.

As you progress through the SMB size scale, a modular design approach using specialized blades that support routing, switching, security, or IP Telephony from a single chassis becomes more preferable and cost effective. A larger SMB size translates into higher capacity and higher port density on fixed-configuration switches or on blades for modular switch units, routers that switch more packets per second, or firewalls that support more simultaneous connections. Modularizing the SMB or even a larger enterprise into distinct units, applying appropriate product categories to those units, and integrating those units via a logically hierarchical topology is a key concept in designing scalable solutions for SMBs of varying sizes.

Business Missions

A business mission, often nicely framed and gracing the walls of the business establishment, proclaims the reason that a particular business exists. It might take a creative imagination to establish a connection between a business mission and a router, a switch, or a firewall humming along on a rack in a telecom closet, a data center, a dusty crawl space, or perhaps even under someone's desk. However, if you choose to accept the premise that a computer network is becoming as important as a common utility, those very devices—if configured and operating properly—are as important to the fulfillment of those flowery mission statements as employees being able to transport themselves to their places of work, the business having reliable power for all of the necessary office equipment (not just the networking gear), and workers being able to communicate via a variety of telephony services.

You ought to be willing to establish a working relationship between a business mission and the networking equipment or solutions. Take a moment to do the following:

- Clearly articulate how the existing network infrastructure and solutions support or detract from the fulfillment of the mission.
- Consider the impact on the business mission if the network or any specific solutions suddenly disappeared and were not going to be available for varying periods of time.

This exercise affords you and all of the stakeholders a bird's eye view of how a new solution is likely to support the mission. And having that bird's eye view provides a necessary refocus during the design stage, when it is easy to lose sight of the ultimate purpose of the design because of the extreme amount of technical detail that must be considered during the design process.

The Pitfalls of the One-Size-Fits-All Approach

Up to this point, the commonality of different SMB types has been stressed in the context of designing a computer network or a networking solution. But even if a network is perceived as a common utility, it is quite obvious that to function properly, the utility delivery systems need to have a proper hierarchical structure to provide effective service— for example, a city water main and high-voltage transmission lines do not terminate at people's homes or at small office buildings. In networking, the logical layers (access, distribution, and core) as well as the level of equipment performance approximate the hierarchies of the common utilities.

The one-size-fits-all approach might attempt to use similar equipment at all network layers and not recognize the need for varying levels of performance of the solutions discussed throughout this book. At one extreme, the pitfall of the one-size-fits-all design approach is overdesign, making the SMB pay for a level of performance or capacity that is much higher than it needs and that is out of range for the business model. This strategy might be adopted so the SMB can use the same equipment models throughout the enterprise. If the SMB makes a conscious decision that the lower support costs resulting from that approach offset the higher equipment costs, there is nothing wrong with this approach. However, this consideration should appear in the design document.

The other extreme of the one-size-fits-all approach is not having sufficient capacity or level of performance at the core or distribution layers. This happens for exactly the same reason as overdesign: The SMB is trying to use the same equipment models throughout the enterprise to save on support and/or configuration costs. Thus, when considering the deployment of either an isolated or an end-to-end networking solution, it is critical to distinguish between the common functions of solutions that span the business sectors, sizes, and missions and the elements of solutions that need to be customized, mostly in terms of equipment models and levels of performance. Common solution functions include the following:

- The generic ability to move information between locations (routing and switching)
- Providing security in terms of confidentiality, information integrity, or prevention of the denial of service
- The ability to support and to integrate with applications

Within each of the preceding common functions, the solution differentiators that must be observed across the spectrum of SMB types and sizes to avoid the one-size-fits-all pitfalls are as follows:

- The level of performance of routers and switches

- The degree of security or the use of integrated versus single-purpose security devices
- The configuration customization that is required to support specific applications

SMB Networking Solutions Design Considerations

The basis of any business transaction is the exchange of perceived value between the transacting parties. Designing a networking solution is not only a technical issue, it is a business proposition and a transaction.

For example, the value of a solution might be found in its sheer novelty, thus creating a perception on the part of an SMB's stakeholders of a business that is innovative, creative, and on the cutting edge of technology. That perception in turn could lead to higher levels of investment or an increase in the customer base that further expands the business. A single converged IP network transcending geographical boundaries and supporting multimedia communications (voice, streaming audio and video, selective video conferencing, and all of the traditional database and resource sharing functions) can be viewed as a trendsetter in ultimate productivity. That kind of perceived value tends to come from early adapters whose business mission (whether formally stated or not) demands that they be perceived as innovative and progressive. The value of a networking solution can also be associated with something that is perceived as a bit more mundane and mainstream, such as an incremental increase in productivity by occasionally allowing an employee to work remotely.

Whatever the SMB's position regarding a networking solution, the value proposition of the solution needs to be clearly articulated because it drives the design process. When considering the design of the solutions in the sections that follow, ponder the fundamental issue of value to the SMB resulting from each solution.

In addition, keep in mind that many solutions are organically grown together. Remote access can be designed for internal employees only, as a part of collaboration with partners, or as a part of customer care. In all instances, it is tied closely to security. Front office/back office integration requires that a solid networking infrastructure already be in place and that the software applications to be integrated are already functioning well.

When designing a networking solution, it is quite easy to be drawn into the process of solving all of the existing network problems that, from your perspective, represent separate issues. However, keep in mind that when it comes to the network, your perception typically has a higher granularity than the view of the executives who have to sign off on the design document and sign the purchase orders for labor and equipment to proceed with deployment. The executives tend to take a more integrated view of the network, in which many issues boil down to a simple question: Will it function well and support the business's goals?

You must always give consideration to the reconciliation of the highly granular versus the highly integrated views of the network. Otherwise, the potential for failure of the design process is high. The executive stakeholders will not sign off on a design that does not give significant consideration to implementation issues.

Network and Data Security Design Considerations

Ponder these questions in the context of considering the deployment of a security solution:

- Has the SMB placed a monetary value on having its computer network inaccessible for varying periods of time, from a few minutes to hours, or even days?

- Is the impact of system unavailability linear as a function of time, or does the impact spiral out of control at a certain point, causing the business to fail or lose a significant market share to competition?

- What is the impact of having employees spend many hours unproductively due to downtime?

- What is the impact of having confidential and proprietary information fall into the wrong hands?

- What is the impact of having mission-critical information imperceptibly altered or outright corrupted?

A key concept to keep in mind while designing security solutions is that a security solution is not equivalent to a security policy. A security solution supports a security policy but is not a substitute for one; that distinction, although it might seem clear, tends to get blurred during the design process if an SMB does not have a clearly defined policy.

SMBs without sufficient resources to afford internal network security staff probably lack a security policy and might be looking to you as a resource for developing it without even necessarily identifying the process in those terms. When you realize that this is happening, you must differentiate between the changing responsibilities: designing a solution to support a policy versus developing a policy that in turn will require one or more solutions to implement it. Although both tasks are valid, developing a security policy might have different legal ramifications than designing a security solution to implement it.

Design considerations for specific security solutions dealing with specific threats and deployment scenarios are discussed in Chapter 5. Chapter 4, "Overview of the Network Security Issues," provides an overview of security issues, including terminology, security threat categories and their respective antidotes, and the importance of developing a security policy before proceeding with any security implementations.

Remote Access Design Considerations

You should consider the following questions before defining the requirements for any form of a remote access solution:

- What is the value of having access to a corporate database anytime and from anywhere?

- Are there any other resources on the corporate network—such as high-performance printers, network management stations, or even individual networking devices—that it would be useful to access remotely?

- Who are the most likely candidates within the SMB's corporate structure to have remote access?
- Who are the least likely candidates for having remote access? Why?
- Is it possible that a mindset has developed that needs to be reevaluated regarding who should and should not have remote access?
- If remote access is offered, what are the acceptable performance criteria for it to be effective?
- What security considerations will accompany any form of remote access?

Answers to those questions drive the design process and determine the specificity of the solution, the remote user categories, the granularity in access levels for different groups of users, and the performance and security criteria for a solution to be effective.

Wireless Design Considerations

What is the value of retaining a connection to the network while maintaining physical mobility? Perhaps mobility in a certain SMB means occasionally carrying a notebook computer from an office cubicle to a conference room and then connecting the notebook to the network in the conference room via a wired outlet in the same manner as it is done in the cubicle. In this case, there probably is not much reason to consider the design of a wireless network.

But what if the work atmosphere at the SMB location is much more dynamic, prewired meeting facilities more limited, and coworkers routinely need to get together to collaborate or to do research on various projects while retaining network access? If a meeting facility has a limited number of wired network connections, it means that a switch might have to be set up locally to provide network access, and cables might snake all over the room—not exactly a scalable or productive environment. What is the value of a wireless solution under those circumstances? Also, consider an automated production facility in which requests for inventory delivery from a manufacturing floor must be transmitted to mobile operators on the warehouse floor. The need for a wireless design in this situation would be greater than in a business that requires only an occasional walk from a cubicle to a conference room.

You need to consider the following questions, and possibly others, when designing a wireless solution:

- Are productivity gains (due to mobility while retaining network access) or savings (from not having to install cabling and cross-connect closets) sufficiently offsetting the cost of design, installation, and maintenance of a wireless solution?
- How secure will the solution have to be, and where will the access points need to be located, to provide sufficient coverage for those authorized to use the wireless local-area network (WLAN) and yet not let it extend beyond the facility to public areas where anyone can tap into it?
- Is the wireless approach considered only for LANs or for WANs as well?

- Will the SMB proceed with a radio frequency (RF) site survey, which is always strongly recommended for larger wireless installation, or will a site survey be skipped, with all of the attendant implications of not identifying potential sources of interference, connection boundaries, and RF dead spots?

The Cisco wireless solution is discussed in Chapter 6, "The Wireless LAN Solution."

IP Telephony Design Considerations

What is the value of deploying an IP Telephony solution if the existing telephone system already works well? You can assume that an SMB will have some form of a telephony infrastructure already in place. There are plenty of questions to ask when considering an IP Telephony solution:

- What is the investment (in terms of time and money) that has been put into the existing infrastructure? Does the high-level design approach require leaving what is already in place (and not changing it in any way), replacing it entirely, replacing it partially, or integrating it with new equipment?
- How old is the existing telephony infrastructure?
- What is its level of depreciation?
- What are the recurring maintenance costs?
- What is the level of expertise required on the part of support personnel for moves, adds, and changes to the infrastructure, and how long does it take to accomplish them?
- How are phone calls made within the enterprise?
- How are phone calls made outside of the enterprise?
- Is the enterprise a single building, or does it encompass multiple locations?
- Are the calls between the locations toll or local calls?
- Is a private data network between the locations already in place? If so, what is the capacity of that network?
- Is the network perhaps already multiplexing traditional Public Switched Telephone Network (PSTN) lines with data?
- Does the SMB have a sufficient number of lines for outside calls, or do employees run into problems when attempting to dial out?
- Does the SMB know if the customers calling in get a lot of busy signals because of an insufficient number of lines, or is it easy to get through?
- What are the features of the current system that are most frequently used? Are there features that nobody uses? If so, why? Is it because they are too difficult or cumbersome to use, or are they simply unnecessary?
- Is there a list of features that users deem desirable that are not available within the current system?

Telephone service is considered a common utility, and overhauling any kind of utility represents an overhaul of an element of the business infrastructure, which can have a significant impact on business operations. When considering IP Telephony, the issue of Voice over IP (VoIP) inevitably comes up. Although IP Telephony is closely coupled with VoIP, to the point where the two expressions are often used interchangeably, there is a difference between them.

VoIP is the enabler for IP Telephony. VoIP represents a technology that encompasses numerous protocols and standards from the Internet Engineering Task Force (IETF) groups and from the International Telecommunications Union Telecommunications Standardization Sector (ITU-T) to allow the transmission of voice traffic over a packet-switched (IP-based) as opposed to a circuit-switched network. IP Telephony refers to the utilization of VoIP to create telephony systems with many advanced features that are not available in traditional circuit-switched telephony installations.

In the context of more than a century of telephony history, VoIP is a relatively recent phenomenon—it is a newcomer that dates to the mid-1990s. However, since its inception, there has been a general consensus in the industry that VoIP has progressed through at least three generations and that its impact has been felt widely in both the carrier and the enterprise markets through ever-more-sophisticated IP Telephony solutions, which are discussed in Chapter 8.

Partner Collaboration Design Considerations

The following questions are just some of the queries that you will need to address to develop a direction for deploying a collaboration solution:

- What is the business value of collaboration with partners?
- What exactly is the manner of the collaboration that an SMB envisions? Is it a matter of one of the following?
  - Providing partners with remote access to internal proprietary tools or knowledge databases on the SMB's network to facilitate problem solving related to the SMB's products that the partners support
  - Having a team of individuals drawn from a group of partners being able to work together effectively for a short period of time on a marketing or an engineering project
  - Setting up an e-mail list to enable the required collaboration
- Is the use of e-mail without even setting up a special list adequate?
- Does the collaboration require exchange of design documents that are subject to strict version control?

Usually, a collaboration solution with business partners, vendors, or even customers boils down to providing them with appropriate access to some of the SMB's internal resources.

That, in turn, can ease the pressure on the SMB's personnel to interact with the relevant parties over the phone, via e-mail, or in person.

The key issues to consider when granting access are as follows:

- What is the level of access to be granted to the partners?
- Does the resulting increase in the SMB's operational efficiency and the savings in personnel time sufficiently offset the resources required to set up the appropriate access levels and to offer the necessary training and technical support to ensure that the setup is being used effectively?

By definition, providing varied access levels from the outside to internal resources implies having to consider the issue of security, which in turn implies a security solution. And the implementation of a security solution should be subject to a security policy. The process of developing a security policy is discussed in Chapter 4.

The mechanics of enabling collaboration with partners, vendors, or customers could require setting up a server on one of the SMB's demilitarized zones (DMZs) or providing virtual private network (VPN) access to the SMB's internal servers residing on the private network. It is entirely possible that SMB's personnel might already have a VPN set up to access the internal network. If VPN access is offered to partners, it becomes a matter of configuring proper authentication, restricting authorization to the relevant resources, and periodically generating reports about their activities. Setting up access to a DMZ server could also take place via a VPN. Alternatively, it could be set up in a more open way, where everyone has access to that server but must log in with a password. More open access to the server on the DMZ could result in greater reliance on the server's operating system (OS) security features to protect it from being breached, which implies that the OS's security level would have to be consistent with the SMB's security policy.

Customer Care Design Considerations

What is the value of an effective customer care solution? It is the lifeblood of a business! Any self-respecting business is well aware that without properly caring for its customers and offering them value for its products and services, it is not likely to stay in business for too long. But what exactly is a customer care solution? Customer care solutions vary as a function of business size and sector.

However unique or standard a customer care solution turns out to be, it is generally enabled via the networking infrastructure. The solution could be as simple as having a well maintained website with routine updates about a company's products or services. The website could be further enhanced with online ordering capability and spruced up with regularly updated links to URLs deemed of interest to the customer base. Customer care might mean regular communication with select customers via e-mail about special offers. Or it could require an IP-enabled call center offering 24×7 technical or problem-resolution support. It could also call for access to internal resources as a function of the customers' relationship with the SMB. Those resources could be digital documentation, technical information relating to the purchased products, or downloads of software updates or bug fixes if the SMB is a software vendor.

Just remember that a key design consideration for any customer care solution is its ongoing availability after it is released to the customer base. If a customer care solution is offered but it is unreliable because it does not work well or it is routinely unavailable, the situation can lead to a high degree of frustration on the part of the customers and can ultimately defeat the very purpose for which the solution was developed.

Front Office/Back Office Integration

Perhaps you are wondering what front office/back office integration has to do with networking solutions to begin with. It is simple—think applications. As mentioned earlier in this chapter, the network routing/switching infrastructure, as well as any of the other networking solutions (security, remote access, or wireless), must support and integrate well with the existing or planned applications.

The applications that customers "interact" with directly that relate to sales and marketing are customarily referred to as *front office* (facing the customer) *applications*. Those applications could include order entry, customer profiles, or general account maintenance in a call center or via a self-service, web-based interface. The applications that support the processes that are not directly seen by the customer (order processing, production, inventory control, or other accounting functions) are typically considered the *back office applications*. The back office applications are also referred to as the enterprise resource planning (ERP) applications.

What is the value of having the front and back office applications integrated into an effective customer relationship management (CRM) system? That is the question that the SMB's executive stakeholders need to answer. Making that decision will probably be a far more complex process than deciding to deploy network security or remote access. However, if the SMB decides to proceed with a custom, in-house integration or an off-the-shelf CRM solution, it must ensure proper connectivity between the relevant locations and sufficient bandwidth and processing power within the networking infrastructure to allow for the exchange of data generated by the CRM solution. Although it might not be absolutely critical for you to understand the specific functions of each of the applications, it is critical to understand the load that they place on the network and their security features.

The integration process might also require a specific functionality, like the support for multicasting within routers and switches or the addition of wireless LAN because a portion of the CRM is useless without the wireless mobility. From a security perspective, with integrated applications, the level of granularity in access and authorization becomes far more critical than with standalone isolated application islands.

Solution Identification and Discovery Process for SMBs

It is hard to imagine that today a successful SMB of any size is going to function without a networking solution, even if it means the most rudimentary file or printer sharing. When prioritizing the spectrum of networking solutions according to their importance and deployment, it is helpful to categorize them in terms of direct versus indirect support of the business mission.

If a wireless solution is a must in a manufacturing facility because of the impracticality of running cables or the exorbitant costs associated with doing so, that wireless solution directly supports the business mission. Forms of remote access in this scenario might be deemed desirable but not necessarily critical to the direct support of the business mission. Security considerations apply to both wireless and remote access deployments. Thus, in this example, the identification process yields that a wireless solution is a must, relevant security in support of it is a must, overall security is a distant second, and remote access is a "nice to have" capability that might happen someday. Following are some of the con and pro arguments for deploying various solutions.

The Case Against and for a Security Solution

The obvious case against a security solution (as well as any other networking solution, for that matter) is that the solution is complex, partial at best, and expensive to implement and to maintain. As discussed in Chapter 5, Cisco security solutions run the gamut in terms of ease of implementation, range of threats that they protect against, and cost.

What any SMB contemplating a security solution ought to know is that a security vendor like Cisco is not in the business of developing specific security policies for SMBs. In the process of attempting to sell a solution, a vendor can offer assistance in guiding the development of a security policy, but the SMB must recognize that without a policy and without the business placing a value on the assets to be protected, it is easy for the SMB to shoot down any proposed solution. So the SMB must clearly communicate to the designer the need for a solution and the degree of required protection before arguing against the solution because of its cost or complexity.

If an SMB has nothing to protect, the case against a security solution is clear-cut: There is no need for one. If an SMB comes to the conclusion that its network and information assets are worth protecting, the case for a security solution is even more clear-cut: It should get one. If the SMB reaches this conclusion, you can begin to determine the appropriate solution from a range of choices.

As discussed in Chapters 4 and 5, implementing a security solution is not a static, one-time event; it is an ongoing process of reexamining the value of what needs to be protected against the well-known and emerging threats to determine if the degree of deployed protection is adequate. The good news is that, as a general rule, security solutions from Cisco are getting easier to deploy, offer an increasingly comprehensive and integrated level of protection against varied threats, and are geared toward a spectrum of SMB budgets.

The Case Against and for a Remote Access Solution

The case against a remote access solution might be as simple as the perception on the part of an SMB that a solution is not needed because the business does not understand the possibilities associated with it. In that case, you should make sure the SMB considers the business possibilities that a remote access solution offers.

Remote access by itself is a generic solution without a face. But what if it translates into the following?

- A flexible work environment, by allowing employees occasionally to work from home, thus boosting employee morale and commitment to the business

- A high degree of collaboration with business partners, thus decreasing time-to-market cycles and boosting productivity

- Improved customer service, by allowing customers to place orders online, view order status, or search through an SMB's databases

These benefits sound like e-commerce, customer care, or just online access, but underneath them is the ability to remotely access SMB's resources. Every time someone logs on to the Internet, it is a form of remote access. Try taking that away from businesses and individuals alike and observe the impact.

The case for a remote access solution is quite compelling if the prospective SMB considers the solution in terms of business activities that it facilitates and the resulting value that it creates for the business. Remote access is the ultimate enabler of modern-day business communications. Strong security that is currently available through VPNs and firewalls adds to the appeal of remote access solutions.

The Case Against and for a Collaboration with Partners Solution

Making the case against or for a collaboration with partners solution depends to a large extent on the existing SMB's network implementation. For example, if an SMB already has an effective VPN solution, then granting outsiders access to internal resources becomes a matter of Authentication, Authorization, and Accounting (AAA). Separate Virtual LANs (VLANs) for different partners on the SMB's internal network might be the result of applying the AAA principle to partner access. If an SMB already has a firewall solution with one or more DMZs, collaboration with partners might also be a matter of providing them with the needed resources on the DMZ networks.

Because any collaboration solution is closely tied to security, an SMB should have a well-developed security policy and update it when a collaboration solution is being considered.

If remote access and, consequently, security solutions are not in place, there might be a stronger case against collaboration with partners because that solution might require a more comprehensive design. It depends on how exactly collaboration with partners is defined. Simple collaboration could be a matter of additional configuration or setup without any new hardware or software. However, remote access and security already in place will ease any collaboration deployment and create a strong case for it, subject of course to SMB's business objectives. Naturally, not every SMB is going to have partners to collaborate with.

The Case Against and for a Customer Care Solution

There is really no effective case against a customer care solution. No magic formula defines such a solution because it is unique to each business, but if this lack of a clear-cut definition is used as an argument against designing and implementing one, it is a weak argument at best.

The case for a customer care solution is simple. Other networking solutions—including IP Telephony, security, wireless, and the well-developed networking infrastructure—all stand in support of developing effective customer care, whether it takes the form of a call center, online banking, or VPN access by customers to internal resources.

The Case Against and for a Front Office/Back Office Integration Solution

The overwhelming case against a front office/back office integration solution is that it is generally a complex process that requires a lot of up-front planning and preparation. Such a process is not something that a typical SMB might be readily willing to undertake given the high level of risk associated with the entire process, the level of project management expertise required to see it through to completion, and the required degree of understanding of the existing applications environment and business processes.

The case for a front office/back office integration solution is equally strong. It can increase revenues and reduce costs through more focused and targeted customer service and the reduction of production overhead or the cost of sales. The availability of high-performance computing platforms and networking infrastructure that is capable of large throughput over long distances facilitates the deployment of complex applications, which an integrated CRM/ERP application suite can certainly be.

Summary

Designing a networking solution with the intent of bringing it to fruition through implementation is a business transaction. It is in your and the design process's best interest if that transaction is perceived by an SMB as valuable.

Business sizes and sectors usually impact the quantity and the level of equipment performance within a networking solution. As a general rule, all SMBs share the need for similar solution functions. Modularizing the enterprise and adhering to hierarchical interconnection of the infrastructure components (routers and switches) become keys to a scalable network design.

Cisco offers a spectrum of products in each solution category to accommodate varying business sizes. Any networking solution must support applications that are unique to varying SMB categories and critical to any SMB's success. Networking solutions do not operate in isolation; there is interdependency between them, with certain solutions being the enablers for others. Each networking solution has pros and cons that should be considered before proceeding with design and implementation.

CHAPTER 3

Network Infrastructure Requirements for Effective Solutions Implementation

In Chapter 2, "SMB Networking Environments and Solutions Design Considerations," I introduced the idea of the network infrastructure as a common utility. This chapter considers the building blocks of that infrastructure, some of the industry standards and protocols that govern it, and the acceptable best practices to make the network utility an effective tool in facilitating solutions that are discussed in the subsequent chapters.

Just as no one can force a homeowner to fix leaky faucets or running toilets, no one can force a small-medium business (SMB) to install and administer networks properly. Therefore, SMBs can have network cables running all over the office floors (subject to being stepped on and damaged), file servers and switches sitting under desks or in cramped quarters (subject to being accidentally shut off and overheating), or routers placed in unsecured locations (subject to being easily disconnected from a WAN service or an Internet service provider [ISP]). The impacts of poor network installation and administration are obvious. They include intermittent problems resulting from damaged or substandard cabling procedures, loss of access to applications for varying periods of time, or disconnection from the Internet and/or a portion of a larger internetwork, with all of the attendant implications.

If an SMB goes to the trouble of setting up a network to support its business operations, it should be in the SMB's best interest to install and to maintain the network infrastructure so that it functions well and is not subject to routine outages—similar to a properly working plumbing or electric service. However, ultimately, every SMB needs to determine the value to the business of a properly functioning network.

Assuming that the value is present and that it is significant, consider the following elements that make up and affect the functioning of an effective network infrastructure:

- Telecommunications (telecom) closets (TCs), with all of the cabling that they terminate and the networking equipment (switches and routers) that they house
- Data centers or computer rooms housing network servers and storage systems
- The user desktop environment, which is composed of workstations and network peripherals
- Network upgrades planning (as part of the design process)
- Applications, choices in e-mail systems, and approaches to network management

The Telecom Closets

According to the TIA/EIA-568 standard, the primary purpose of a *telecommunications closet (TC)* is the termination of the horizontal cable distribution. In the cabling hierarchy, horizontal cables feed the data outlets in the *work areas*, which are defined as the locations where the network users reside. In multi-TC environments, a TC also terminates *backbone cabling* (intrabuilding cabling between TCs) and facilitates the horizontal-to-backbone cabling cross-connection. Generally, TCs are real closets or rooms that should be physically secure and supplied with adequate power and ventilation.

The following are common sights in TCs:

- Patch panels (terminating horizontal cables)
- Numerous patch cables (extending from the patch panels to the networking equipment)
- Power protection equipment
- Rows of racks that house switches, routers, firewalls, VPN concentrators, uninterruptible power supplies (UPSes), CSUs/DSUs (channel service units/data service units)
- Other network gear

WAN services and Internet feeds usually terminate in the TCs as well. In larger enterprises, cable feeds from multiple TCs aggregate in the intermediate cross-connects (ICs), with the cabling between the ICs forming an interbuilding backbone. Figure 3-1 illustrates the generic components of a telecom closet.

Newer office buildings that were designed with computer networking in mind probably observe cabling standards. However, there are numerous network installations where, for whatever reasons, an SMB is not able to adhere to the industry cabling standards and still have the network work. If there are no data outlets in the walls, the horizontal cabling might be snaking along the floors, in the plain sight of the users, and going directly from the end-user devices into a switch that is under someone's desk. A firewall, router, or any other network equipment might not be far removed. In those cases, the telecom closet assumes more of a logical and an informal meaning.

Effectively, the network gear and the real estate that it occupies become a TC. Placing switches, routers, firewalls, or any other network gear outside of the physical TC (or at least a consciously designated area approximating a TC) is not the recommended approach to installing and maintaining a solid network infrastructure. However, a designer is bound to bump into such scenarios eventually while attempting to design a security, wireless, or an IP Telephony solution at an existing installation. In the short run, a network can continue to work without the adherence to the industry-recommended cabling and equipment placement standards. Over a longer period of time, though, such a network's scalability is bound to suffer as expanding or troubleshooting the network gets more and more labor intensive.

Figure 3-1   *Generic Components of a Telecom Closet*

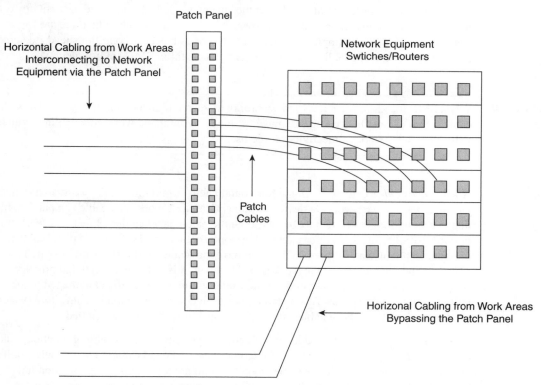

Consider now the three key components of a typical TC. They correspond to the bottom three layers of the Open Systems Interconnection (OSI) reference model:

- Patch panels and cabling (Layer 1, physical)
- Switches (Layer 2, data link)
- Routers (Layer 3, network)

The following sections discuss these three components and many of the associated design issue and protocols.

Patch Panels, Horizontal Cabling, and Work-Area Cabling

Patch panels are wiring intermediaries that relieve the strain on the cables that connect the end-user devices to the network equipment (typically switches). Effectively, they are static switchboards. Incoming horizontal cables from the user work areas are permanently punched down in the back of the patch panels and extended via patch cables from the ports on the front of the patch panels to the appropriate networking equipment. With patch panels, it is easy to redirect horizontal cables to different network equipment ports simply by moving the patch cables.

The use of patch panels in TCs is an accepted and standardized practice. However, the realities of data networking are such that the acceptable industry practices are not always followed. And because there are not necessarily code requirements (like there are for an electrical service, for example), the pressure of various business conditions leads to some creative approaches in cabling and equipment placement in SMB environments.

WARNING   When SMB locations are not cabled according to the recommended industry standards, the cabling that is most likely to get damaged is the horizontal and work-area cabling, which will result in network connectivity problems.

A *work-area cable* extends from the horizontal cable termination in the work area (a data jack in a wall) to a networking device in the work area. A work-area cable is a patch cable that is usually longer (10 feet to 14 feet) than the patch panel cables (3 feet to 7 feet). It is possible to collapse a work-area cable, a horizontal cable, and the TC patch panel cable into one (one cable instead of three cables) and have that cable go directly from a switch in a TC to an end-user device in the work area. However, it is not a recommended practice because the connectors at both ends of the cables are more likely to get damaged by being pulled through tight spaces. Alternatively, in-house connectorization might follow (watch out for the quality of those cables!) if any unconnectorized cables are pulled.

If an SMB installation cannot adhere to the industry-recommended cabling practices, take extra measures to ensure the safety of the otherwise deployed cables. They should not lie unprotected in heavy traffic areas, be wound around hot water pipes, or share conduits with electric wires. Try testing the cables for continuity and, if possible, for adherence to relevant standards (such as Category (Cat) 5, Cat 5e, or Cat 6).

Any respectable cabling installation that follows industry standards should be accompanied by test results and documentation for the entire cable plant. Optionally, consider going wireless if industry-standard cabling installation is not possible and a creative but a substandard cabling installation is not acceptable. The Cisco wireless solution is discussed in more detail in Chapter 6, "The Wireless LAN Solution."

Switches

Ethernet switches are now the mainstay of the LAN infrastructure. Switch deployment considerations should include the following:

- Modular versus fixed-configuration switches
- Switch port density and speeds
- Number of virtual local-area networks (VLANs) required per installation
- Switch trunk ports and trunking

- Switch uplink ports and uplinks
- Use of the Spanning Tree Protocol (STP) optional features

Modular Versus Fixed-Configuration Switches

The decision to proceed with a modular versus a fixed-configuration switch model should depend on the following:

- The SMB's topology
- The number and type of current users
- The anticipated future demand for additional switch ports

For a single location with a stable number of users and no foreseeable need for interconnects with other networks, a single fixed-configuration unit with the appropriate port density is probably the most appropriate and economical choice.

Cisco offers several fixed-configuration switch product lines, including the 1900, the 2900, and the 3500 series. The Catalyst 2948G and 2980G models from the 2900 series are fixed-configuration units with a port density of 48 and 80, respectively, port speeds ranging from 10 to 1000 Mbps, and a backplane switching capacity of 24 Gbps.

Consider an existing network installation at an SMB with a demand for 60 switch ports that is currently accommodated via a combination of several small hubs and switches from multiple vendors. The current setup results in poor performance, and the multivendor device-level management of switches is becoming a headache for the network administrator. This combination of factors is having an adverse financial impact on the SMB.

A single 2980G Catalyst unit would offer 2-Gbps ports for server connections and 80 10/100-Mbps autosensing ports for the network users or other devices, leaving room for at least 30 percent growth in the number of users. This single fixed-configuration switch solution would eliminate crossover cables, multivendor device-level management, the potential for Ethernet loops, and a high level of collisions that results in marginal performance.

Modular switch models are available in the 2900 series and the 4500 series as well as in the Cisco flagship product line, the 6500 Catalyst family. The 6503, 6506, 6509, and 6513 Catalysts come with chassis of 3, 6, 9, and 13 slots, respectively. As a function of the SMB's requirements, 6500 series Catalysts accommodate 10/100/1000 switching, routing, firewalling, VPN, and IP Telephony solutions.

Switch Port Density and Speeds

A general rule of thumb is that at brand-new installations, the number of unused spare ports should be about 20 percent of the total number of switch ports available. This guideline accommodates reasonable growth without leaving a business with undue investment in equipment producing no immediate return on investment (ROI).

Calculating the number of required switch ports should be one of the easier aspects of the design process. Follow these steps:

1 Count the number of users and/or devices that need to plug into the switch.

2 Make allowances for trunking and uplink ports.

3 Consult the switch data sheets to calculate the available number of switch ports.

   On a fixed-configuration switch, the number of ports is usually reflected in the switch model.

   On a modular switch, there are plenty of module choices to populate the switch. Count the total number of switch ports required versus the maximum number of ports that a switch can support when fully populated. From there, you can decide what port density modules to plug into the switch and whether or not to leave slots available for future expansion.

4 Allow for 20 percent growth, and you will have an idea of how many switch ports will be needed.

As an example, consider the 4500 and 6500 series switches. When fully populated, the highest-end models support 240 and 576 10/100/1000BASE-T ports, respectively. Assume that a designer already knows the network topology and the required number of switch ports for the entire installation. A summary chart with maximum port density and available speeds for all switch models under consideration would allow the designer to make decisions about which switches to consider for deployment and where, and which ones to eliminate. A building with a requirement for 350 switch ports would not be well served by even the highest-end single 4500 series switch.

Number of VLANs Required per Installation

In the nonswitched, legacy, Ethernet internetworks, which are composed of routers that interconnect shared-media and nonbridged LANs, the routers automatically break up the internetwork into collision domains and broadcast domains. For each collision domain, there is a corresponding broadcast domain of the same size, and both domains encompass the same group of LAN devices. In this type of scenario, the growing size of the collision domain (and the resulting degradation in network performance from the increasing level of collisions) would normally drive the process of ongoing network segmentation with routers.

In the modern-day switched Ethernet LANs, the size of each collision domain is reduced to a single device that is plugged into a switch port, thus making collisions and collision domains irrelevant in the context of network design. However, all of the devices still participate in a single broadcast domain, which, in turn, can lead to a performance penalty if the broadcast domain gets too large—but only if the switch or switches are configured with a single rather than multiple VLANs.

Technically speaking, VLANs exist to define Layer 2 broadcast domains. In switched LANs, from the perspective of network performance, the growing size of a broadcast domain (rather than the size of a collision domain) often determines the need for further network segmentation with additional VLANs.

Before you create multiple VLANs, you should be clear about the technical and business reasons for their existence and the implications of their use. Although having multiple VLANs can improve network performance, it can also present administrative challenges.

The following reasons might be a sufficient deterrent to jumping on the multi-VLAN bandwagon without a solid reason. Simply put: Do not define multiple VLANs at any installation for the sheer joy of it; be mindful of the attendant implications.

- Intern-VLAN communication requires that traffic between VLANs be routed.
  - Having to route traffic between VLANs might require additional funds for external routing equipment if switches do not support the routing function. Routing-capable switches are preferable to using an external router, but they also might cost more.
  - Additional configuration is required to set up inter-VLAN routing.
- Multiple VLANs might require you to develop a greater granularity in the IP addressing scheme than would otherwise be needed.
- Multi-VLAN, multiswitch environments require trunking and the configuration of trunk ports. Trunk configuration requires that you understand the VLAN encapsulation methods, the trunking modes, the acceptable combinations of trunking modes, and several additional protocols related to trunking.
- In general, to minimize errors, the multiswitch, multi-VLAN configuration requires considerably greater care and configuration expertise than a single VLAN environment.

Even though VLANs were not created for the purpose of providing security, they enhance security by isolating traffic between broadcast domains. From a business point of view, the primary purpose of VLANs is likely to be the isolation of traffic between different areas of the SMB's operations, which minimizes the potential that unauthorized personnel will intercept sensitive traffic or access restricted resources.

The combination of technical and business considerations ought to determine the specific number of VLANs at any SMB installation. The key technical consideration is performance. VLANs can keep the size of broadcast domains manageable so that the level of broadcast traffic does not interfere with critical network applications and employee productivity.

In a small SMB installation, using a single default VLAN might be adequate as long as the level of broadcast traffic does not cause a noticeable performance degradation and there are no requirements for isolating traffic between groups of users. However, a different installation of identical size might have one or more broadcast-intensive applications that need their own VLANs and a requirement for isolation between varying user groups. Going through the requirements process as outlined in Chapter 1, "Effective Networking Solution Design Process," should help determine the number of VLANs that any SMB will require.

Switch Trunk Ports and Trunking

Trunking implies the presence of multiple VLANs in a multiswitch environment. Trunking design considerations include the following:

- The type of VLAN encapsulation method to use to facilitate it (ISL or 802.1q)
- The mode to use to configure the trunk ports (on, off, auto, desirable, or negotiate)
- What additional protocols to use as a function of the VLAN encapsulation type or the approach to VLAN management

Additional protocols that you can use in conjunction with trunking include the VLAN Trunking Protocol (VTP), Dynamic ISL (DISL), and the Dynamic Trunking Protocol (DTP). VTP facilitates more effective VLAN management by allowing the separation of switches into domains (VTP domains) and then communicating the creation and deletion of VLANs on any switch throughout the entire domain. DISL and DTP facilitate automatic negotiation over a point-to-point link between Catalyst switches to enable or to disable ISL.

ISL, which is advisable in Cisco-only switching environments, is the Cisco proprietary protocol for multiplexing VLAN traffic over a trunk port. 802.1q is an IEEE standard that facilitates trunking between switches from different vendors. However, to avoid potential problems with interoperability because of variation in the protocol implementations, the designer should also consider not creating trunks between switches from multiple vendors. Instead, consider confining VLANs to single switches (or groups of switches from the same vendor) and then routing between VLANs that would otherwise be part of the same VLAN if trunking were employed.

Switch Uplink Ports and Uplinks

The meaning of the term *switch uplink ports* varies as a function of the network topology.

- In a topology that differentiates between the core, distribution, and access layers, the uplink ports represent the lower-layer switch ports that are used to link with the higher layer switches. The uplink represents the connection between the switches.
  - If all three layers were present, the uplink ports would be configured on the access layer switches to connect to the distribution layer, and on the distribution layer switches to connect to the core layer.
  - In a more condensed topology without the distribution layer, the uplinks would connect the access to the core layer.

- In the collapsed single-layer topology, there would be no need for uplink ports to connect the layers, but there still might be a need for uplink ports to interconnect individual switches operating at the same layer.

What differentiates an uplink port from a trunk port is that an uplink has a broader meaning, which technically could encompass a trunk port. An uplink can exist between switches that belong to the same VLAN. An uplink can also be a routed point-to-point link between the topology layers, if, for example, the design calls for all of the traffic coming from the access layer into the higher layer(s) (distribution or core) to be routed at Layer 3. In that case, the uplink would probably require its own IP subnet.

A key design consideration for uplinks is redundancy, which translates into the number of physical ports that need to be allocated for the uplinks and the ability of the switch software to switch between uplinks in case of failure.

Use of the STP Optional Features

At first glance, use of the STP in switched internetworks might appear to be an option. After all, Radia Perlman developed the protocol for bridged networks while at Digital Equipment Corporation (DEC) (when DEC still existed) at the time when bridges were making their mark in the networking arena. Today, bridges are a legacy technology, yet STP has since been standardized by IEEE and is of paramount importance in switched networks.

The purpose of STP is to ensure a single path between any two devices in Ethernet networks—in other words, to prevent Ethernet loops. Activating STP can be avoided in smaller networks through diligent administration, but the reality of today's switched Ethernet internetworks dictates its deployment.

The leap in performance when you use switches instead of bridges is undeniable, but, theoretically, switches are multiport bridges. This makes STP as relevant or more relevant in modern switched environments than it was in the legacy, bridged networks. To experience the effects of not having operational STP, have multiple paths between switches belong to a single VLAN or multiple links from a hub go into a switch.

The design issues for STP do not deal with whether to deploy it or not; instead, such issues include which version to deploy (802.1d is common), whether to influence the root bridge section through configuration, and what optional features to configure. Cisco offers a number of optional STP features, including PortFast, Bridge Protocol Data Unit (BPDU) Guard, UplinkFast, BackboneFast, Root Guard, and Loop Guard. When configured properly, all of these optional features increase the switched network stability by decreasing STP convergence times (when new devices are introduced into the network or failures occur) and by reducing the potential for creation of temporary loops. Given the importance and complexity of STP, it benefits you, as a switched network designer, to understand the operation of STP before proceeding with design decisions regarding configuration.

Routers

In SMB environments, routers interconnect VLANs, facilitate access from private LANs to the Internet, and allow for the creation of WANs. Over the past decade, the implementation of the routing function has evolved significantly. The following are router deployment considerations:

- Modular versus fixed-configuration routers
- Dedicated routers versus integrated appliances
- The choice of a routing protocol
- Logical IP addressing for the internetwork
- Internet connectivity and WAN services

Modular Versus Fixed-Configuration Routers

As a general rule, lower-end access routers tend to have fixed port configurations, whereas mid-range and high-end routers are modular. The purpose and size of the SMB's internetwork determine the type of routers that an SMB needs. To determine which type of routers to deploy, consider where and why the routing function is needed:

- Is the routing required between VLANs at a single office building? How many VLANs are there?
- Is routing required because the private network is geographically dispersed and branch locations require access to the headquarters data? What is the topology of the private network, and how many locations are there that must be connected?
- Is routing required for Internet access only? What type of Internet service is the SMB providing? Is the SMB a local or a regional ISP with a sizable number of Post Office Protocols (POPs) aggregating traffic to a central hub that has a high-capacity WAN connection to a Tier 1 provider?

Several techniques are available for routing between VLANs. Some of these include the traditional routing with a dedicated router interface connected to each VLAN, connecting (and configuring properly) a single router interface to a switch trunk port, the use of the route switch module (RSM) in switch product lines that support it (5000, 6500), or the use of the appropriate Cisco IOS image on the 4500 series supervisors.

In the case of a trunk-connected router interface, the router IOS must first and foremost support one of the trunk encapsulation methods. Next, the physical router interface would be configured with subinterfaces assigned to each VLAN that needs to be routed. The RSM allows for the defining of virtual VLAN interfaces that are assigned to each VLAN.

Each of the inter-VLAN routing techniques has advantages and limitations; see Table 3-1.

Table 3-1   *Advantages and Disadvantages of Inter-VLAN Routing Options*

Option	Disadvantage	Advantage
Single router interface per VLAN	Not very scalable	Allows for integration of certain legacy routing equipment into a switched internetwork, which might be economically advantageous
Trunk-connected routers	Might suffer from performance problems because all routing takes place over a single physical interface	Improves scalability
RSM	Available only in the higher-end switch product lines	Offers an integrated high-performance solution

Now, consider an SMB with fewer than 100 users, a single VLAN that occupies one physical location, and a T1/E1 or other broadband type (digital subscriber line [DSL], cable) access to the Internet. A single access router from the 800 series or the 1700 series accommodates the routing requirements in this scenario. Other design decisions might include what type of IOS feature (firewall, IP Security [IPSec] for VPNs) to purchase in case of a fixed-configuration unit (800 series), or what additional modules and type of IOS to configure in case of a modular unit (1700 series) to take maximum advantage of the initial investment required for the routing function.

On the other hand, an SMB with multiple VLANs, multiple geographical locations that need to be linked together with headquarters (via a private network or through the use of VPNs over the Internet), and with a need for Internet access at each location faces completely different routing requirements. Assume that there are 8 branches and 12 VLANs at the headquarters in this scenario. Although one or more of the access routers from the 800 or the 1700 series might be suitable for each branch location to accommodate the requirements of having its own Internet access as well as the connection to headquarters, the central location (headquarters) requires a higher-capacity router to aggregate all of the branch feeds and perform routing between the VLANs. A modular unit is needed for the central location.

An Internet-based VPN rather than a private leased-line network should be used to link the branches with the headquarters because the use of a VPN offers the greatest flexibility in WAN connectivity. What might be needed at the headquarters is a dedicated router that is equipped with a sufficient number of Ethernet ports (to accommodate the inter-VLAN routing) and a sufficiently high-capacity WAN port to connect to the Internet and to communicate with all of the branches. This requirement is met by a 7200 series (7204 VXR) router with a couple of eight-port Ethernet 10BASE-T port adapters (for the inter-VLAN routing) and a large number of WAN port adapter choices for the Internet connection.

However, if the SMB already has a 6500 series Catalyst switch for its headquarters' LAN users, there is no longer a need for a separate dedicated router. The 6500 series

Catalyst supports an RSM (as a daughterboard or integrated into the supervisor engine to accommodate the inter-VLAN routing), a FlexWAN module that shares WAN port adapters with the 7200 series routers to accommodate a wide range of Internet connections, and an IPSec/VPN module to accommodate the VPN requirement. This is a powerfully integrated network appliance.

Dedicated Routers Versus Integrated Appliances

The continuous propensity toward integration in the networking arena has led to more and more functionality being incorporated into each networking device. Consequently, a single physical unit (either fixed configuration or modular) can incorporate routing, switching, firewalling, and VPN functions. Integration reduces the number of discrete devices, simplifies cabling, and often eases administration. The downside of integration, compared to the use of dedicated discrete devices, might be poorer performance or less functionality in some areas.

When you consider dedicated routers versus integrated appliances, once again, the business model should drive the network design. An ISP that falls into the category of an SMB likely uses dedicated routers at its POPs and deploys other equipment to perform the firewalling, VPN, and LAN switching functions. On the other hand, an office with more than 50 employees might well benefit from integrating multiple functions into a single unit.

The Choice of a Routing Protocol

Routing is implemented within an internetwork via static routes or through the use of a dynamic routing protocol. Choose a routing protocol with the following design considerations in mind:

- The scalability of a protocol in the context of the current or anticipated size of the internetwork.

- The protocol convergence time, which affects performance and network availability.

- The protocol interoperability. This is applicable in multivendor environments because some protocols are proprietary whereas others are open standards.

- The IP addressing scheme. It is critical to determine if Variable Length Subnet Masking (VLSM) will be deployed because some protocols do not support it.

- Ease of configuration, which affects the level of expertise required for protocol deployment and subsequent management.

If an SMB has a single logical network and a single router connecting it to the Internet, a static route should suffice. When multiple routers are deployed within the SMB's internetwork, static routing becomes less and less scalable as the internetwork grows and there are more subnets to interconnect.

Routing Information Protocol (RIP) and its Cisco companion, Interior Gateway Routing Protocol (IGRP), are the simplest to configure. However, because they are distance-vector protocols, they converge slower than a link-state protocol like Open Shortest Path First (OSPF) or Cisco Enhanced IGRP (EIGRP) and do not scale well in larger internetworks.

RIP version 1 and IGRP are also poor choices if there is pressure on the IP address space because they do not support VLSM, which helps to optimize the effective use of the IP address space. RIP version 2, EIGRP, and OSPF all support VLSM. OSPF is an open Internet Engineering Task Force (IETF) standard (RFC 2328), whereas EIGRP is proprietary to Cisco. In Cisco-only environments, EIGRP is the preferred routing protocol. It is scalable, bandwidth efficient, and converges faster than RIP or IGRP. In multivendor environments, OSPF is preferable. Coexistence of multiple dynamic routing protocols is possible through redistribution.

Logical IP Addressing

The following are the design considerations for deploying an IP addressing scheme for an SMB:

- Use of private versus registered addresses
- Number of IP devices
- Number of logical networks/subnets
- Growth accommodation

As a general rule (which is naturally subject to exceptions), most SMBs do not need registered addresses for their internal networks. At the same time, most SMBs need access to the Internet, which requires registered addresses.

Private IP addressing (RFC 1918) alleviates the pressure on the registered address space and offers enterprises a flexible IP address deployment scheme. If access to the Internet is needed from the private network, Network Address Translation (NAT) needs to be deployed and configured properly. A private Class B offers 256 Class C subnets, which should accommodate the needs of even the largest SMB. If all of the addresses from a single Class B were used, the SMB would have more than 65,000 users or devices in need of IP addressing. That is stretching the SMB definition a bit!

Recall from Chapter 1 that an SMB is defined as having from 1 to 500 employees. To calculate the required address space, make the worst-case scenario assumption that an SMB has 500 employees, and then consider a scenario with the following requirements and how they will impact the choice of an addressing scheme:

- Two IP addresses are needed for each employee (one for a network device and one for an IP phone).
- There are 12 VLANs accommodating all of the users. They range in size from 20 to 80 ports. A separate, larger (more than 500 ports) voice VLAN exists for all of the IP phones.

- One IP-addressable network printer exists on each VLAN.
- There are 23 servers within the enterprise, a dozen of which are multihomed with dual network interface cards (NICs) to two VLANs.
- Thirteen LAN switches require one address each for management purposes.
- Routing takes place between all of the VLANs through the use of one RSM (rather than trunk-connected external routers or a dedicated router interface) per VLAN.
- One external router connects the enterprise of the Internet.

The logical network topology in this scenario uses two layers: an access layer and an aggregation layer, which combines the distribution and core layers into one. You can go through the calculations and add up the numbers to come up with the exact number of addresses and subnets required. You can then proceed to size up the subnets and develop an addressing scheme that is extremely efficient. Or, if you are going to use private addressing, you can adopt an addressing scheme beforehand that might not be the most efficient from the address usage point of view but that will accommodate significant growth and be easy to administer.

In SMB environments with addressing requirements similar to those of the preceding scenario, the efficiency of the address usage is quite irrelevant when private addressing is used. Of course, in large enterprises that fall outside the scope of an SMB definition, attention still has to be paid to efficient use even of the seemingly inexhaustible private address space. Examine the process of calculating the required addresses and trying to make the address space efficient versus coming up with an addressing scheme and using it to accommodate the addressing needs.

Calculating the number of the required addresses yields 1074 (1000 for the users + 12 for the printers + 35 for the server NICs + 13 for LAN switches + 13 for inter-VLAN routing + 1 for connection to the Internet router = 1074). Technically, five Class C addresses (5 × 256) offer more than sufficient address space—but, of course, that statement is totally meaningless unless the number of required subnets is also known. How many subnets are needed? From the preceding requirements, the number of subnets corresponds to the number of VLANs, which would be 13.

The voice VLAN requires 500+ addresses, with the remaining VLANs requiring between 20 and 80. The address space of two Class Cs accommodates the voice VLAN. Without trying to squeeze blood out of a turnip, assume that all of the remaining VLAN subnets are the same size, which would mean that each of them would need to have at least 80 addressable hosts. Half a Class C for each VLAN (128 less 1 or 2) will do, making the total requirement of eight Class C addresses. So much for the gymnastics of IP address space calculations.

Given that a Class B address is subnetable into 256 Class Cs, you could use a Class B address here, giving each nonvoice VLAN a /24 (a Class C) and the voice VLAN a /22 (four Class Cs). Doing so would leave plenty of room for any further expansion, both on individual VLANs and additional VLANs within the enterprise.

As a rule of thumb, the registered address space is tight, and the method of calculating the address requirements and then making the most efficient use out of the available space is a proper design approach. In the preceding calculations, if the addresses used were from the registered ranges, it would have been foolish to allow each VLAN to have up to 128 addresses rather than using VLSM to a greater extent and matching more precisely the number of addresses needed with the subnet size. However, with private addressing, getting involved in extensive calculations might be a waste of time.

Follow these steps when using private addressing:

1 Make a reasonable estimate of the number of subnets.

2 Estimate the size of the largest subnet.

3 See if a Class B with /24 subnetting will accommodate both the number of subnets (256) and the number of devices on each subnet (254).

   Or

   Just use the needed number of actual class Cs from the private range for all of the logical networks within the enterprise.

4 If more than 254 devices need an IP address on the same subnet, use a Class B with VLSM, creating a needed number of subnets with /23 or /22 subnetting to allow for 510 or 1022 addresses respectively on those subnets.

This process is probably the most effective way (least time consuming and easiest to administer) to approach the addressing needs when deploying private addressing.

Remember, though, that if a subnet needs more than 1000 addresses, you might want to reexamine the design because performance might become an issue. The additional benefit of a larger and more flexible private IP address space is the ability to embed into it information about the network topology.

Using private IP addressing in a multibuilding, multifloor environment with Class B /24 subnetting could mean using the subnet numbers (certain ranges from the third octet) to designate building locations and WAN links, while using the host IPs within certain ranges from the fourth octet to designate floors within a building. Certain addresses within each floor range could be designated for certain types of peripherals, such as printers. Embedding topology or administrative information into an IP addressing scheme is an individualized process and depends to a degree on a network administrator's understanding of IP addressing as well as his or her desire for consistency in network administration.

Internet Connectivity and WAN Services

Internet access considerations for SMBs include the following:

- Capacity of the Internet connection
- Security measures to be taken to protect the internal network from outside intrusion

- Deployment of any publicly accessible servers
- Level of integration of the Internet with the SMB's operations

An SMB might outsource all of its Internet-related operations to an ISP (another SMB) that specializes in web hosting and providing Internet access. With the exception of e-mail use, that SMB might not have further Internet access requirements. Compare this scenario to the ISP with multiple POPs and hundreds of customers. If one SMB is an Internet user and another facilitates that use, the relationship of their networks to the Internet will be drastically different. That difference will manifest through the network topology (one will be LAN-centric, the other WAN-centric), the type of equipment and security solutions (one or a few routers and/or firewalls versus a larger number), and the capacity and type of the connection(s).

From the Internet user SMB's perspective, the connectivity considerations include the type of service (DSL, cable, Frame Relay, or a dedicated leased line), the choice of bandwidth capacity within those services' typical ranges, and the use of a dedicated router and a firewall versus an integrated security appliance.

From the Internet provider SMB's perspective, the connectivity considerations include the number of POPs that must be connected and the associated topology (hub and spoke, full mesh, or something in-between), the type and capacity of the links between the POPs, the uplink capacity to a higher-level ISP (multiple T1s, T3, OC-3), potential peering/interconnection considerations with other ISPs, the choice of a routing protocol, Domain Name System (DNS) and firewalling, the hardening of routers against intrusion, and the stress of allocating the normally tight registered address space.

Typical WAN services for building private SMB networks overlap with the Internet services (leased lines, Frame Relay), but they also include emerging technologies. Gigabit Ethernet is extensible into the WAN arena at distances of up to 2000 kilometers through the use of fiber-optic transmission media and long-haul dense wave division multiplexing (DWDM) systems. Long Reach Ethernet (LRE) leverages older legacy wiring (Cat 1/2/3) over distances of up to 5000 feet (approximately 1.5 kilometers).

The traditional distinction between LANs and WANs—LANs operating over short distances (500 meters) at high speeds (10 to 100 Mbps) versus WANs operating at long distances (up to hundreds of kilometers) at lower speeds (64 Kbps to 1.5 Mbps)—is now completely blurred. Technologies exist to accommodate a wide spectrum of bandwidth capacities at just about any distance. (Consider 1000 Mbps up to 2000 km!) From a design perspective, the choice of WAN service is most often driven by its availability in a given geographical area.

Data Centers or Computer Rooms

Design considerations for the data centers or computer rooms and their contents include the following:

- Physical security of the facility
- Fire protection

- Adequate ventilation to dissipate the heat that is generated by the equipment that is stored there
- Power protection
- Disaster planning and recovery in the event that an unforeseen catastrophe should affect those critical locations

All these considerations facilitate the proper functioning and protection of what makes networks so indispensable to begin with: application servers and storage devices that accumulate more and more of the SMB's data. Data centers might house some network gear, like routers and switches, but primarily they house servers, extended storage, and backup equipment.

Network Servers

Early vintage network operating systems (NOSes)—and the servers on which they were installed—supported basic file sharing and print services across the network. As NOSes have continued to evolve, they have incorporated more and more network services functions in addition to providing the required robust platforms for complex vertical applications. The network services include DNS, Dynamic Host Configuration Protocol (DHCP), remote access, routing, security (such as Remote Access Dial-In User Service [RADIUS], Terminal Access Controller Access Control System Plus [TACACS+]), and more. Numerous applications and database servers now populate data centers. They use a range of hardware platforms and operating systems (such as Windows, NetWare, and Solaris) to support critical business functions.

However, setting aside the applications for a moment, from the network infrastructure perspective, design considerations relating to servers boil down to the following:

- Will the servers be single or multihomed? That is, how many NICs will they have?
- What will be the connection type and speed between the servers and the switches? Will the servers connect to a switch at a predetermined speed? That is, will the connection parameters be hardcoded on both the server and the switch, or will they be negotiable? Is the number of servers at the site sufficient that a policy regarding server-to-switch connectivity might be necessary?
- What VLAN or multiple VLANs will the servers belong to?
- Will any of the server connections be a trunk?
- What are the server availability requirements?

Server Multihoming

Multihoming applies if you need to connect the server to multiple VLANs. Consider a scenario with three VLANs that share no other resources except a single server. There would not be a need for routing between the VLANs if the server were equipped with three NICs, each connecting to one of the VLANs.

Server Connection Speed and Parameters

There are no absolute standards for whether to allow parameter negotiation between a server and a switch. With the spectrum of Ethernet connections now ranging from 10 Mbps to 10 Gbps, with the 100/1000 Mbps being in the mainstream, it is advisable for servers to use the highest available speed. Experience dictates that at higher connection speeds (1000 Mbps or more), it is preferable to hardcode the parameters at both ends of the connection instead of allowing them to be autonegotiated.

Server VLAN Membership

The purpose of the server determines which VLAN or multiple VLANs it will belong to. If a server connects only to a single VLAN but needs to be accessed from other VLANs as well, remember that routing between the VLANs is required and that server traffic will be crossing multiple VLANs. Perhaps in this situation it might make better sense to use a single VLAN.

Server Trunk Port Usage

Connecting servers to VLAN trunk ports is possible (and has already been mentioned earlier in this chapter), but the server OS in combination with the NIC must support trunking.

Server Availability Requirements

Network services servers like DNS or DHCP have become an integral component of effective network infrastructure and administration. These servers must typically be more available than even the specific application servers. Whereas network services functions can reside on the same server as the business applications (and many times they do), consider a more robust design, in which they would be separate. Bringing down an applications server for maintenance, upgrade, or any other reason should not shut down key network services functions. In multilayer topologies, local servers (network services or applications) are typically plugged into the access layer switches. They tend to have lower availability requirements than enterprise servers, which are typically connected at the distribution or core layers. You should also consider having redundant hardware for enterprise servers.

Network Storage

A staggering evolution has taken place in mass storage technologies since the early 1990s. Storage capacities have increased dramatically while their physical size and power requirements have gone down. The capacities of storage solutions are now measured in terabytes (TB) as opposed to megabytes (MB), which represents an increase of six orders of magnitude. Gigabyte (GB) capacities are sandwiched between the megabytes and the terabytes.

Two approaches emerged to address the explosive demands for mass storage in network environments: storage-area networks (SANs) and network-attached storage (NAS). In addition to these two storage technologies, SMBs should not entirely overlook the more traditional direct-attached storage (DAS) approach, in which large-capacity disk drives are installed directly in the NOS servers. Those drives can be in the hundreds of gigabytes, which might be sufficient to meet the needs of enterprises with less demanding storage requirements.

SAN and NAS solutions should be viewed as distinct but complementary tools in the arsenal of a designer confronted with developing a storage solution for an SMB as part of the overall network design. Nothing prevents SAN and NAS from harmonious coexistence on the same internetwork.

Storage-Area Networks

A *storage-area network (SAN)* can be defined as a dedicated network whose primary purpose is to transfer data between computer systems and/or storage elements. The generic components of a SAN include a communications infrastructure (the network part), a management layer (configuration and control software), storage elements (disks, backup tapes), and computer systems (servers). The storage elements and the servers are interconnected via the network component or the communications infrastructure, which most frequently, but not always, is implemented with Fibre Channel switches. The products in the Cisco 9000 series family of Multilayer Directors and Fabric Switches (MDS) are aimed at supporting the SAN technology. SAN solutions are available from multiple vendors, including IBM, EMC Corporation, Hewlett-Packard (HP), and Dell.

Because they have to do with networks, SANs invite almost an intuitive understanding on the part of network professionals, even though they might not necessarily be directly involved with storage solutions. Those who have dealt with networks know well that despite the many commonalities, it is hard to find two networks that are the same; similarly, SANs can differ drastically from one another while still fulfilling their primary purpose of providing an enterprise with large amounts of storage.

Many of the design considerations for SANs are generically similar to those for LANs, WANs, and the internetworks that combine them. A few of these considerations follow:

- **The geographical layout of the SAN or the topology**—SAN topology affects the network technologies that will be used to interconnect the storage elements and servers, especially if long distances are involved. For example, the MDS 9000 series switches support optical interface modules with shortwave or longwave options that can extend Fibre Channel or Gigabit Ethernet up to 500 meters or 10 kilometers, respectively.

- **Data locality**—The location of the data on the SAN and the associated access paths between the storage elements and the servers impacts performance. Data access patterns between the servers and the storage elements need to be analyzed, and the relevant servers and storage elements should be interconnected with maximum possible bandwidth between them to ensure adequate performance.

- **The storage capacity of the SAN**—Large storage capacity is the reason that SANs are deployed in the first place. The SAN's capacity should reflect the business requirements that were identified through the design process. SAN total storage can be increased through the addition of new storage elements or the upgrading of existing ones to larger capacities.

- **Business continuance policies**—Backup and restore procedures, and requirements for overall data availability, can translate into considerations for designing redundancy. The level of disaster tolerance (complete or partial loss of the SAN) can translate into a consideration for designing data replication.

Network-Attached Storage

NAS and SANs share a common purpose: to accommodate the demanding storage requirements of many SMBs and large enterprises. Whereas SAN is its own network, interconnecting servers and storage elements, NAS is a storage system that attaches to a LAN. Figure 3-2 illustrates the difference between a NAS and a SAN in the context of logical network topology. As a mnemonic to help you closely relate SAN and NAS technologies, remember that when you spell SAN backwards, you get NAS.

Figure 3-2 *Differences Between a SAN and a NAS in the Context of Logical Network Topology*

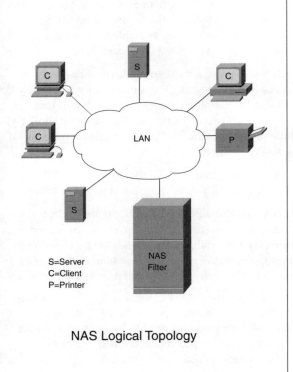

S=Server
C=Client
P=Printer

NAS Logical Topology

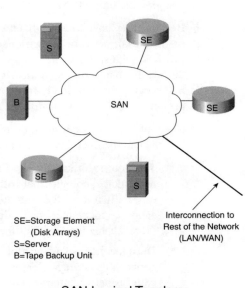

SE=Storage Element
   (Disk Arrays)
S=Server
B=Tape Backup Unit

Interconnection to
Rest of the Network
(LAN/WAN)

SAN Logical Topology

The heart of a NAS solution is typically a *filer*, which is a dedicated high-performance file server with its own optimized operating system that controls multiple disk arrays. The filer is equipped with one or more high-speed (typically Gigabit Ethernet) interfaces to the network. The filer services data I/O requests using standard higher-layer protocols like the Network File System (NFS) in UNIX environments or the Common Internet File System (CIFS) in Windows-based environments. NAS appears to be simpler to deploy than SAN because it is effectively a storage product. In contrast, SAN is considered an architecture. Logically, NAS is positioned between the application server(s) and the file system, whereas SAN can be thought of as being positioned between the file system(s) and the underlying physical storage elements.

From the design perspective, another way to think of a NAS is that it is a high-performance extension of the application server(s) that unburdens them from the bandwidth-intensive I/O tasks, instead allowing them to concentrate on the processing of data. Designers should also consider SAN and NAS for developing effective network backup solutions. SANs support the tape backups. A NAS can also serve as a backup for SAN contents, or vice versa. Multiple NAS filers can be used as backups for one another.

It is common for SAN vendors to offer NAS solutions as well. HP, IBM, and Sun Microsystems all offer NAS products. Cisco switches from the 4000 or the 6500 series are well suited for NAS interconnection, and they have proven their reliability in performance tests with NAS products from Network Appliance Corporation.

Power Protection

Reliable power is part of any effective network design. The ability to provide uninterruptible or stable power to critical network components affects the level of network availability, which is always a key design consideration. Proceed with the following steps when designing power protection for a network installation:

1 Identify all network components to be protected.

2 Determine each component's power requirements.

3 Determine the aggregate power requirements and the amount of time that the equipment needs to remain operational.

4 Make a decision regarding type of power protection equipment to be deployed (such as UPSes, generators, line conditioners, isolation transformers).

5 Look at data sheets from companies that offer power protection products. Identify devices that match the requirements.

6 Consult as necessary with the network vendors on the most appropriate power protection solution for their products to ensure compatibility between the selected power protection equipment and the network gear to be protected.

Uninterruptible Power Supplies

Uninterruptible power supplies (UPSes) are rated in volt amperes (VAs). VAs are derived by calculating the following formula:

operating equipment voltage × number of amps drawn by the equipment

The voltage is typically 110 or 220. Vendors normally identify the amp rating on each piece of equipment. Repeat this exercise for each piece of equipment under consideration.

Alternatively, you can get the watts rating from each piece of equipment. If you follow the watts route, remember to convert watts to VAs after you come up with the total number of watts for all of the equipment. Dividing the number of watts by a square root of 2 over 2 (or approximately 0.7) yields the number of VAs. The UPS VAs can also be converted to watts in the event that they are not already specified. Simply put, be consistent and work either with watts or VAs.

Next, you need to determine the UPS operational times under various power load levels. The higher the load (that is, the higher the aggregate VA or watts number of the equipment to be protected), the shorter the duration of UPS operation when the device is disconnected from utility power.

Another design consideration for UPS deployment is whether to deploy a single larger unit or multiple smaller ones. Multiple units offer greater mobility and ease of power protection distribution. However, they will likely end up being more expensive than a single higher-capacity unit and, over time, more difficult to manage.

When deploying UPSes, develop a plan for periodic battery testing and replacement. Doing so enables you to avoid the surprise of watching a UPS fail when you are most in need of it.

Other Power Protection Equipment

Generators, line conditioners, and isolation transformers can complement the deployment of UPSes in the following ways:

- Generators tend to be crucial in health care (hospitals) or utility services environments, where loss of power and the subsequent loss of network connectivity or access to critical data can be life threatening.

- Line conditioners maintain stable voltage levels during *brownouts* (voltage dips) and *overvoltages* (voltage spikes) but do not continue to supply power during an outage. They tend to be less expensive than UPSes of comparable ratings. You need to make a pragmatic design decision whether to deploy a line conditioner or a UPS. UPSes offer line conditioning as well.

- Isolation transformers might be most applicable in manufacturing and laboratory environments or, in general, in environments in which heavy electrical machinery needs to coexist and operate side by side with more sensitive networking or other SMB-specific equipment. Isolation transformers eliminate ground loops and noise that can impact network equipment operation.

The User Desktop Environment

The most powerful routers and fastest switches can end up being of little value if the SMB's desktop environment is not configured and maintained properly to take advantage of this increasingly robust network infrastructure. If it were not for the innate desire on the part of humans to communicate in a faster, more expressive, and more graphic manner, we might not have routers, switches, or even the Internet. Thus, the front end to this communications infrastructure, whether it is an SMB's private network or the global Internet, needs to be set up, configured, and properly maintained. That front is the desktop environment, which represents all of the devices in the user work areas that connect to the network and with which the network users interact most directly. These devices include workstations, printers, IP phones, scanners, sorters, or any other specialized peripherals.

Workstations

End-user workstations are likely to be the primary consumers of LAN switch ports. Given the reliance on commuting power for all aspects of SMB activities—for example, creating architectural designs, video or audio editing, construction administration, or performing research in any of the fields of science—the range of computing power, operating systems, and applications are going to make the collective SMB workstation environment as varied as the SMB field itself.

Fortunately for network designers, from the network infrastructure perspective, the workstation OS, the workstation hardware, and the applications are less important than the workstation's interface to the network—that is, the kind and the number of NICs that a workstation is equipped with. The OS, naturally, has to support the NIC(s) or at least be compatible with the drivers for the NIC(s) if they are required. A design consideration for workstations is whether to nail (explicitly define) the workstation's NIC parameters (speed, duplex, flow control) or whether to allow the switch port and the workstation NIC to negotiate them.

Experience in this area dictates that a consistent policy for interfacing workstations to the network is important, but it is not necessarily a one-size-fits-all approach. Because they need to manipulate large amounts of data, specialized, high-powered workstations with large bandwidth requirements might have to connect to higher-speed switch ports (1000 Mbps/10 Gbps) in a manner similar to the servers. In these cases, it might be preferable to hardcode the communication parameters at both ends. Other workstations that are used for more routine customer service-based applications, e-mail, and Internet access could be allowed to negotiate their parameters on lower-speed (10/100 Mbps) switch ports. If performance problems develop, the workstation interface to the network is an area to investigate.

For higher-end workstations that plug into the Gigabit or 10 Gigabit Ethernet ports, it is also critical to know the cabling requirements for those standards. Whereas fiber dominates at those speeds, Gigabit Ethernet is supported over twisted pair. The 803.3ab standard specifies Gigabit Ethernet over Cat 5 cabling with distances of up to 100 meters.

CAUTION	The only word of caution here is to ensure that the cabling does indeed meet at least the Cat 5 requirements. As a general rule, the higher the transmission speeds, the more sensitive the technology is to substandard cabling.

Network Printers and Other Peripherals

IP-addressable printers with built-in or installable high-speed NICs or print servers are the norm in modern SMB networks. These kinds of printers are normally accessible and configurable over the network via a web browser.

A unique design consideration for printers in a switched internetwork is its placement within the network as a function of its use. High-speed, high-volume printers are functionally comparable to servers. In a multi-VLAN network, they should be located on the VLAN from which most of the print requests originate. This setup minimizes the routing of large volumes of print-related traffic. Consistency in printer NIC parameter negotiation or hard coding is also advisable. From the network administration perspective, consider simplifying network administration by assigning static IP addresses to printers rather than having them come from the DHCP pool.

Network peripherals other than printers include scanners for document imaging systems, document copiers, specialized sorters required for the processing of checks in financial institutions, specialized medical equipment, IP phones, and even IP-based video surveillance systems. And the number of network-attachable peripherals or subsystems (most of which only a decade ago would have been perceived as having nothing to do with data networks) will only continue to grow. This is by and large thanks to the drastically increasing availability of high-bandwidth technologies (over longer and longer distances) combined with high-capacity network storage.

For example, Ethernet, which since its inception back in the 1970s has been considered a LAN technology, has recently been extended into the metropolitan area network (MAN) and WAN arenas. Full-duplex Gigabit or 10-Gigabit Ethernet operating over fiber-optic media has no inherent distance limitation, although practical physical limits and distance recommendations are given by the standards bodies (IEEE in this case). When these kinds of transmission capacities are combined with the storage capacities of technologies like SAN or NAS, the field is ripe for growth in the number of network-attachable peripherals.

The sheer number and diversity of the peripherals only reinforce the concept of the network infrastructure as becoming a common utility. Operation of each type of peripheral and subsystem might require specialized training that is outside the scope of a network designer's expertise. However, as long as you can draw a line between the mechanics of the peripheral's operation and its interface to the network, you will be able to incorporate into a network design every device that has a NIC or IP address.

Network Upgrades Planning

The almost relentless forward progress in networking technologies and CPU processing power means that networking equipment is subject to obsolescence at faster rates than many other modern appliances or necessities, such as cars, refrigerators, or dishwashers. When designing a network, whether from scratch or as part of an overhaul of an existing network, you should consider future upgrades that will be made to keep the network infrastructure from becoming obsolete. Without upgrades planning, it is just a matter of time before the network becomes unresponsive to ongoing business requirements, which usually become more demanding over time.

Network unresponsiveness can occur in small increments. First it appears as longer response times to routine queries, more time spent managing disk space, backups taking longer, and the occurrence of first-time security breaches. Although these small degradations do not appear significant in and of themselves, their cumulative effect might lead network administrators and users to perceive that the network is no longer working. When this happens, it is time for an upgrade.

Network upgrades can be gradual and ongoing, or they can occur all at once, in a more dramatic "forklift" style. The issues that are likely to confront most SMBs regarding upgrades are classic:

- **Who?**—Who is going to do them?
- **When?**—When will they happen?
- **How?**—How will they impact the business operation?
- **How much?**—How much will they cost?

Sources of Upgrades Expertise: The Who

Assuming that an SMB has dedicated in-house information technology (IT) staff, the sources of upgrades expertise include the in-house IT department, IT consulting companies, and, of course, the equipment vendors and their partners. The in-house IT departments are frequently so overwhelmed with day-to-day operations and responding to varied user requests that planning and executing a major upgrade is often not possible for them. Hiring an IT consulting company to perform upgrades might be deemed by an SMB as too expensive. Vendors usually offer technical device-level support, but they are not necessarily of much use when problems arise with systems integration or in multivendor environments.

It almost seems like a no-win situation when it comes to network upgrades and who is going to do them. However, that condition occurs only because of a lack of understanding on the part of an SMB that network upgrades are not painful, expensive, and completely unexpected events that occasionally must be endured. Rather, upgrades are an integral part of a long-term strategy for maintaining an effective network infrastructure. Human and financial resources should be consciously allocated to future upgrades planning and implementation as part of any network design.

With an up-front allocation of resources for future network upgrades, who is going to perform them is hardly even an issue. As a function of the SMB's size and the existence of internal IT staff, an effective team for planning and performing upgrades is composed of the following:

- Internal IT representatives who understand the peculiarities and quirks of the SMB's current network

- Outside contractor(s) to provide additional manpower, second opinion, or subject matter expertise

- Technical support personnel from the equipment vendor

The exact formula for the composition of an upgrades team is as varied as the spectrum of SMB types and sizes, but the principle is that a diversified team approach to upgrades planning and implementation tends to be the most effective.

Upgrades Timing: The When

What all of the network upgrades have going against them is that while they are in progress, they are going to cause a disruption—either to the SMB (and its operations) or to those who perform the upgrades. Upgrades timing depends on these factors:

- **The SMB's system usage cycle**—Ideal times for performing upgrades are when an SMB is shut down for normal operations. That might mean late nights, weekends, or holidays. However, some SMB sectors (such as ISPs or e-commerce sites) simply never shut down, or at least would prefer not to ever shut down. Minimum system usage periods are the next best choice if an SMB never shuts down its operations.

- **The extent of the upgrade and the potential for its success or failure**—Always plan for the best and prepare for the worst when it comes to performing network upgrades.

- **Vendor plans for the release of a new feature or bug fixes that must be implemented as quickly as possible**—When a security fix comes along, the risk of not implementing it as quickly as possible might far outweigh the cost of any disruption to the SMB's operation while the fix (upgrade) is being performed.

When performing upgrades, whenever possible, observe the fundamental principle of not burning your bridges behind you. If the new IOS or a server OS does not work as expected, if configuration or data is accidentally lost or erased, if a new switch proves unstable, if Internet access no longer works, or if one of myriad other unexpected events affecting network operation occurs, make every effort to be in a position to restore the network to the condition it was in before the upgrade was attempted.

Upgrades Impact: The How

Every network upgrade should have a beneficial impact on the SMB's operations. The benefit of the upgrade will vary. It might be faster and more effective customer service due to an overall better network performance. It might be a higher operational efficiency because of an increase in the capacity of a storage solution for SMBs involved in digital audio, video, or graphic arts production. It might be more sales as a result of more incisive marketing, made possible by a greater availability of customer data and more business intelligence.

Generically, the benefits of a network upgrade are measured in reduced operational costs, better customer satisfaction, higher sales, better business intelligence for strategic decision making, or even improved employee morale. The benefits ought to be anticipated and then measured against established benchmarks in the appropriate areas, in part as a justification for the ongoing upgrade process.

When upgrades go awry, a temporary disruption to SMB's operations will likely result. Consequently, to minimize potential negative impact of the upgrade process (caused by equipment incompatibility, unanticipated bugs, or configuration errors), planned upgrades should be tested offline to the greatest extent possible before going live with them.

Upgrades Cost: The How Much

Network upgrades carry a price tag, which tends to loom large when an SMB is confronted with the upgrades prospect without anticipating it. However, the upgrades price tag is more manageable when upgrade planning is incorporated into the network design process from the start. When a new network is being installed, the SMB should consider leasing instead of buying.

Cisco Capital, for example, facilitates the lease process. Leasing might result in a program in which critical network components (such as routers, switches, firewalls) are replaced with the latest comparable models at the end of each lease period. This arrangement allows for an ongoing (every few years) network refresh at fixed monthly costs.

Alternatively, where the equipment volume does not warrant a lease program, a cumulative monthly or quarterly budget for upgrades can also prove effective. It can spread the cost of the upgrade process over a period of time rather than having it hit all at once. Because network upgrades are a fact of life, SMBs need to learn to live with them in a way that minimizes the potential for any large and sudden financial impact.

Applications, E-Mail, and Network-Management Tools

Applications, e-mail and network-management tools might not seem like components of the network infrastructure, but they are definitely a part of any end-to-end network solution. Applications and e-mail, which could be considered an application itself, are the main reasons for any network's existence. And networks tend to degrade when left unattended with no oversight or management.

Consider then as part of any network design the impact of applications, the choices in e-mail system, and the fundamental approaches to network management.

The Impact of Applications

Each SMB is going to have a unique set of core business applications that rely on the proper functioning of the network infrastructure. Given the layered nature of network architecture, well-designed applications are insulated from the network infrastructure components and protocols in terms of compatibility but not in terms of the impact on the network bandwidth and the network devices' processing power.

The impact of applications on the network bandwidth has lessened with the transition from shared media to switched networks, but it is still a key design consideration. How bandwidth intensive are the applications? Are there large volumes of data that move across the network as a result of the application usage? Who are the application users, and where are they located on the network with respect to where the application program resides? Do the applications generate broadcast traffic? Do they require multicast support? Network design applications considerations can be reduced to bandwidth consumption and CPU cycles, but those in turn affect VLAN design decisions, storage solutions, WAN bandwidth provisioning, and the switching capacities of LAN switches.

E-Mail Options

The e-mail options for SMB operations include internal e-mail only, which does not integrate with Internet e-mail; an integrated e-mail system (internal and Internet) that is supported by an internal SMB-administered server; the use of a provider's e-mail server; or the use of web-based free e-mail services like Yahoo or Hotmail. Given that e-mail has become a "killer app," and the degree of reliance on e-mail communication is typically noticed only when the capability to use it disappears, it benefits any SMB to consider building a high degree of redundancy into its e-mail system. That redundancy applies in terms of access to the Internet for external e-mail communications (multiple providers), procedures for quick restore of an e-mail server in the event of a crash, and having a backup e-mail system for critical communications in the event of the primary system's prolonged failure.

Network-Management Methods

A well-designed network is also a well-managed network. Effective network management can pinpoint bandwidth bottlenecks, insufficient storage space, intermittently failing switch ports, or attempts at unauthorized intrusions. In general, as a function of an SMB's philosophy, networks can be managed proactively or reactively:

- **Proactive management**—Tends to prevent crisis caused by outright outages, security breaches, or poor performance.

- **Reactive management**—Relies on a problem staring an SMB in the face before corrective action is taken.

Aside from the management philosophy, another network-management design consideration is whether to use a centralized (system-wide) or device-level approach.

- Centralized management tools might be more expensive up front, but they will likely significantly reduce administrative costs in the long run. They provide a singular and more comprehensive view of the entire network than can be gleaned from individual devices.
- Device-level management can still be effective in smaller installations, but it is more labor intensive on the part of the network administrator.

Summary

This chapter explored the data networking infrastructure and addressed design considerations relating to its key elements. Those elements include telecommunications closets and their most common components (cabling, switches, and routers), network servers and storage solutions, power protection, and the user desktop environment (including workstations and other network peripherals). Cabling, switching, and routing encompass the bottom three layers of the OSI model and are accompanied by numerous standards and choices in equipment and protocols, offering you the opportunity to accommodate a wide range of SMB infrastructure requirements.

Network servers and storage solutions were discussed in the context of their interface to the network, topology, and impact on the network bandwidth. The user desktop environment, which includes workstations and other network peripherals, was addressed in a similar context. The "Power Protection" section considered the available tools and the process of calculating the requirements. Network upgrade planning was then discussed, with an emphasis on making it part of any effective network design process from the start. This chapter concluded with a discussion of the impact of applications, choices in e-mail systems, and approaches to network management.

PART II

SMB Networking Design Solutions

CHAPTER 4

Overview of the Network Security Issues

Writing about network security is tricky when compared to writing about other network-related topics. Because effective security implementations rely on a high degree of secrecy, there seems to be an inherent contradiction in the process of openly discussing security issues. I've heard people say that those who thoroughly understand security simply don't or can't talk about it, and that those who do either don't know what they are talking about or are leaking sensitive and confidential information.

Applying this kind of an argument to the extreme could easily translate into an information blackout regarding network security solutions, thus depriving a small-medium business (SMB) of readily available means to protect network resources and information assets. That certainly would be foolish. Yet this type of argument is valuable in that it is true that not all of the information out there regarding network security is reliable. Moreover, after a security solution has been implemented by an SMB, only designated personnel should know the specific implementation details, and they should not discuss them openly.

The recommended middle-of-the-road approach regarding network security seems to be that available security solutions should be openly promoted—their features, capabilities, and perhaps even shortcomings clearly articulated. However, the specifics of each solution's implementation ought to be tightly guarded. Of course, those who provide security solutions should not make available for public consumption any proprietary algorithms that are inherent within their hardware or software.

SMBs need to be aware that implementing a security solution is not a static, one-time event. As technology advances and new threats emerge, you can't always rely on what worked yesterday to protect you from today's threats. Deploying network security is a process that involves an initial design and implementation followed by ongoing monitoring of the solution's performance, reassessing of existing and emerging threats, and keeping up with technological advances that might affect the viability of the existing solution.

In the extreme, perhaps, there is no such thing as achieving perfect security on a computer network as long as people must manage and use the network, and the network has to interface with other networks, including the Internet. However, an SMB can take numerous security measures to present a formidable challenge to any potential intrusion attempt from the inside or the outside.

Consider one aspect of a network security breach that many fear the most: disclosure of sensitive information. Through the global reach of the Internet and the 24×7 news coverage, information can be propagated almost instantaneously to large audiences. The act of wide dissemination of information that ought to be held close to an SMB's vest can be damaging, regardless of whether that information is ridiculously frivolous or highly proprietary and confidential. That is only one reason why doing nothing about network security places a business at risk.

Managing risk levels is the crux of dealing with network security. An SMB must be willing to take the time to determine the degree of risk that the business is willing to tolerate. If an intolerable risk level is reached because of security threats against the SMB's network and information assets, the SMB must proceed with prudent steps that will reduce the threat.

TIP   When an SMB decides to take steps to protect the business from threats against its computer network, those threats need to be clearly identified and prioritized. Does it sound like there is an implication here of having a security policy? Indeed!

At a small enterprise, a security policy might be an unwritten policy that consists of information in someone's head (hopefully, the person who is responsible for network security). However, it is preferable for an SMB to create a network security policy in writing with input from the groups of stakeholders identified in Chapter 1, "Effective Networking Solution Design Process."

A definition of a security policy and an example conclude this chapter. However, because the security vernacular tends to be cryptic, security threats need to be articulated in a language that is understandable to the network design professional and layman alike before a security policy is defined and developed. Those threats then need to be translated into a visible, understandable impact, from which security risk assessment analysis can be performed. An understanding of internal versus external security threats has to follow. Finally, the antidotes to the various threats need to be defined.

This chapter addresses all of the following issues:

- The broad security threat categories
- The meaning and impact of specific threats in SMB environments
- Which to fear more: internal or external security threats
- The security threat antidotes
- The importance of having a clearly defined security policy

Specific security solutions representing the various antidotes are the focus of Chapter 5, "Cisco Security Solutions." When you read about those security solutions in Chapter 5, you should understand which threat category they address and how to make them fit effectively into a security policy.

Categories of Security Threats

Security threats against an SMB's network fall into the following broad categories:

- Information corruption
- Information disclosure
- Repudiation and lack of authentication and authorization
- Denial of service (DoS)

These threat categories are neutral when it comes to the source of the threat, the motive behind it, and the manner in which the threat is executed. Consider a drastic example of information corruption: An SMB's database is destroyed, and there is no backup from which to restore it. From an operational point of view, it almost does not matter who performed the act of destruction, why, and how. It might matter from the legal point of view, but that is a separate topic outside the scope of this publication.

However, when the specific threat mechanisms are identified within each of the preceding categories, the threat's origin, the motivation behind it, and the manner in which it is carried out need to be considered for the purpose of developing an effective security policy and selecting the appropriate antidotes. Figure 4-1 depicts an effective network security framework. The threat mechanisms emanating from each of the threat categories are unable to reach and to disrupt the network resources and information assets because effective antidotes neutralize them. Refer to Figure 4-1 as the discussion of security threats and antidotes proceeds.

Figure 4-1   *Effective Network Security Framework*

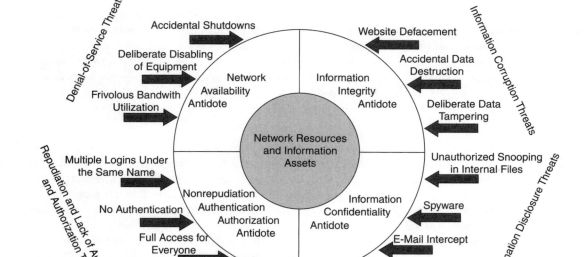

Information Corruption

The act of information corruption translates into some form of data modification or destruction. It might be a deliberate act of malice perpetrated against a business by those seeking to disrupt its operations, or it might be an accident that occurs in the course of an entirely constructive endeavor, such as an operating system upgrade or an application program installation.

Accidental data modification or destruction might become immediately obvious to those involved in the activities leading to such an occurrence. It is also possible that the fact that data has been modified or lost might go undiscovered for quite some time until another accident, a customer complaint, or an audit brings that knowledge to light.

Information Corruption Resulting from an Unverified Backup

Drastic cases of information corruption in the form of outright destruction are normally discovered fairly quickly. I had the misfortune of participating in one accidental act of data destruction during an innocuous installation of the Personal Information Manager (PIM) utility on a network's server. The PIM's installation program chose to wipe out the contents of a certain DATA folder and fill it with its own files. Unfortunately, that folder contained critical data files used by an accounting program. The deleted files could not be recovered through the use of any of the operating system's undelete or restore utilities. It was time to head for the backup tapes but, as fortune would have it, several of the most recent backups had failed, unbeknownst to anyone at the business. Ultimately, the data that was restored was almost two weeks old.

The data destruction caused a major disruption in business operations and produced a less-than-pleasant situation for all parties involved. The lesson here is simple: Any program installations on network servers should proceed only when a verifiable backup of critical business data exists. Of course, not every program that is installed on a network server is going to wipe out critical accounting data on the server, but it certainly can happen, and it is wise to be prepared for that possibility.

At first glance, the example presented in the sidebar might not seem like a security issue— but indeed it is. When a malicious virus is planted on a network server with the intent of destroying all or select data at some future time or upon the execution of a certain program, the effects are basically the same as what I experienced when an installation program wiped out the contents of a mission-critical folder. The motives in those two scenarios are entirely different, and the means of protection would differ as well. But a security-conscious network administrator (or a security administrator, if an SMB is fortunate enough to have one) should remember that well-meaning consultants can be as dangerous to the health of their network as malicious hackers.

Consider another case of data destruction, in which the physical hard drive is simply stolen from the network server. Although the data has not been literally destroyed, it is still considered data destruction because, from an operational point of view, the data is not there.

WARNING   What do networking consultants, nasty viruses, and high-tech thieves have in common? They can all destroy (make unavailable for use) an SMB's mission-critical data.

Of course, when a hard drive is stolen, another potential problem besides data destruction is that data will be disclosed to unauthorized users, which is discussed in the next subsection.

Data destruction does not need to be a wholesale erasing of entire folders or hard drives. If contents of select data files are destroyed, it can have an equally disruptive impact on business operations. When an application program presents an interface that displays data from multiple files or tables, having the contents of one of those tables completely overwritten with a random binary pattern would certainly qualify as a form of data destruction. Network users would likely detect this form of destruction fairly quickly. But it might be a lot harder for users to detect data modification. The question is this: When does data destruction turn into data modification, and vice versa?

Consider the following criterion in differentiating between data destruction and data modification. Whereas data destruction is outright wiping out or removal of information, data modification involves alteration in which the modified data masquerades as the valid data. Assume, for example, that a few zeros were somehow added to the figure representing the balance in one's customer checking account at a local bank (which, according to its size, qualifies as an SMB). No actual deposit took place, which means that some backdoor method was employed. Because nothing was destroyed through the activity—in fact, money was created out of nothing because the balance increased—this is a clear case of data modification. It is likely to distress the bank, but it will bring a great deal of satisfaction to the fortunate customer.

Now, turn this scenario around. Suppose instead that a malicious virus removed all of the zeros from the balance figures for a select group of customers that meet the twisted virus's selection criteria. You happen to be one of those customers. If you did not have any zeros in your balance, consider yourself fortunate. But if your balance happened to be $10,000.73, you are looking at a drastic reduction of your portfolio to $1.73. Is this a case of data modification or destruction? It is certainly a case of destruction of your finances, but from a technical and security point of view, it would still be a case of data modification. Both the original and the modified figures are valid because they represent money amounts.

As you can see from the preceding examples, data modification can be more insidious and perhaps more difficult to detect than data destruction. Although a security solution can protect an SMB against infestation by malicious viruses that attempt to tamper with critical data, periodic data audits (either automated or by competent professionals) need to be part of the antidote arsenal to guard against malicious or accidental data modifications.

Some forms of information corruption can result in denial of service (DoS), a threat category that is discussed later in this section. The goal of denial-of-service attacks is to slow or to entirely shut down business operations. As the discussion of the threat categories proceeds, it will become obvious that there are overlaps between them. But whether a threat is classified as information destruction, disclosure, lack of authentication, or denial of service, in the final analysis, its effect is the same: undermining of an SMB's mission through disruption, slowdown in operations, and appearance of incompetence, all of which can definitely affect an SMB's bottom line.

The means and mechanisms that facilitate information corruption can be partially synthesized as follows:

- Malware (trojans, viruses, logic bombs)
- Intentional or unintentional tampering with information by employees or contractors
- Intentional tampering with information by unauthorized outsiders who have gained unauthorized access to the network
- Absence of database administration
- Poor data backup procedures

To ensure data integrity, each of the preceding can be countered effectively with specific tools and procedures, as discussed in the "Security Threat Antidotes" section later in this chapter.

Information Disclosure

The threat category that most SMB executives I have known associate with a security risk is information disclosure. If company data is destroyed but can be restored from a backup, it is at most a temporary disruption to the business operation. Data modifications can often be resolved through effective audits after the discrepancies are discovered. However, if proprietary or confidential information leaves a company's protected environment, there is no way to restrict it again to the group of individuals who were supposed to be the only ones privy to it. At best, the source of the disclosure can be identified and action taken against future disclosures. At worst, the disclosures might continue, indicating a mechanism that evades detection and for which an effective antidote has not yet been implemented or even designed.

As with information modification or destruction, information disclosure can be either accidental or deliberate, with the source of disclosure either inside or outside the business. For example, take an act of information disclosure deliberately perpetrated by someone from outside the business. This kind of disclosure can result in an instantaneous worldwide broadcast of confidential information through the use of the news media or the Internet. Perhaps the information is something sensational or of a scandalous nature, which catches everyone's attention for a time and then fades away. The business that is the object of the disclosure becomes aware of the security breach quickly.

However, a disclosure can also mean gaining access to confidential and proprietary information by unauthorized individuals without the business being aware that it is happening. *Industrial espionage* is one term for this kind of disclosure. Over a period of time, the effects of spying can be far more devastating than the one-time sensational blast heard 'round the world.

TIP For the purpose of developing a security policy, an SMB needs to place a value upon the different types of information and consider the implications of having it disclosed.

Information disclosure encompasses more than just gaining access to static information, such as proprietary data about a specific product, the company's payroll, or confidential memorandums outlining a company's business strategy. There is now a whole array of tools—collectively referred to as *spyware*—that concentrates on behavioral disclosure in addition to content disclosure.

A person subject to spyware is probably unaware that it operates on his or her PC because spyware installation is frequently a byproduct of installing or downloading other software or even visiting certain websites. This statement is not intended to set off panic alarms in anyone's mind. When an SMB purchases a commercial accounting package, it probably will not come bundled with spyware. But when an employee at an SMB decides to download a program for free file swapping, that employee's PC might become infested with spyware. Or if an employer decides to start monitoring all of an employee's computer activity, that employer will likely resort to installing a commercial spyware package on an employee's machine without the employee's knowledge. However, just as employers can resort to spyware to monitor employees' computing activities, employees with access to their bosses' PCs can and probably do install spyware.

Spyware tools range in utility and sophistication, but they can be broadly categorized into monitoring and advertising spyware. *Monitoring spyware* keeps track of all of someone's computer activity, for whatever purpose. Needless to say, monitoring spyware is intrusive at an individual level. Both commercial and freeware versions of monitoring spyware software are readily available. Because everything that is typed in on a PC—including passwords, letters, credit card numbers, customer information, or e-mail—might stealthily be captured and viewed by unauthorized personnel, SMBs should consider protective measures against monitoring spyware. Just as there are numerous antivirus packages to protect against viruses, there are both commercial and freeware packages to detect and remove spyware installations.

Advertising spyware is less intrusive than its monitoring sibling and is intended to detect response patterns to the ads and popups that routinely grace web surfers' screens. Aggregate information collected by advertising spyware can help companies that use popular websites as an advertising medium for their products develop marketing and advertising strategies.

Repudiation and Lack of Authentication and Authorization

One meaning of the verb *repudiate* is to reject as being untrue. The concept of repudiation is closely tied to those of authentication and authorization. *Authentication* allows users to prove that they are who they claim to be. *Authorization* allows users to carry out certain restricted activities, such as viewing confidential information, updating a database, or performing physical acts related to network maintenance.

Repudiation and Nonrepudiation

Under normal circumstances, a legitimate user authenticates onto the network and carries out authorized activities. However, what if a user authenticates and carries out authorized activities, but then it turns out that the user was not the person whom he or she claimed to be via the authentication mechanism? In a username/password authentication system, this scenario can easily occur if another person knows a legitimate user's password and username combination. The compromise of usernames and passwords effectively sets the stage for the stealing of any legitimate user's network identity.

Let's say that the real user in this scenario can prove he did not authenticate onto the system at the recorded time and place—that is, someone else was performing activities under his or her name. This is an example of weak security. The legitimate user is able to repudiate (prove as being untrue) the act of carrying out activities under his or her name.

The converse of repudiation is nonrepudiation. Security is considered to be strong when activities that are carried out following an authenticated access to the network cannot be, at a later time, repudiated or denied by the person assigned the authentication mechanism. The more unique the authentication mechanism, the harder it becomes to repudiate the act of authentication. Passwords, of course, are a common means of authentication, but password administration requires a degree of care and education to minimize the potential for repudiation.

Assume that an unauthorized individual can easily steal or, through devious means, solicit passwords and usernames from legitimate users for future network access. Usage logs that are viewable only by the company's information technology (IT) and internal auditing staff begin to detect unusual patterns of updates to the company's databases. The activity continues for several weeks. It's highly probable that under these circumstances, the legitimate users, by cooperating with the alert IT and auditing staff, will be able to repudiate the updates ascribed to them, and the imposter will be caught. This result is more favorable than if the illegitimate activity goes undetected, but it still reflects a weak level of security that has not been hardened to the point of nonrepudiation.

Poor Authentication

The following are drastic examples of poor security practices in the area of authentication that allow users to repudiate any allegations of illegitimate activity on the network:

- Absence of any password use at all
- Allowing multiple logins into the network under the same login name

These practices are quite common among SMBs with small or null IT budgets. An additional complication is that in situations in which authentication is weak, authorization tends to be weak as well. An example of weak authorization is absence of any granularity in access rights to the network. All users have the same—usually powerful—access rights to all network resources.

Lack of Security Education

What if the actual authentication and authorization mechanisms are strong, yet, due to lack of education, users are unaware of security procedures? When users freely share passwords, badges, or other authentication mechanisms among themselves and even with perfect strangers, the security administrator enjoys a false sense of security, and repudiation remains a given.

Denial of Service

Denial of service (DoS) means preventing the use of network resources for their intended and legitimate purposes. More specifically, DoS can mean an actual shutdown or crash of key network components like routers, switches, and servers.

Whether an attack is viewed as a DoS attack is a matter of semantics. Generally, when the network is somehow disabled, and the cause of the disability is deliberate and external to an SMB, it is perceived as a DoS attack. However, when the network is disabled as a result of internal activities, it is usually viewed as an accident. And, of course, a network can be disabled as a result of external accidents.

When a network is deliberately targeted via a DoS attack, the result might be the maximum exploitation of the network bandwidth, a server's memory, or a router's CPU for a frivolous, useless purpose. When the network resources are tied up passing large volumes of uninvited traffic, responding to frivolous requests, or being stuck in endless processing loops, legitimate requests from legitimate users receive no attention, thus denying them the service that a network is supposed to offer. From the point of view of a network user, it matters little what causes the network to be disabled or unavailable for legitimate use. However, discovering the cause of a network's disability is important; doing so helps determine whether or not it falls under the security umbrella or was the result of other network-related activities. If a security issue is involved, figuring out the cause helps determine what antidotes need to be deployed to defeat DoS and to ensure network availability.

TIP   For the purpose of developing an effective security policy, you should think of DoS not only in terms of an SMB being subject to an external attack but also in terms of keeping the network available for legitimate use.

Let's revisit the issue of determining whether or not network disability falls under the security umbrella. If servers tend to crash because of poor quality of utility power and lack of adequate power protection, is it a network management or a security issue? If, in the course of considering network security, an overlap develops with other network-related areas, statements to that effect can be incorporated into the SMB's security policy.

If a natural disaster strikes and key network components are damaged or destroyed, making the network unavailable for a prolonged period of time, is it a disaster recovery, a network management, or a security issue? Again, it matters little from the operational point of view. What if key network components reside in easily accessible areas and are either being accidentally turned off or—perhaps worse—they sprout legs and walk? This scenario has a good chance of being considered a security issue. But what if the network is simply badly managed, resulting in a bleak response time and an inability to perform legitimate tasks? By now, the security envelope is getting stretched really thin.

An all-encompassing view of security can lead to overall better network management practices if those practices are poor to begin with. In and of themselves, certain activities affecting the network and its ability to properly serve legitimate users might not be considered security issues. However, when the effects of those activities are comparable to the results of a security threat, perhaps it's time to pay less attention to semantics and to concentrate on the real purpose that the network is supposed to serve.

What Security Threats Mean to an SMB

SMBs have varying levels of understanding of security threats, depending on their experience with security breaches and their implications. When an SMB has experienced the impact of security breaches (for example, DoS attacks or disclosures of confidential information), its view of developing a security policy and implementing security solutions is tempered by those experiences.

For example, take an Internet service provider (ISP) that offers a wide range of Internet-related services to businesses and individuals. This ISP experienced a DoS attack that was intermittent and that lasted several days. Many of the ISP's business clients were frustrated because their communications were severely disrupted.

The ISP's network engineers experienced their own high levels of frustration while trying to determine the source of the attack and how to stop it. (It was probably not the best time for the ISP to be recruiting new clients through glitzy marketing campaigns advertising the high degree of reliability of its services.) The upshot of such an experience is that, in the future, as compared to other ISPs who have never experienced a DoS attack, this ISP will be in a much better position to assess the cost of similar attacks versus the cost of the solution to protect against them. Perhaps the unfortunate ISP lost a few clients, and the salaried staff had to work overtime. But after the frustration subsided, the cost might not have seemed so large.

Trying to determine the actual cost of a security breach is a tricky business. A fundamental principle regarding security is that the cost of a security solution should be less than the cost of recovery from a security breach. The decision of whether to deploy a security solution should be clear, then, if the two costs can be easily compared. But the problem with that fundamental principle is that it is difficult to figure out what the actual cost of a security breach is. An SMB cannot look simply at the immediate monetary cost of a security breach. What about the long-term effects on the SMB's reputation and credibility when the services it offers are disrupted as a result of poor security?

There is no magic bullet to figure out the cost when it comes to intangibles like credibility, trust, or reputation. But decision makers need to consider these types of costs when developing a security policy and considering appropriate security solutions.

Consider the scenarios in the following subsections. They are presented in the form of questions that anticipate different types of security breaches. Each of the scenarios represents a manifestation of a threat from one of the broad categories of security threats discussed earlier in this chapter.

Given the wide range of businesses that fall under the SMB umbrella, the impact of these scenarios—if they occur—will vary from one SMB to another. However, in preparation for the discussion in the section "The Importance of Having a Security Policy" later in this chapter, I attempt to raise issues that are universally applicable across the SMB spectrum and that must be considered when developing a security policy. Without a security policy (explicitly defined or at least implied), an SMB will likely be paying lip service to network security rather than taking it seriously.

What if My Website Is Defaced?

A defaced website can make people laugh, or it can make them lose confidence in the website owner's ability to conduct business. A defaced website represents a form of information corruption. It is also a statement to the whole wide world that someone other than the business has control over the manner in which the business is presenting itself to the public via the Internet.

When faced with the issue of website defacement, consider the following:

- The extent of the defacement
- How long the defacement lasted before being discovered
- Whether or not the defacement had a visual impact only or an operational impact as well

If an SMB uses its website as a glorified business brochure but conducts no business transactions over the web, the defacement is at best a temporary embarrassment. No confidential client information was lost, and no normal activity was disrupted as a result of the defacement. But if an SMB's e-commerce website is defaced, and in the process, confidential client information is stolen and business operations are disrupted, the situation presents an entirely different challenge. There is likely to be an immediate monetary loss and perhaps long-lasting consequences resulting from the compromise of sensitive information.

In general, the perspective that needs to be maintained regarding websites is that they are extremely dynamic. Numerous websites are in a constant state of being updated, revised, and revamped. If someone were to take a really broad view of the concept of website defacement, they might even argue that websites that simply malfunction, point to nonexistent pages or URLs, or present viewers with misleading information are defaced. There is no need for an attack to deface them.

Because the Internet permeates all aspects of modern-day life for individuals and most businesses alike, there is a degree of understanding that websites, just like printed matter (books, newspapers, or magazines), will contain some errors and have navigational problems regardless of any effort made by someone to deliberately deface them. Viewers (browsers, surfers) have developed a degree of familiarity against these conditions. Consequently, unless defacement is absolutely spectacular, the tendency on the part of today's surfers is to take it in stride.

High-Profile Website Defacement

When hackers defaced the home page of the Central Intelligence Agency (CIA) in 1996, changing the name of the agency to Central Stupidity Agency, it certainly caught the attention and imagination of the public, bringing a chuckle to many. However, the CIA does not fall into the category of an SMB and presents more of a high-profile challenge to the hacking community than, let's say, a local hospital, a car dealership, a community bank, or a grocery store.

It is also important for an SMB to ask who would want to deface its website. Would it be a hacker, a competitor, or a criminal? Although exact statistics are not available, there are orders of magnitude more websites out there than there are hackers willing to spend time defacing them. Competitors attempting defacement run the risk of being more easily discovered because they most likely do not have the hacking expertise to cover their tracks. And criminals usually need a motive other than a desire for mere fun and a rush of adrenaline.

It takes work on somebody's part to deface a website, and a general human tendency is to want material compensation or at least emotional satisfaction for work performed. So if an SMB is selected for defacement, at least it's a sign that it attracted someone's attention to such a degree that the person felt compelled to exert effort to deface the website.

Because the sport of defacing websites is becoming rather passé, if an SMB's web server implements basic security measures, the odds of being selected for defacement are small. However, the risk still exists and should be taken seriously. Implementing all of the web server's operating system security features and keeping up with ongoing updates is the absolute minimum action that an SMB ought to take to minimize the potential for having its website defaced. Also, having a current backup of all of the HTML files that compose the website allows for its quick restoration after the defacement has been discovered.

What if My Website Is Inaccessible?

Web browsing is a process that is now taken for granted. Every time an SMB's customer accesses its website, myriad low-level events transpire to facilitate that process.

Unless an SMB is an Internet provider, it is going to rely on one or more ISPs for access to the Internet. When an SMB's website becomes inaccessible to some or all of its customers, it's time to engage in a troubleshooting process to determine the cause of the problem. Although website inaccessibility is a form of DoS, having this problem does not mean that the SMB is experiencing a DoS attack. In fact, it's far more likely that the inaccessibility is caused by an equipment malfunction or a traffic jam somewhere along the path between a customer and a web server rather than any form of a security breach.

Consider the potential causes of website inaccessibility:

- Web server down due to operating system crash
- Web server down due to hardware malfunction (hard drive or NIC, for example)
- Problem with router/switch to which a web server is connected. This occurs either at the SMB's or a hosting company's site.
- Failed WAN link from the SMB's ISP to the rest of the Internet
- DoS attack specifically against the SMB's web server
- Major disruption of Internet traffic due to failure of DNS root server(s)
- Worm attacks against numerous Internet servers, causing a collective slowdown or near shutdown of Internet activity

An SMB can take reasonable measures to protect against DoS attacks targeting its server(s) or increase website availability by having multiple providers. However, the SMB needs to realize that when you're dealing with the Internet—which consists of more than a hundred thousand networks and millions of computer hosts linked via a vast array of digital pathways—glitches are to be expected.

It is a tribute to the technology companies that manufacture Internet-related equipment and software and to the countless individuals who design the protocols, configure the equipment, and maintain the vast and complex infrastructure that the Internet works at all. Given the magnitude of the Internet as a collective enterprise and the degree of interoperability and cooperation that is required between the numerous ISPs, consider it a kind of a miracle every time it works. Then, when a website becomes temporarily unavailable, it can be perceived as nothing more dramatic than a temporary power blackout, a freeway traffic jam caused by an accident or just a lot of traffic, or being out of range for a cellular phone.

What if Someone Intercepts and Reads My E-Mails?

Ah, the illusion of privacy! Just consider the nature of e-mail. After you click the Send button, that e-mail message must pass through the outgoing mail server and be received on the incoming one. It might also linger in the mailbox of the person who sends it as well as the mailbox of the receiver, and it passes through countless routers and networks in between. If someone wants to read your e-mail, the intrusion can happen at the sending or receiving workstation, at the mail server, or while the e-mail is in transit.

When creating a security policy, you should assume that all unprotected e-mail is potentially subject to inspection by unauthorized prying eyes. If an e-mail sender feels comfortable with his or her message being widely publicized, there is little case for strong security measures relating to e-mail. However, if strict confidentiality must be maintained in an SMB's e-mail communications, stronger confidentiality antidotes like encryption might have to be implemented. Information confidentiality is discussed in the "Security Threat Antidotes" section later in this chapter. SMBs with multiple geographically dispersed locations that are concerned about the confidentiality of internal e-mail communications should consider a virtual private network (VPN) solution.

When considering e-mail confidentiality during the development of a security policy, consider the risks of having e-mail messages exposed to various groups of individuals. Who could possibly want to spy on e-mail communications, what benefit would they derive from it, and what are the consequences to the SMB? If a hacker wants to get into someone's e-mail for the sake of personal satisfaction, the business fallout from that kind of hack is likely to be minimal. But if a competitor gains access to an SMB's e-mail communications, business implications change drastically—for example, planned mergers might fall through, bids could be underbid, and product announcements might be preempted.

What if My Customers Can't Send Me E-Mail?

A poorly maintained in-house mail server is a serious vulnerability for an SMB. If an SMB relies on an ISP's mail servers, it is less vulnerable because the ISP has probably taken steps to harden those servers against attacks and to ensure a degree of redundancy and reliability that would minimize any lengthy e-mail service disruptions.

But what if an SMB gets a domain name and sets up an internal e-mail server that perhaps doubles as a web server? The SMB must take the following reasonable steps to minimize e-mail communication disruptions: maintain the server with all of the latest security updates to the operating system, back up the server and ensure that it can be restored quickly under any circumstances, and place the server in the demilitarized zone (DMZ) of a firewalled network. If the SMB does not take these steps, watch out!

By now, you are probably thinking that if customers can't send you e-mail, it is the result of a DoS attack. And that could certainly be the case. But if it is a DoS attack, it is probably directed against the customers' ISPs, of which there could be many. Coordinated DoS attacks occur, but they require effort and motive on the part of somebody or multiple somebodies.

If an SMB is not receiving e-mail from customers, there is probably a problem with the SMB's ISP or the SMB's incoming e-mail server. If such an event happens, the SMB's IT staff needs to ascertain the following: Are *all* of the SMB's customers not able to send e-mail to the SMB? Or, better yet, is the SMB able to receive any e-mail? The silver lining in this situation might be the relief on the part of the SMB's employees from unsolicited e-mail, also known as spam.

Loss of e-mail communications, whether incoming or outgoing, can represent a serious disruption to business operations and should be considered a form of denial of service, even if not a DoS attack. However, you always need to maintain the perspective that loss of e-mail communications is typically a temporary problem and that, despite the popularity of e-mail, there are still numerous other means of communicating, even if they are more traditional.

What if Unauthorized Personnel Gain Access to My Internal Databases?

Unauthorized access to internal databases—whether that access is by employees or not—is serious business. It represents a form of information disclosure, and the severity of the compromise depends on the degree of confidentiality of the information being viewed. The degree of damage to the SMB resulting from the disclosure also depends on whether or not the information being viewed can be copied and taken off the SMB's premises for future use.

Two of the broad security threat categories are involved here: information disclosure and lack of authentication and authorization that facilitates repudiation. Consider a scenario in which an outsider with a malevolent intent gains access to the internal databases as a result of gullibility on the part of an SMB employee or, perhaps even worse, as a result of an employee's cooperation. This is not an intercept of an e-mail about the date and time of the next marketing meeting; trade secrets and confidential customer information are at stake. The authentication mechanism that has been compromised relied on strong passwords. What went wrong?

Authentication that cannot be repudiated should be considered by an SMB when the stakes are extremely high regarding sensitive internal information. Although strong password management combined with user education can harden authentication, passwords are inherently problematic:

- Easily remembered passwords are also easy to guess and to crack.

- More robust passwords that are hard to remember are likely to be written down someplace that an unauthorized individual can find easily.

- Using a single password is certainly more convenient than trying to remember a complex password for each system. However, if an individual within an SMB has access to many systems requiring passwords, having the same password for many systems compromises multiple systems.

- Employees share passwords for seemingly valid reasons.

If you combine all of the potential problems with passwords, you might conclude that something stronger than passwords is needed when really sensitive internal information needs to be protected.

The trend that is emerging in the area of authentication is biometrics. Not every SMB needs to employ biometrics for network authentication, but it should be considered in high-security environments. Biometrics relies on extremely unique characteristics of an individual, such as fingerprints or retinal pattern. Biometric authentication is considered strong compared to passwords, but you need to clearly understand one thing: With cooperation from authorized individuals, any authentication mechanism, regardless of how sophisticated it is, can be cracked.

What if Unauthorized Employees Get into My Payroll Files?

Human nature being what it is, unauthorized peeking into the payroll files probably happens more often than is actually reported. The danger to an SMB is potential embarrassment if the information is made public, especially if there is a great disparity between salaries of different categories of employees. Conceptually, this is no different from unauthorized access to internal databases. The difference lies in the type of information being compromised.

Even though peeking into the payroll files is often cited as a breach of internal security, the damage to the business from this act of curiosity is likely to be minimal. Should this activity be detected, however, it could indicate that other, perhaps far more sensitive and confidential, information than payroll is being compromised as well. As is the case with gaining unauthorized access to internal databases, snooping around payroll files combines the threat categories of information disclosure and weak authentication.

Which to Fear More: Internal or External Security Threats

Opinions vary as to whether internal security threats are more serious than external ones. A scan of the security landscape leads me to believe that among security professionals, the trend is to consider internal threats more deadly and costly, whereas SMB chief information officers (CIOs), chief executive officers (CEOs), and system administrators have a tendency to view external threats as being more serious. The issue of which type of threat is more serious will probably never be definitively resolved. However, what an SMB needs to be aware of is that both types of threats are real, and both need to be considered when developing a security policy and implementing security solutions.

TIP

Network security is not just about technology. An astute human resources director can be invaluable by properly screening potential employees and by keeping them happy and loyal to the company that they work for.

When considering threats from the outside, remember that unless an outsider just wants a feeling of satisfaction from penetrating a network's defenses, he or she is actually trying to become an insider. When an SMB considers network vulnerabilities from the perspective of a malicious insider, the overall security plan that will be implemented will most likely be stronger than if the SMB viewed vulnerabilities only through the lens of external threats.

Employees and contractors who have access to sensitive information who are either contemplating leaving the company to join the competition or who are considered for termination are perhaps the most common sources of internal security threats. Those threats range from information corruption and disclosure through DoS to disabling of equipment, destruction, or theft.

As a measure of protection against these threats, an SMB should consider having procedures in place that prevent access to the network and physical locations with sensitive equipment after an employee has been notified of a termination. The individuals being terminated might perceive security-minded termination procedures as being perhaps less than humane. They probably are. Losing a job is a traumatic event in one's life that can arouse hard feelings and result in a great deal of emotional turmoil. A decision to do something foolish at this difficult time—such as an act of destruction or theft—can complicate life for both parties. Legal safeguards in the form of strong nondisclosure agreements can also protect against internal security breaches from employees or contractors whose relationship with a business might be drawing to a close.

Employees who enjoy a healthy relationship with an SMB can also pose a variety of security threats, both accidental and deliberate. Those threats can be minimized through the use of the following:

- Strong authentication that minimizes the potential for repudiation
- Granularity in authorization
- Restricting network access to typical work hours
- Use of physical security
- Encryption of sensitive information
- Network segmentation
- Application of commonsense security procedures that are important to an SMB's success

Strong Authentication

Strong authentication that allows for bulletproof nonrepudiation is difficult to achieve. But even if the most common and inherently flawed form of authentication—that is, passwords—is being used, authentication can be enhanced by having a strong password use policy.

A strong password policy forbids the exchange of passwords between employees, specifies use of strong passwords (a combination of a minimum of seven or eight alphanumeric and special characters), and does not allow the use of the same password for the same individual to access multiple networks, servers, or devices. A strong password policy might be perceived as inconvenient and a nuisance from the users' point of view.

Granularity in Authorization

Granularity in authorization means that everybody does not have access to everything. Providing granular access to the network for different categories of users requires planning and ongoing administration, but the effort is worthwhile because it can prevent highly confidential information from being exposed or destroyed. Rights and permissions management of folders and individual files is a standard feature in modern operating systems. Unfortunately, that and many other OS security features often are not well understood or are completely unused on SMB networks.

Restricting Network Access

Restricting network access to typical work hours can foil snooping attempts by completely unauthorized personnel or those with lower levels of authorization. As an example, suppose that the username and password of an employee who has a high level of authorization have been compromised. The SMB's network permits only one login at a time under that username, and the employee remains logged in continuously during normal business hours. If an unauthorized person attempts to log in under the compromised username after the employee has left the office for the day, that attempt will fail. It might also result in a log that could alert a security administrator that someone is trying to hijack a username that can access restricted information.

Physical Security

Physical security can prevent unauthorized personnel from entering sensitive facilities, whether purely by accident, out of curiosity, or with a malicious purpose in mind. But even when equipment is housed in sensitive areas like data centers, key network components should be physically protected and properly placed so that those authorized to be present do not damage them by accidentally kicking, unplugging, or showering them with coffee or soft drinks.

Encrypting Sensitive Information

Some SMBs opt to deploy internal VPNs to facilitate encryption and thus protect the confidentiality of highly sensitive internal communications. A decision to deploy an internal VPN should result from consideration of threats while an SMB is developing a security policy and should be subject to the design process discussed in Chapter 1.

Consider that when an encryption is required on an internal network, it means that there is the potential for intercept and reconstruction of the information while it is in transit over that network. Although capturing and decoding packets might be a routine procedure for IT personnel, it is generally not the favorite pastime of many other employees. However, in a high-tech, highly sensitive environment with a workforce that is technically savvy, strong encryption might be a key to the protection of confidential information.

Network Segmentation

Physical network segmentation, where certain resources (servers, for example) are on entirely separate networks, is an effective security mechanism as long as it does not interfere with normal business operations and necessary communications. There is generally a price to pay in terms of extra inconvenience as the level of physical security increases, whether in networking environments or elsewhere.

Having operational networks within an SMB that are entirely disconnected from each other can reflect one or more of the following:

- The SMB is security minded and maintains highly sensitive information on an internal network that is not connected to anything else. Access to this network is limited to a select group of personnel.

- The SMB does not have the internal expertise or a sufficient IT budget to get outside help and to integrate its networking infrastructure.

- Multiple separate networks might be the result of haphazard growth over a period of years where generations of networking equipment and operating systems somehow coexist and hang together to facilitate basic day-to-day operations. Although this kind of infrastructure lacks scalability, it also, ironically, can be more resilient to a security attack than a more uniform infrastructure.

Security Procedures Important to SMB Success

Having good security is not a guarantee that an SMB will be a successful business enterprise. However, having good security can enhance an SMB's image in the eyes of the public and its customers, provided that an SMB's other business practices are sound.

Consider SMBs that are privy to a lot of confidential customer information. Examples would be a health care facility or a financial institution. Suppose that someone with a bit of determination to test an SMB's security envelope walks into a bank, sits down at a logged-in, unattended workstation, and starts using the bank's software applications. This is unlikely to happen at any respectable bank or financial institution, regardless of its size.

Suppose, however, that someone walks into a bank with a notebook computer and attempts to tap into the bank's wireless network. Is the bank prepared to deal with that eventuality? Did the bank consider security concerns when it implemented a wireless local-area network (WLAN)? Also, what if that person spots an RJ-45 jack in the bank's waiting area and plugs a notebook into it? The person might not be able to log in immediately into the bank's network, but if the notebook computer is equipped with a protocol analyzer that captures all network traffic flying by, the intruder could fairly quickly capture passwords and login names to be used at a future time for less than honorable purposes.

Common sense dictates that if a person who is reasonably knowledgeable about computer networks and security and has a reasonable amount of determination to glean confidential information or disrupt network operations is not able to do so in a reasonable amount of time, the SMB has implemented a level of security that ought to inspire a degree of confidence in the eyes of the public and customers. That is not to say that other security measures should not be taken against the more determined security envelope testers rather than the hypothetical reasonable one.

Following are just a few commonsense procedures that when diligently adhered to should enhance an SMB's potential for success with respect to security:

- Under all circumstances, employees should turn down requests for passwords and login names coming from other employees, contractors, or perfect strangers.

- Unattended workstations should be logged off or turned off completely.

- Any unused access jacks to the network should be *dead* (not patched into a network production switch).

- Data centers should not be accessible without going through one or more layers of physical security—that is, locked doors with combination codes.

- Equipment within a data center should be located in a manner that prevents accidental shutdowns.

Security Threat Antidotes

Newton's third law of motion—frequently paraphrased as: For every action, there is an equal and opposite reaction—can be easily applied to the area of network security. For every security threat, there is an equally effective antidote.

Of course, network security is not the well-established field of classical physics; networking technologies are dynamic and continue to evolve at a rapid pace. It's a given that new security threats will emerge as a function of time. But it's also a given that over a period of time, if not immediately, those threats will be countered with effective antidotes. The following generic antidotes counter the four broad threat categories identified earlier in this chapter:

- Information integrity (counters information corruption)

- Information confidentiality (counters information disclosure)

- Nonrepudiation, authentication, and authorization (counters repudiation and lack of authentication and authorization)

- System availability (counters DoS)

Within a generic security antidote for a specific threat category, there can be numerous security solutions that implement a wide range of protocols and algorithms.

Information Integrity

Information integrity means that data or information remains unaltered, during transmission and storage, from the original value intended by its creator. (This statement does not imply anything about the integrity of the intent of the data creator, which is a separate issue.) Examples of the principle of data integrity are obvious and numerous.

If an SMB employee sends an e-mail message to a group of customers, data integrity means that the message will be delivered exactly as it was sent. Subtle changes will not be introduced into the message during its transmission. (If the message accidentally contains information that was not supposed to be sent to customers, the boss might wish that the message could be changed during transit, but that is a different issue!) Whether the contents of a message are proper or not, if they remain unchanged during transit, the principle of data integrity applies.

The extreme case of lack of data integrity in the case of an e-mail transmission is the nondelivery of the message or a delivery with the contents of the message being null. Information integrity in the case of data being transmitted is closely coupled with nonrepudiation and encryption. Encryption minimizes the potential for outsiders to tamper with the data, whereas nonrepudiation ensures that the transmitter is whom she or he claims to be.

Here are some examples of lack of information integrity:

- Application program installations or operating system upgrades that result in alterations to the system other than those intended by the vendor
- Viruses that change or destroy data
- Website defacements

Specific tools and procedures that are commonly used to enforce data integrity include the following:

- Use of encryption and digital signatures for e-mail transmissions. Both techniques also enforce data integrity when dealing with information disclosure and repudiation.
- Firewalls with regularly updated virus-scanning software to prevent virus infestations and unauthorized access to the network from the outside. It is vital that the security administrator keep up with upgrades to the firewall software.
- Strict procedures regarding installation of software applications and operating system upgrades. These procedures must ensure that the preinstallation state of the server or workstation can be quickly restored in case of the device crash or data destruction during the installation. For example, all installations could be tried first on an offline server or workstation before being attempted on a production unit.
- Data audits to detect discrepancies between the actual and the intended data. (Don't be alarmed if this seems like an accounting function. Comprehensive network security encompasses many types of functions.)
- Verifiable backup procedures. Backup procedures are verified by simulating complete data destruction and performing a restore from a backup device. Backup procedures are not verified when the backup software says that it successfully completed a backup. (Again, no need to be alarmed if this procedure seems like it has more to do with network administration than network security. Consider the final result of the procedure and decide for yourself under which umbrella to place it.)
- Disaster recovery plan. (Linking information integrity with disaster recovery is perhaps stretching the security envelope thin and getting more and more controversial, so it's time to stop. But again, no need to get hung up on semantics. The final goal is data integrity under all circumstances.)

Information Confidentiality

As stated earlier in this chapter, whenever an SMB's CEOs and CIOs think about network security, information confidentiality is probably their greatest concern. Information confidentiality needs to be enforced through technology as well as commonsense procedures.

The proactive approach to maintaining information confidentiality is, as a default, to deny everyone access to all of the confidential information, and then to permit access for authorized individuals as a function of their need to know. This concept is the basis for the use of firewalls and access control lists (ACLs). Access to information is denied unless explicitly granted.

Generic tools that facilitate the enforcement of information confidentiality include these:

- Use of firewalls to secure the network from unauthorized outside penetration. Firewalls must be properly configured, the logs they generate must be monitored, and they must be subject to ongoing maintenance with upgrades to their software. Use of firewalls can be defeated from the inside if an authorized access point to the network is created that bypasses the firewall—for example, if an SMB's network is protected by a firewall, use of a modem or a digital subscriber line (DSL) on one or two workstations can bypass the firewall.

- Use of encryption for confidential internal and external transmissions. If a transmission that is encrypted with a long key (128 bits or more) is intercepted either internally or externally, it is nearly impossible to decode it without access to extremely powerful computing resources.

- Use of strong internal authentication to minimize the potential for repudiation. If access to information—and, consequently, its disclosure—cannot be repudiated, individuals who are contemplating malicious action might reconsider because they might not want to face the consequences of disclosure.

- High granularity in authorization to minimize the degree of damage and compromise after a disclosure occurs. By maintaining granularity in authorization, even if a deliberate disclosure occurs, the damage is limited to only the information the individual was authorized to see rather than all of the SMB's confidential information.

Nonrepudiation, Authentication, and Authorization

Not being able to deny an act of authentication under any circumstances is equivalent to nonrepudiation. This is easier said than done, so why bother with nonrepudiation? Even hardened network security will sooner or later encounter individuals who are entrusted with a high degree of authorization who can't resist sharing secrets with others. Nonrepudiation offers the means to tie an individual to an act of authentication and possibly other activities that follow—which could include information disclosure or corruption.

Nonrepudiation in and of itself does not prevent someone, except as a deterrent, from creating security breaches by disclosing information, engaging in acts of data destruction or modification, and performing other acts that result in DoS. But in select high-security environments, nonrepudiation backed up by strong legal and financial consequences is nonetheless a desirable security antidote against all of the security threats discussed in this chapter.

An SMB must consider the cost of implementing a high degree of nonrepudiation compared to the cost of taking other security precautions. In such a situation, a security policy comes in handy.

Following are some recommendations for SMBs to ponder while pursuing the goal of a high degree of nonrepudiation, authentication, and authorization on their networks:

- Consider biometric authentication for highly sensitive areas housing critical network equipment.
- Clearly spell out in the security policy the consequences of deliberate or even accidental security breaches that can be conclusively tied (beyond repudiation) to an individual.
- Take advantage of all the authentication and authorization mechanisms that come with modern network operating systems.

System Availability

Network or system availability should be a design consideration in every networking solution, as discussed in Chapter 1. In the context of network security, the system availability antidote counters the threat of DoS. This antidote means that network security is sufficiently robust to defeat all attempts to bring the network down through any means other than the authorized and scheduled shutdown procedures.

System availability can be hardened in the following ways:

- Use of firewalls and a server operating system configuration capable of detecting and ignoring DoS attacks
- Uninterruptible power in the form of uninterruptible power supplies (UPSes) or generators for critical network components
- Strong physical security for data centers, telecom closets, or any location housing a network server, a switch, or a router

- Standby spares of critical components
- Presence of verifiable up-to-date backups in case a restore is required following information destruction or unrecoverable failure of data storage devices

The Importance of Having a Security Policy

Implementing security solutions without having a security policy (either explicitly defined or at least implied) represents at best a haphazard approach to addressing network security issues. It is preferable to have a network security policy in writing, with input into the policy coming from the groups of stakeholders identified in Chapter 1. Figure 4-2 depicts the impact of security policy on implementation of security solutions.

Figure 4-2   *Impact of Security Policy on Security Solutions Implementation*

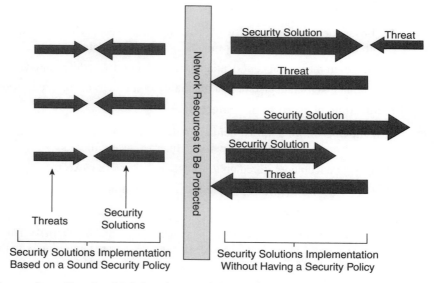

A security policy should define the security goals that an SMB aspires to with respect to its computer network or, in a broader sense, all of its information and technology assets. This definition of security goals creates a framework for the full development of a security policy by facilitating the following:

- Identification of assets to be protected
- Delineation of threats against the protected assets
- Review of the available responses—that is, security solutions—to counter the perceived threats

- Creation of rules that users are obliged to follow with respect to the utilization of the protected assets
- Development of an action plan in the event of a security breach
- Identification of a baseline against which compliance with security procedures can be measured and monitored on an ongoing basis
- Identification of trigger mechanisms for updating and reviewing the policy

Based on this framework, a sample security policy follows for a hypothetical SMB called XYZ. XYZ employs a total of 150 people, has two locations in metropolitan areas separated by a distance of about 120 miles (approximately 200 kilometers), and its primary line of business is the design, development, and production of components and subsystems utilized in the space program. XYZ is highly dependent on its network.

The network security policy for XYZ follows.

Security goals:

- Ensure network availability 99.9% of the time. There will be approximately 45 minutes of downtime per month for scheduled maintenance.
- Maintain maximum confidentiality of production schedules and design documents.
- Maintain a high degree of confidentiality of all internal communications.

Identification of assets to be protected:

- Entire networking infrastructure within XYZ's facilities (cabling, network switches, engineering and production servers, Internet access routers).
- Design documents stored on a storage-area network (SAN).
- Ongoing communications regarding business strategy.

Delineation of threats:

- Denial of network usage through any means (internal or external). This includes virus and DoS attacks as well as accidental and deliberate tampering with the network infrastructure by unauthorized employees.
- Loss of confidential design documents.
- Interception of e-mail communications by unauthorized employees.

Security solutions to counter perceived threats:

- Firewalls with virus-checking software deployed at multiple Internet access points to counter external penetration and to ensure redundancy in Internet access.
- An external VPN to ensure confidentiality of communications between the two locations.

- An engineering network, with access to the SAN that stores the design documents, that is completely isolated from the Internet and the production network. Access to the production network from the engineering network is allowed only for the purpose of large file transfers. A special-purpose server becomes disconnected from the production network and is temporarily connected to the engineering network.

- Select use of internal VPNs to ensure confidentiality of internal e-mail communications.

- Strong authentication, including a strong password policy, use of badges, and biometric authentication. All routers and switches are password protected. Router privileged mode is password protected. ACLs allow access to the routers only from select workstations on the network.

- Strong physical security at all servers, SAN, router, and switch locations that requires biometric authentication for access to the designated areas where those devices are kept.

- Spare servers, routers, and switches on standby in case of unrecoverable crash.

- Power protection for all servers, routers, switches, and select workstations.

- High granularity in authorization as a result of effective determination of each employee's network activity.

- Intrusion detection scanner to help with development of a baseline for network traffic levels.

Rules regarding protected assets:

- No password disclosure or badge swapping is permitted under any circumstances.

- No computing devices such as notebook computers, modems, routers, or switches can be brought into the facility without clearance from the IT director.

- Any maintenance on critical network components that must performed by an outside contractor has to be done in the presence of an authorized IT staff member.

- Use of the Internet and downloading of files is subject to a separate acceptable use policy (AUP) for Internet access.

Action plan in the event of a breach:

- Attempt to identify the compromised asset or information as quickly as possible.

- Isolate the compromised devices from the rest of the network.

- Communicate the situation to people in executive management and keep them apprised of its progress.

- Alert local law enforcement if criminal intent is suspected.

Identification of baseline:

- Develop a historical baseline using network management tools that identifies traffic levels and device utilization as a function of time.

- Develop a baseline of network usage by employees, including login duration, number of login attempts, and hours of usage.
- Develop a baseline of any security incidents and their frequency.

Identification of trigger mechanisms for policy review or update:

- Emergence of what is considered a new threat, which would typically be reported in the media.
- Security breach incident.
- Elapse of fixed amount of time—for example, three months.

This policy is based on the components of a security framework that has been developed throughout this chapter. Because each SMB has unique security requirements, this skeletal policy should be tailored to a specific SMB's needs.

An Additional Policy Reference

The informational RFC 2196 titled "A Site Security Handbook" is an excellent source that offers extensive guidelines regarding the development and implementation of a security policy. The RFC defines a security policy as follows: "a formal statement of the rules by which people who are given access to an organization's technology and information assets must abide." Addressing the purposes of the security policy, the RFC further states: "The main purpose of a security policy is to inform users, staff, and managers of their obligatory requirements for protecting technology and information assets. The policy should specify the mechanisms through which these requirements can be met. Another purpose is to provide a baseline from which to acquire, configure, and audit computer systems and networks for compliance with the policy. Therefore, an attempt to use a set of security tools in the absence of at least an implied security policy is meaningless."

RFC 2196 is recommended reading for anyone who is involved with developing a network security policy at an SMB. Note the emphasis that the RFC places on the principle of having rules and informing the users and staff of those rules.

Summary

This chapter stressed the importance of having a security policy, and it culminated with a definition and an example of such a policy. If an SMB does not have a policy that identifies assets to be protected and that considers the cost of solutions versus the cost of recovery from a security breach, its approach to network security will be at best haphazard.

Generic categories of threats to an SMB's information and technology assets were introduced and clarified. Those threats include information corruption, information disclosure, repudiation coupled with lack of authentication and authorization, and DoS. Specific threat mechanisms that exemplify one or more of the preceding categories were discussed in the context of numerous scenarios.

The issue of internal versus external security threats was addressed, as were the following generic threat antidotes to the security threat categories: information integrity, information confidentiality, nonrepudiation coupled with strong authentication and authorization, and system availability. This chapter also emphasized that implementing network security is an ongoing process that must be responsive to changing technology; it is not a static, one-time event. Specific technology solutions for implementing network security are discussed in Chapter 5.

CHAPTER 5

Cisco Security Solutions

An effective security solution should counter one or more of the security threats that have been identified in a security policy as having the potential to impact the operations of the small-medium business (SMB) in a drastic, adverse manner. All of the security solutions presented in this chapter can be used either standalone or in a complementary manner to oppose one or more of these threats.

Ideally, the choice of a solution should result from the process of defining a security policy and should depend on the type of threats (see Chapter 4, "Overview of the Network Security Issues") and their damage potential to the SMB's network resources and information assets. But if the ideal of having a well-defined security policy cannot be realized, you still need to find a security solution.

Firewalling an SMB's internal network, which is also connected to the Internet, is a given, even if the SMB chooses not to engage in a formal process of formulating a security policy. As the security solutions become more versatile, easier to deploy, and counter more and more of the common threats in a single integrated security appliance, securing a network of the future might eventually become a "plug-and-play" operation. Everyone involved in the development of security solutions should aim for that goal.

Meanwhile, existing security solutions, even if they are getting easier to deploy, require a degree of design and configuration planning. The solutions presented in this chapter include the following:

- Virtual private networks (VPNs)
- Firewalls
- Intrusion detection systems (IDSes)
- Router security features

These security solutions offer effective antidotes for many of the specific threats in all of the security threat categories discussed in Chapter 4. They facilitate the enforcement of information confidentiality through multiple encryption algorithms while data is in transit across the network. They also secure the network parameter and prevent outsiders from gaining access to the internal network and its resources through stateful firewalling. In addition, they detect hundreds of network intrusion signatures—including denial of service, worms, and application attacks—and either alert a security administrator to a possible intrusion or mitigate it. They also facilitate consistency of configuration, network monitoring, and traffic analysis, and, consequently, the enforcement of security policies through integrated management platforms and individual device managers.

In addition, identity services in the form of user Authentication, Authorization, and Accounting (AAA) are integrated with the security solutions either at a local device level or in a centralized manner via dedicated servers. Collectively, and especially when deployed in a complementary manner, Cisco security solutions facilitate a flexible modular end-to-end approach to securing a network that raises the bar for network access to include only those who are indeed authorized to have it. In turn, secure network access and communication in today's dynamic business environment translates into enabling new sources of revenue and productivity gains by eliminating the traditional distance and time boundaries between the SMB's partners, customers, and employees. Now, let's consider each solution in more detail.

Virtual Private Networks

A *VPN* is typically defined as a private network operating over a shared infrastructure. By definition at least, a *private network* implies highly restricted access to authorized personnel only, transmission over the network that is secure from outside intrusion, and a quantifiable level of performance. *Shared infrastructure* potentially implies just the opposite: free-for-all access, lack of secure transmission, and no guarantee of performance. When a VPN is deployed over the Internet, a private network is operating over an insecure public network.

Given the success of the VPN technology, it's clear that the benefits associated with the private network have prevailed over the shortcomings of the shared environment. This outcome was possible thanks to the many varied security protocols and technologies, wide-ranging global advances in the public communications infrastructure, ease of deployment, and high-performance routing/switching techniques, including the following:

- Strong user authentication for remote access VPNs that can leverage an existing authentication server like Remote Access Dial-In User Service (RADIUS), the Cisco Terminal Access Controller Access Control System (TACACS/TACACS+), an NT domain, or an internal authentication server that is configured on the VPN 3000 series concentrator.

- The use of the IPSec (Internet Protocol Security) protocol suite with the attendant Internet Key Exchange (IKE) protocol and encryption options, such as 56-bit Data Encryption Standard (DES), 3DES or the Advanced Encryption Standard (AES), to ensure a high level of authentication and data privacy in site-to-site VPN deployment scenarios.

- Flexibility in deployment options, meaning that VPNs can be constructed through the use of VPN-capable firewalls, VPN-capable routers, or dedicated VPN concentrators to suit the needs of a wide range of SMB topologies and business requirements.

WebVPN or Secure Socket Layer (SSL) VPN further adds to the flexibility in VPN deployments by eliminating the need for dedicated VPN client software or hardware and by allowing clients to use SSL-enabled browsers.

- Increasing robustness and geographical pervasiveness of the public network infrastructure that facilitates widespread VPN deployment and through the economies of scale makes the VPN products and services more and more affordable to a typical SMB.

- Increasing availability of higher bandwidth to the established places of business, residential home offices, and various travel transit locations (for example, hotels, airports, cafes), which translates into an ever-improving VPN performance and introduces a high degree of flexibility for a company's mobile or geographically dispersed workforce.

- Adaptation of the Multiprotocol Label Switching (MPLS) technology, which facilitates simplified Layer 3 routing at Layer 2 switching speeds in peer-to-peer VPN deployments in the core of provider networks.

In combination, the preceding factors make a strong case for VPN deployment by any SMB, especially if the maintainance of effective and secure communication between locations, employees, partners, vendors, and customers is part of the SMB's overall business strategy.

VPN Deployment Considerations

Despite the many factors listed in the preceding section that have effectively made VPNs a part of the mainstream vernacular, deploying a VPN solution by an SMB is not necessarily a given like firewalling an internal network would be.

Solid security that VPNs offer represents the absolutely necessary but not necessarily sufficient condition for deployment. Whether the VPN is deployed as remote access only or site to site in the various topologies, it needs to provide an SMB, first and foremost, with new (and secure, of course) communications options, or it needs to replace or enhance the existing ones. So the first order of business is to prove that a VPN offers a solid means of communication, and the second is to ensure the security of that communication.

Here are some specific design considerations that you should take into account when contemplating VPN deployment for an SMB:

- The SMB's existing or proposed network topology and the expected or required performance level, as determined by the applications, workforce distribution, mobility, and projected growth

- Potential for significant cost savings if a VPN solution ends up replacing a private network based on leased lines, Frame Relay, or Asynchronous Transfer Mode (ATM)

- Introduction of new lines of secure communication for employees, SMB executives, and business partners, which leads to higher productivity and greater operational efficiency

- Ease of implementation of a VPN solution without disrupting the ongoing SMB operations, in the event that a VPN is going to replace a well-functioning but more expensive existing private network

- Reliability, resiliency, and scalability of a VPN solution that ought to be comparable to that of a private network, in case an SMB decides to switch completely from a private network to a VPN

- The ease of configuration and management of a VPN solution during and following deployment

- The delivery of a comparable or higher level of security than what an SMB has been accustomed to in the private network

VPN Network Topologies and Workforce Distribution

Potential VPN deployment is often driven by the static geographical distribution of a company's workforce and facilities. However, in today's mobile and Internet-driven economy, when considering VPN deployment, an SMB should look not just at the physical location of its workforce and facilities but also at the communication trends among all of its stakeholders. The communications to consider include the following:

- SMB and customers

- SMB and vendors

- SMB and partners

- Intracompany

Suppose that an SMB has only one brick-and-mortar facility, and a good portion of its workforce is mobile. Would the SMB benefit from a VPN deployment? Absolutely! If the road warriors need to access confidential information on the corporate network to be effective in their work, a remote-access VPN solution will facilitate those communications in a secure manner.

Suppose that an SMB needs to communicate on an ongoing basis with a few of its major clients. No SMB employees are physically located at those clients' sites, but the nature of the communication entails mutual database access in addition to e-mail and file transfers. Security of those communications is critical to the SMB and its clients. This is a clear-cut case for an appropriate site-to-site VPN deployment, regardless of whether the clients are a few miles or thousands of miles away.

What if the SMB needs secure communications internal to its network? Suppose that two subnets on the internal network need all of the communications between them to be encrypted. In this case, the remainder of the SMB's private network effectively becomes a public network with respect to those two subnets. Those subnets can be placed behind VPN-capable firewalls or routers, and a VPN tunnel can be formed between them to accommodate the internal security requirement. In this scenario, because communication between the two subnets was already established, the security aspect of the VPN would be the primary reason for VPN deployment; the established line of communication did not meet the security requirements specified in the SMB's security policy prior to the VPN deployment.

The preceding scenarios illustrate only partially the versatility of VPN solutions, which are able to accommodate a wide range of network topologies and workforce distributions. Whether the requirement for secure communication is by remote users, between two or multiple sites, or even internal to the SMB's private network, a scalable VPN solution can be deployed to meet the demand.

With integrated VPN capability in the key components of the network infrastructure (routers, firewalls, switches, dedicated VPN concentrators, and hardware clients), Cisco has VPN solutions that are uniquely positioned to fulfill the diverse VPN requirements that arise in the many and varied SMB scenarios. And SSL VPNs further ease VPN deployments on the client side.

All of the VPN deployments can be broadly categorized as being either remote access or site to site. Within these categories, the use of the IPSec protocols facilitates the construction of the following designs, depending on topology and configuration:

- Fully meshed or hub-and-spoke site-to-site with static addressing
- Hub-and-spoke site-to-site with static addressing at the hub and dynamic addressing at the spokes
- Fully meshed on-demand site-to-site with Tunnel Endpoint Discovery (TED)
- Dynamic-multipoint site-to-site with Generic Routing Encapsulation (GRE)
- Cisco Easy VPN remote access

Site-to-Site with Static Addressing VPNs

Fully meshed or hub-and-spoke site-to-site VPNs with static addressing rely on the use of static crypto maps during configuration. For the fully meshed option, the addition of a new location means the reconfiguration of all of the routers or devices involved in the creation of IPSec tunnels. It also means that as the number of sites increases, configuration does not scale well.

The cutoff in the number of sites becomes a matter of a designer's individual preference. For example, for 20 sites, a router at each site would have to have 19 static crypto maps. The configuration would be a lot more manageable for five sites, where a router at each site would have only four static crypto maps.

For the hub-and-spoke option with static addressing, addition of a new spoke does not require the reconfiguration of all of the other spokes. But the hub router needs to be reconfigured if a new spoke is added, and the number of static crypto maps that are configured on it will correspond to the number of spokes.

Static and Dynamic Addressing VPNs

The hub-and-spoke option with static addressing at the hub and dynamic addressing at the spokes scales better with respect to configuration than the static addressing equivalent because it relies on the use of dynamic instead of static crypto maps. A single dynamic crypto map can be used on the hub instead of multiple static ones. However, the limitation of this configuration is that only the spokes can initiate the IPSec tunnels after they authenticate with the hub. One authentication method works by configuring the same preshared key on all of the spokes.

On-Demand Site-to-Site with TED VPNs

The fully meshed on-demand site-to-site VPN with TED scenario is intended mainly for topologies in which static configuration is not practical because of the large number of sites. However, nothing prevents a smaller SMB from deploying this kind of VPN if the SMB anticipates significant growth in the number of sites. In addition, the designer should think modularly, which means that a large enterprise could be broken down into smaller units, each of which could be considered an SMB.

The benefit of the on-demand TED feature is that dynamic IP addressing can be used at all sites, and configuration is greatly simplified because each site can be configured with only one dynamic crypto map. However, the TED feature relies on probing of the attached LANs, which require IPSec protection, and the addresses of the LANs must be routable. If this configuration is implemented over the Internet, it means that the LAN addresses must be globally routable and cannot be NATed.

Dynamic-Multipoint Site-to-Site with GRE VPNs

The dynamic-multipoint VPN with GRE can be deployed in scenarios in which a combination of static and dynamic tunnels is desirable to optimize an SMB's communication requirements. For example, if the communication pattern for an SMB is mostly hub and spoke, but there is also a need for communication between the spokes without placing undue processing burden on the hub router(s), the dynamic multipoint solution can be deployed. The formal name for this solution is Dynamic Multipoint IPSec VPN (DMVPN).

DMVPN relies on the Multipoint GRE/Next Hop Resolution Protocol (mGRE/NHRP) to detect peer addresses and to establish dynamic tunnels. DMVPN supports the use of dynamic private addressing at the spokes, which adds greatly to the flexibility of this VPN deployment approach.

Cisco Easy VPN

Cisco Easy VPN remote access solution is intended mainly for telecommuters and small branches. Its architecture consists of Cisco Easy VPN server, which terminates tunnels from the Easy VPN remote clients. The Easy VPN server can be a dedicated VPN 3000 series concentrator, an Internetwork Packet Exchange (IPX) firewall, or an IOS router.

Cost Savings Resulting from VPN Implementation

Suppose that an SMB has multiple branches and links them with the central location via private leased lines in a hub-and-spoke topology. The security advantage of a VPN solution might not be the biggest selling point in this situation because the private network already offers adequate protection. However, if the locations are separated sufficiently, and each needs high-speed access to the Internet, it is almost a given that a VPN solution would result in significant cost savings for the SMB.

When designing a VPN solution in this scenario, you must have access to the costs for the leased lines. Then you need to research the broadband access to the public network at all of the branch locations. Needless to say, broadband access needs to be available. Often, the provider that offers the leased lines is the same provider that would offer broadband Internet access.

Comparing the recurring costs for leased lines to those for Internet broadband access can quickly demonstrate if there are grounds for pursuing a VPN solution for cost-saving reasons (assuming that all of the remaining factors, such as performance and reliability, are the same or better).

CAUTION   Here's something to watch out for: Monthly prices for leased lines might be tied to a long-term contract. Getting out of the contract could result in costly disconnect charges that would at least temporarily offset the potential cost savings resulting from switching to a VPN.

VPNs as Enhancements to the Existing Communications Infrastructure

In the multisite hub-and-spoke scenario from the preceding section, suppose that an SMB decides not to implement a VPN because the cost savings resulting from a proposed VPN solution are not sufficient to warrant an initial investment in equipment upgrades or to sustain a potential operations disruption resulting from the switch. This could be the case if the SMB's facilities are fairly close together geographically and the cost of leased lines is comparable to the cost of broadband Internet access.

However, when several of the leased lines subsequently fail, the SMB becomes painfully aware that the private network has no redundancy whatsoever. A VPN solution suddenly reappears on the radar screen and could be introduced as a backup for one or more of what the SMB considers its most critical branches.

A backup VPN solution can be readily implemented in parallel with an existing private network. To be effective, the solution must include a well-documented procedure for switching from the private network configuration to the VPN if a private network failure occurs.

As part of a backup solution, suppose that VPN-capable routers and broadband Internet access are deployed at the central location and two of the branches. This setup allows an added bonus: It becomes possible to establish a direct line of communication between the branches without going through the hub. As this scenario scales, it might become obvious that a VPN solution is more flexible and resilient than a private network based on leased lines. And, in general, experience dictates that providing broadband access to the Internet is a lot easier and faster than providing point-to-point leased lines, which might increase the desirability of expanding the VPN instead of the private network as the SMB adds new branches.

VPN Implementation Issues

From an implementation point of view, a major logistical consideration is whether the VPN deployment is creating a new network or replacing an existing operational one.

If the deployment is a replacement, two additional deployment variables to consider are the following:

- Testing the VPN reliability in parallel with the exiting network.

- Minimizing any operational disruptions resulting from the switch. If the existing network works well, it is even more important to ensure that the VPN solution works equally well before going live with it.

Any new deployments of networking solutions or switching between communications systems or infrastructure of any kind are generally not without glitches or the need for users to learn new operational procedures. You should take this into account by doing the following:

- Allocating the time to work out unanticipated glitches

- Offering effective user education

VPN Reliability, Resilience, and Scalability

In a multisite hub-and-spoke topology, there might be minimal or no difference between the equipment required for a private network and a VPN. In a private network, two main topologies are applicable at the hub: a single router with multiple WAN ports aggregating all of the incoming lines from the outlying locations, or multiple routers with a single WAN port dedicated to each of the locations. As a function of the size of the network, an in-between option is also available in which several routers at the hub aggregate multiple lines, each router from a group of outlying locations.

In any of these topologies, the aggregating router(s) or the individual routers would be plugged into a switch that is interfaced with the remainder of the SMB's network at the hub location. To minimize the amount of equipment, cabling, configuration, and management required, the router(s) should be equipped with built-in channel service units/data service units (CSUs/DSUs) that are required to interface to a provider's leased lines.

Similar equipment and topology could potentially be used if an SMB decides to deploy a VPN instead of a private network. Instead of having a point-to-point leased line from each branch to the hub, each location would have a leased line to the Internet. The hub would likely require a higher-capacity leased line than the branches to accommodate the aggregate traffic from the branches.

VPN Reliability

The big difference between the private network and the VPN solution is in the IOS features and the actual configuration of the routers. An outside observer just looking at the equipment might be unable to determine whether a certain network is a private network or a VPN. However, to a designer familiar with the Cisco product lines, the determination would be easier. If the router(s) happen to be from the 7100 series, a VPN solution is probably in place, and if the router(s) are from the 7200 series, it is most likely a private network. At the branches, the router models might vary depending on the required WAN interfaces.

The preceding comparison between a private network and a VPN demonstrates that from an equipment point of view, the reliability of the VPN is going to be comparable to that of a private network because similar Cisco equipment enables both solutions. However, neither a private network nor a VPN is going to be immune from downtime, which is often a result of the communications lines going down rather than VPN-equipment failures. In either a private network or a VPN scenario, you should have a contingency plan in the event that a portion of the network fails.

VPN Resilience

The superior resilience of a VPN solution when compared with that of a private network stems from the fact that a VPN solution allows for spoke-to-spoke communications if the hub location sustains prolonged downtime. With a leased lines private network, a serious problem at the hub location would isolate from one another all of the branches that were communicating through the hub. With a VPN solution that's using broadband access to the Internet at each branch, even if the configured lines of communication between all of the locations mirror a hub-and-spoke topology, you need to understand that it's only a logical topology resulting from a particular kind of VPN configuration. A contingency set of configuration files could be readily deployed at the spokes to create spoke-to-spoke communications capability if the hub experiences downtime.

VPN Scalability

When considering a VPN from the scalability perspective, you face the challenge of selecting the best solution from the large number of available options, given that VPN capability has been built into diverse networking equipment. The key to minimizing this challenge is to be aware of the primary purpose of each VPN-capable device and the degree of VPN scalability that is built into it.

Scalability of VPN Concentrators 3000 Series   As a general rule, you should consider remote access concentrators like those in the Cisco VPN 3000 series, with the appropriate models depending on the number of users. VPN 3005 or 3015 would be an appropriate choice for smaller enterprises (with up to 100 users), whereas the VPN 3030 is recommended for medium-size and larger businesses (with up 1500 users). The VPN 3000 series concentrators work in conjunction with the VPN software or hardware client. In addition, the 3000 series concentrators support SSL VPNs.

Scalability of VPN 3002 Hardware Client   The VPN hardware client (VPN 3002) is ideal for groups of users at locations where, for policy reasons, the VPN client software (or any other software, for that matter) cannot be installed on workstations. The workstation operating system (OS) is transparent to the hardware client, which means that a single hardware client can support a wide variety of workstation operating systems, including Windows-based, DOS, UNIX, or Mac.

The VPN 3002 is an almost plug-and-play device because it requires only a minimal initial configuration, with the remainder of the configuration supplied by the concentrator. Because of the ease of configuration, the VPN 3002 hardware client also works well in scenarios in which technical resources are scarce at the deployment locations. Although you could argue that because it is a dedicated piece of hardware, the VPN 3002 is less portable than the software client, you should not confuse being less portable with not being portable. The hardware client is ideal for offices or temporary meeting places that allow for an Ethernet interface to a provider's equipment (cable modem, digital subscriber line (DSL) modem, or an IOS-based Cisco router).

Scalability of VPN Software Client   The VPN software client naturally has the benefit of being able to be used from anywhere that a desktop PC or a notebook has access to the Internet, including dialup. Its additional benefit lies in being able to facilitate enforcement of certain policies. Suppose that the software client is used from behind an 800 series router that needs to have its IOS upgraded to a more recent version. The VPN software client will detect that condition and will require that an upgrade be performed before the VPN session is established. In addition to the client software, consider the SSL VPN if the deployment includes the VPN 3000 series concentrators at the main VPN sites.

Scalability of VPN-Capable Routers   In contrast to the VPN 3000 series concentrators, VPN-capable routers are best suited for setting up VPN tunnels, where all of the participating devices across the tunnel transparently become part of the same network. However, that is only a general statement. Cisco offers a wide range of VPN-capable routers, ranging from the lower-end 800 series through the higher-end 7100 series. Although the lower-end access or edge router located at a small branch or a home office might be ideal to set up a tunnel to a 7100 unit that is located at a central location, the 7100 can also accommodate hundreds of remote VPN sessions.

Scalability of VPN-Capable Firewalls   A firewall's primary purpose is to stop undesirable traffic from entering or leaving the SMB's network. However, firewalls can be used to set up tunnels and to offer VPN concentrator service, provided that performance considerations are taken into account when maxing out all of the security capabilities on an integrated appliance like the PIX. If you consider that the higher-end PIX firewalls beginning with 515E offer concentrator services that support up to 2000 remote users, it's a given that VPN accelerator cards will be needed to maintain reasonable performance.

When small numbers of users are involved, an integrated appliance that performs all of the security functions (firewalling, intrusion scanning, or a VPN) might be appropriate as opposed to using dedicated boxes for each one of those functions. For example, a lower-end firewall like the PIX 506E can support up to a maximum of 25 remote users through its VPN concentrator service. If you add to it a subset of IDS signatures in addition to the stateful firewalling capability, the integrated appliance becomes a perfect solution for an SMB with a dozen or so employees, some of whom periodically need to access the network via a VPN. For advice on the type of solution to use depending on the number of users, remember that when getting down to the nuts and bolts of specifications, the *Cisco Products Quick Reference Guide* is a helpful resource.

VPN Management

The issue of how to manage a VPN is a classic design decision. Scalability, performance, and financial considerations (as discussed in Chapter 1, "Effective Networking Solution Design Process") all play a role in the decision of what form of management to deploy.

Device-Level Versus Integrated Management

The choice that a designer is normally confronted with is between a device-management platform and an integrated-management software package. Because an integrated platform is going to be more expensive, the issue becomes how much value an SMB places on avoiding potential problems stemming from misconfigurations. Such pitfalls can include accidentally passing confidential traffic over the Internet or having a firewall allow all or most unauthorized outside traffic to penetrate the internal network, causing expensive disruptions.

In the health care industry, for example, the issue of confidentiality is extremely critical because inappropriate disclosure of patient information has serious legal and financial implications. The choice of management software often boils down to a "pay now or pay later" principle. If an SMB is willing to gamble with the legal or financial implications of having confidential information disclosed or network operations disrupted, a more expensive integrated-management platform might be a difficult sell.

VPN Management Offerings from Cisco

Whatever the decision regarding management software, Cisco offers an integrated platform in the form of the CiscoWorks VPN/Security Management Solution (VMS), which facilitates the management of VPNs, firewalls, and IDSes. VMS is modular, which allows you to choose the appropriate modules as a function of the security devices present in the network. You can also use device-management software such as the PIX Device Manager (PDM) or the browser-based VPN concentrator graphical user interface (GUI), especially in the much smaller enterprises where cost considerations are paramount.

Of course, you have the option of performing all of the configuration and device monitoring directly from the command-line interface (CLI). However, this scenario requires a significant skill level and often tends to wrap the management aspect of a network around an individual, which is not necessarily the healthiest approach to network administration and management.

VPN Security

Provided that VPNs are configured properly, security and VPN are effectively synonymous. Although data encryption is possible over a private leased line or Frame Relay network, it is not always practiced because a private network is assumed to provide adequate security.

However, consider that even a private network is not as private as it might seem. The leased lines go through multiple central offices (COs) and physically snake through many cables. In addition, if the unencrypted data sneaking along the private network can be intercepted someplace along the way, it is subject to easy deciphering. The same holds true for a Frame Relay network, where the provider offers emulated leased lines over the provider's network cloud. Frame Relay networks are sometimes referred to as overlay VPNs.

When you consider the security that private networks offer through their physical characteristics of isolation versus the security offered by VPNs through encryption and tunneling, it becomes obvious that even the private networks could benefit from the VPN security capabilities.

VPN Deployment Scenarios

Although various VPN scenarios in isolation were useful in the context of discussing the deployment considerations, the purpose of this section is to summarize some of the typical scenarios in the form of case studies, with reference to specific topologies and equipment.

Branch Office Connectivity via the Internet

A typical multibranch private network with a central location is implemented either via point-to-point leased lines or Frame Relay in either hub-and-spoke or a partial-mesh topology. The hub-and-spoke topology works well when all of the branches need to communicate with the hub but don't necessarily need to communicate with one another. Extensive communication between branches in a hub-and-spoke topology can place considerable pressure on the routers at the hub.

Let's consider a case study that involves a financial institution with a central location, 11 branches, and 250+ employees. All of the branches have between 12 and 15 employees, whereas the central location houses 100+. The institution expects to see growth through acquisitions. The current topology is hub-and-spoke point-to-point leased lines. Management is wondering how the high cost of the leased lines can be reduced, especially as new branches are added.

A VPN is the natural answer to alleviate management's concern about the high cost of maintaining and upgrading the private network. The challenge is choosing the options that are needed for this VPN deployment from all the possibilities. After defining the user requirements, the design team comes up with the following:

- All of the branches need to communicate with the central location. The bandwidth requirements for that communication have been estimated at approximately 1 Mbps for each branch.

- Three of the branches have significant exchanges with one another, with an estimated bandwidth requirement of 500 Kbps for each pair. This translates into an additional 1 Mbps of bandwidth per branch for the interbranch exchanges between the three branches.
- The institution would like to allow a few of its employees, including the internal auditor, to work from their respective homes.
- Security of all communications is absolutely critical.

Given these requirements, the design team develops following recommendations:

- All branches that do not have significant communications with one another are to provision a single dedicated leased T1 pipe to the Internet.
- The three branches that communicate with one another are to provision two dedicated leased T1 lines to the Internet. All traffic will be load balanced over the two lines.
- Each branch will have a modular lower-end VPN-capable router and a lower-end PIX firewall.
- The central location will provision a dedicated T3 line to the Internet and will deploy a high-end VPN router and a higher-end dedicated firewall. Intrusion detection will be integrated into the high-end router.
- The logical topology (VPN tunnels) will be hub and spoke between all of the branches and the central location, in addition to a full mesh between the three branches that communicate with one other. Static addresses and static crypto maps will be used to configure the VPN tunnels.
- 3DES encryption will be used for all communications.
- VMS with the Management Center for VPN routers and firewall modules will be deployed.
- Small access routers along with VPN client software will be provided for telecommuters who need to work out of their home offices.

The specific equipment recommendations follow.

Branches:

- 1700 series modular routers with IP and IPSec 3DES IOS features and two WAN slots (1721 model, for example).
- A single T1 WAN interface card (WIC) for the branches communicating only with the hub.
- Two T1 WICs for the branches communicating with the hub and one another.
- PIX 506E firewall.
- Existing switch and cabling.

Central location:

- Cisco 7140 with IP and IPSec 3DES, FW, and IDS IOS feature set.
- A T3 serial port adapter with an integrated CSU/DSU.

- A PIX 515E firewall with four-port Ethernet module to allow setup of demilitarized zone (DMZ) networks. This firewall will also be used to offer VPN concentrator service to the telecommuters.

- VMS with the VPN router and firewall modules.

Telecommuters:

- All telecommuters already have broadband Internet service at their locations terminating with a cable or DSL modem from the provider.

- Cisco 831 broadband access router.

- VPN software client.

The obvious question might be this: Is this the only possible VPN solution for this particular SMB scenario? The obvious answer is no; you could consider numerous permutations, mostly as a function of budget considerations. For example, not all branches have to follow the same identical bandwidth-provisioning pattern if their bandwidth requirements are sufficiently different or a leased T1 service is not available.

The enumerated solution ensures the desired level of performance, meets the security requirements, allows for consistency in device configuration and management, and facilitates scalability as a result of anticipated growth. The solution also ensures that there is plenty of capacity for additional telecommuters to start using remote VPN access.

Being Frank Costs Less

If the preceding solution seems a bit like overkill to begin with, I have my own experience and the words of others to back it up. When a major project is undertaken, it's easier to get the necessary funds initially than to keep going back for additional appropriations within a short period of time following the installation.

When a designer overstates the capability of a lower-end solution to satisfy a tight budget, everybody suffers in the end. The designer's business might later have to perform an upgrade at a reduced rate, and the customer experiences frustration with performance problems after spending considerable funds to begin with. Brutal frankness about a solution's capability and the associated costs is often a designer's best friend.

Communication with Partners via an Extranet

Now, consider a scenario that entails a collaborative effort between a software developer SMB and three of its partners in the development efforts. User requirements reveal that secure and fast communications are of paramount importance. In addition, it is the SMB's responsibility to ensure that no communication is allowed between the partners through the SMB's network(s). The required level of access by the SMB to each partner's network is comparable to the required level of access by each partner to the SMB's network. Access requirements translate into a number of VPN tunnels, which are independent of each other and which need to be established between the relevant networks.

The principals at all four companies want to ensure that the design team makes every effort to leverage the existing equipment. The SMB already has a VPN-capable PIX 525 series firewall with ten 10/100 Ethernet interfaces and a non-VPN 7200 series router. The SMB has provisioned 12-Mbps high-speed Internet access via a fractional T3 line. Partners have no inherent VPN capability, but each partner has a PIX 515E firewall with six 10/100 Ethernet interfaces. Partners have pipes of between 3-Mbps and 6-Mbps bandwidth to the Internet.

Given the requirements and the existing equipment, the design team makes the following recommendations:

- The VPN will be based entirely on VPN-capable firewalls.

- The SMB and each partner are to place the resources to be shared in one or more DMZs. Tunnels will be established between respective DMZ subnets on the SMB's and the partners' networks.

- Partners are to upgrade their 515E firewalls to VPN capability.

- All of the DMZ networks that contain resources to be shared will be globally routable, which is possible because all companies have registered subnets available.

- Static crypto maps will be used to set up the VPN tunnels using 3DES encryption.

- VPN configuration and management will be done locally at each location via PDM.

The same question as in the previous scenario comes to mind: Is this the only possible solution? You know the answer.

Mobile Users and Telecommuters

Some people become telecommuters by their own choice, and some are driven into that role by the realities of available workspace at an SMB's site. I recently interviewed the Vice President of Technology of a multisite financial institution with 290+ employees (and still growing) regarding information technology (IT) issues that he faced associated with the tremendous growth of the institution, through acquisitions and sound business practices.

The network topology at the institution is a classic private network hub and spoke based on leased lines. Although VPN technology has been around a long time, the private network provided secure communication between the branches, so there was no need to start looking at VPNs until shortage of space provided that trigger. Given VPN access, certain employees will be able to work either from home or from smaller satellite offices that are less expensive and easier to rent or purchase than a larger facility.

Although the SMB does not want to consider a VPN solution to replace the private network, the SMB is ready for a remote access VPN. The user requirements are simple. Allow a few employees to work from home initially, with the potential for those numbers to increase to about 25 over the next 12 months.

The recommendation is simple as well. Use the VPN 3015 concentrator at the central location, and equip each user with a VPN client software and 837 series router with a four-port Ethernet switch, given that all of the users already have asymmetric digital subscriber line (ADSL) access from their anticipated telecommuting locations.

Intraorganizational VPNs

Intraorganizational VPNs can be treated as an SMB solution even if an organization in aggregate does not meet the strict SMB criteria because of its large size. It's safe to assume that within the organization, routing is functioning properly, and all destinations are reachable.

Setting up a dynamic multipoint VPN between the identified subnets sitting behind VPN-capable routers is natural given that the LAN addresses need to be routable. If the internal routers do not have built-in VPN capability, they could either be upgraded or additional units deployed, depending on the capacity required for the VPN traffic.

The Cisco VPN 3000 Series Concentrator Family

Following the discussion of the Cisco 3000 series VPN concentrators in the context of VPN deployment earlier in this chapter, it's almost anti-climactic to take it up as a topic in and of itself, especially when detailed data sheets are available on the Cisco website and you are equipped with the Cisco Products Quick Reference Guide. However, I thought a brief summary would be helpful.

VPN 3000 concentrator models range from the entry-level 3005 and 3015, with support for up to 100 simultaneous users, to the 3080 model, which is optimized for large enterprises of up to 10,000 simultaneous remote access connections. Applying the principle of modularity, even a large enterprise with tens of thousands of users can be logically broken into segments, business units, or departments, which allows for the deployment of equipment that is intended mainly for SMB use.

As a general rule, the VPN concentrators are meant for scenarios demanding optimized remote access. As discussed previously, this is not to say that a VPN-capable firewall or router cannot be used to fulfill the same purpose, but always keep in mind that a router's primary purpose is to switch or route packets, whereas the primary purpose of a firewall is to inspect incoming and outgoing traffic against the criteria in an SMB's security policy, as configured on the firewall.

Overview of Capabilities

The 3000 series concentrators work in conjunction with all of the Cisco VPN products (such as routers and firewalls) and with the VPN software and hardware clients. When combined with the software client, the Cisco VPN 3000 series solution allows for access to the corporate network from anywhere that an Internet connection is available.

A VPN software client is free to holders of a Cisco SMARTnet contract. The VPN 3002 hardware client represents a more expensive client solution, but, given its ease of configuration, the fact that there is no need for software installation on workstations, and the workstation OS transparency, the VPN 3002 is ideal for the following workgroups:

- Those with diverse operating systems
- Those with minimal technical resources
- Those with no ability to use the software client for policy reasons

In addition to being optimized for remote access, the VPN 3000 series concentrators can also be used for LAN-to-LAN connections for a single or multiple users, supporting from 100 to 1000 connections between the various models. The encryption method is software based at the low end (3005 and 3015) and hardware based at the higher end (3030, 3060, and 3080), with the throughput ranging from 4 Mbps for the 3005 models to 100 Mbps for the 3080 units. Lower-end units are field upgradable for greater capability. For example, the VPN 3015 is field upgradable to the VPN 3030, and the VPN 3030 is field upgradable to the VPN 3060.

Positioning Within the Network and Configuration Methods

Physically and typically, the concentrator, like a firewall, connects to the internal (private) and the external (public) network. Figure 5-1 illustrates a typical 3000 series concentrator positioning in conjunction with that of a firewall, an IOS router, and several types of client setups.

Figure 5-1 represents a composite scenario. Not all of the components in the figure will likely be present at every deployment. However, the figure accentuates the flexibility of the 3000 series concentrators and the Cisco VPN solutions.

At first glance, Figure 5-1 looks a bit busy, but consider that the composite SMB leverages the maximum VPN capability of the Cisco equipment, as follows:

- There is a group of users with varied operating systems using the VPN 3002 hardware client from a location that already has broadband cable access to the Internet.
- All of those remote users communicate with the headquarters through the VPN 3015.
- A single user behind a DSL modem and a group of users behind a cable modem and a broadband 831 router (with a built-in four-port switch) all use the VPN software client to communicate with headquarters.
- A dialup user can get into the headquarters network by using the VPN software client.
- Between the branch and the headquarters, a LAN-to-LAN tunnel can be configured either between the firewalls or from the branch firewall to the VPN 3015.

Figure 5-1 *Composite VPN 3000 Series Deployment Scenario*

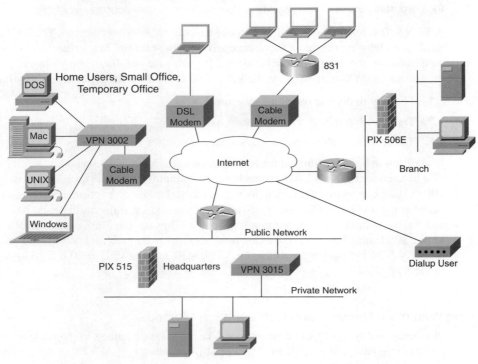

The VPN 3000 series concentrators can be configured in one of three ways: from the CLI (one command at a time), by using a web browser that uses the VPN 3000 series (one device at a time), or via the VMS platform (a whole deployment at a time). Whereas an experienced network administrator might choose the CLI option for larger, more complex deployments, VMS is highly recommended. The web-based configuration manager represents a free, middle-of-the road approach that offers a lot of guidance to an administrator who is less skilled with typing in individual CLI commands. Figure 5-2 shows the initial configuration screen of the 3000 Concentrator Series Manager.

On the left side of Figure 5-2, the collapsible menu offers a glimpse into the capabilities of the manager that fall into the three broad categories of configuration, administration, and monitoring.

VPN-Capable Routers

A degree of VPN capability spans almost the entire Cisco router product line, with certain models being optimized for VPN performance. Software-based 3DES encryption is available even in the entry-level small office/home office (SOHO) 90 series models, like the SOHO 91, 96, and 97.

Figure 5-2   *Configuration Screen from the VPN 3000 Concentrator Series Manager*

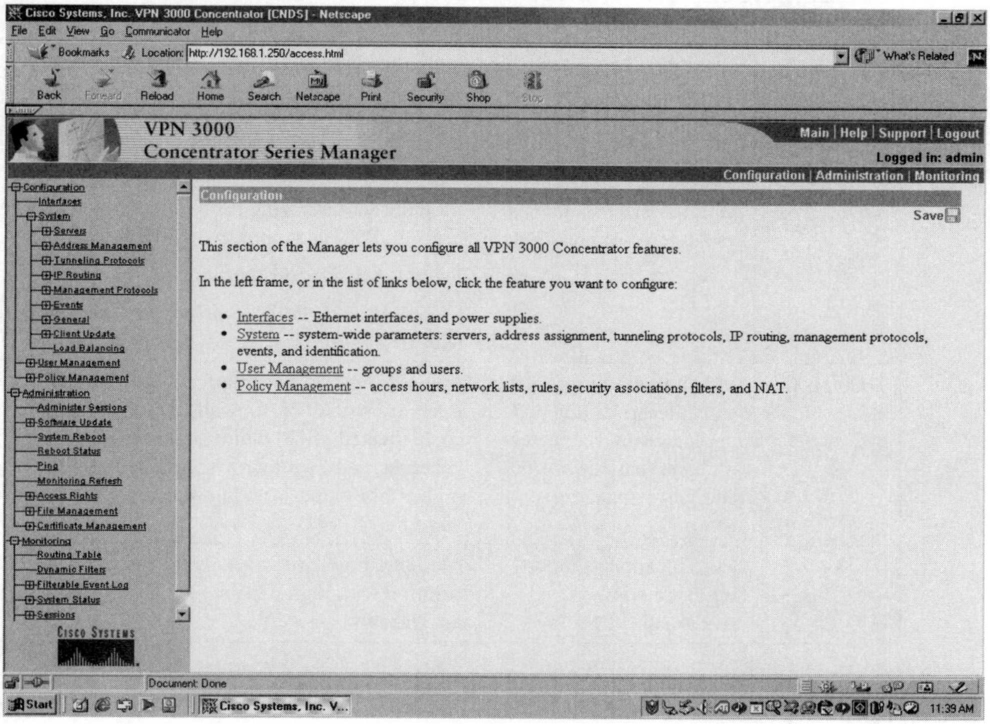

The progression continues through the 800 series, which is designed for small offices and telecommuters; the 1700 series modular integrated access platforms, aimed at SMBs and branch offices; the 2600, 3600, and 3700 multiservice platforms, which also facilitate extensive Voice over IP (VoIP) solutions; into the high-end 7100 series integrated VPN-solution platforms. IOS images with IPSec support are available even for the 2500 series workhorses.

Table 5-1 offers general deployment guidelines for Cisco VPN-capable routers and lists some of their characteristics. When designing a networking solution, the reader is encouraged to refer to the current Cisco data sheet for each model for the most up-to-date information about device characteristics and configuration options.

Table 5-1   *General Deployment Guidelines for VPN-Capable Routers*

Series	Deployment Area	General Characteristics
90	SOHO	Integrated appliance (firewall, 3DES software-based encryption)
		Fixed LAN: 4-port switch
		Fixed WAN: ADSL or Ethernet

continues

Table 5-1 *General Deployment Guidelines for VPN-Capable Routers (Continued)*

Series	Deployment Area	General Characteristics
800	Telecommuters, small offices	Integrated appliance (firewall, IPSec, AES) Fixed LAN: Ethernet port or 4-port hub Fixed WAN: Integrated Services Digital Network, serial, ADSL, Ethernet
1700	Medium-size businesses and enterprise branches	Modular unit allowing for the integration of VPN, firewall, IDS, and extensive VoIP options Fixed LAN: 1-port Ethernet Modular WAN: Point-to-point or Frame Relay T1 with CSU/DSU, ISDN, serial, asynch serial, ADSL
2600/3600/3700	Medium-size businesses and enterprises demanding increasingly greater multiservice integration and performance levels	Modular multiservice platforms facilitating integration of VPN, firewall, IDS, increasingly sophisticated VoIP solutions, wireless, Gigabit Ethernet, and Layer 2 switching, at progressively higher throughput with high-capacity WAN support, including ATM
7100	Core locations supporting large numbers of site-to-site VPNs	Modular, high-end, optimized VPN, firewall, IDS solution with high-capacity LAN and WAN interfaces

Firewalls

Gone are the days of trust on the Internet. Even as the Internet facilitates widespread connectivity and almost instantaneous global communications, it also represents a potential source of danger to an SMB whose network has not been hardened against outside intruders.

The motives for outside intrusion range from malicious play to commercial gain to a full-scale industrial espionage carried out by agents of a foreign government. A properly deployed firewall in the context of comprehensive end-to-end security implementation helps to secure a network from those dangers.

Whatever reasons have been identified in a security policy for securing a network's parameter via a firewall, firewalling an SMB's network that is connected to the Internet is a must. The real issue is not whether to install a firewall solution; rather, it is how to design and to deploy one.

Firewall Deployment Considerations

A well-designed firewall solution should consider and provide for the following:

- Appropriate physical connectivity to the outside WAN, the inside LAN, and the DMZ network(s)

- A desired level of protection from intruders for the inside and the DMZ network(s) as well as the detection and negation of common denial of service attacks
- A high degree of access availability from the inside to the outside and the DMZ, and from the outside to the DMZ
- A high degree of scalability with no or minimal degradation in performance should either of the following conditions be true:
  - The SMB's internal network continues to grow, with the volume of outbound traffic increasing significantly
  - The need arises to have more of the SMB's resources accessible from the outside on the DMZ network(s)
- A reasonable cost that is not a budget buster for an SMB
- A solid integration with the remainder of an SMB's security implementations
- The possibility of additional security services in the form of VPN access, virus protection, or intrusion detection integrated into the firewall
- An easy-to-use but at the same time sufficiently granular method of configuration
- An effective means to manage the device, either standalone or as part of the overall network management system

Firewall Physical Connectivity Options

By design, firewalls separate the inside networks from the outside networks while interfacing to both of them. Logically, the outside network is a WAN/LAN/Internet cloud that is connected to the "outside" interface of a firewall.

Physically, the outside network often begins with a WAN connection to the Internet. The physical characteristics of the WAN interface depend on the type of service that an SMB provisions from an ISP. The WAN service could be a dedicated leased T1 or E1 line, a Frame Relay (somewhat unlikely), a DSL, a broadband cable, or a wireless. If a firewall is to be connected directly to the service provider's WAN, the firewall must have an appropriate WAN port.

Most of the firewalls from different security vendors, including Cisco, do not come with a wide range of WAN interface options; they mainly come with Ethernet-only interfaces for the inside, the outside, and the DMZ networks. This means that, most likely, a router is needed to connect a firewall to the WAN. In those cases where a firewall cannot interface directly to the service provider's WAN, the cost of a router with an appropriate WAN interface and sufficient throughput capacity needs to be factored into the design of a firewall solution.

Figure 5-3 illustrates a Cisco PIX 515 firewall (also referred to as the *PIX Security Appliance*) with Ethernet-only interfaces connecting to the Internet via a 1700 series modular access router. The SMB relies on two dedicated leased T1 lines for Internet access.

The small subnet between the router and the firewall that is created as a result of this physical configuration needs to be taken into account when allocating address space and configuring routing.

Figure 5-3   *Firewall's Physical Connectivity Example*

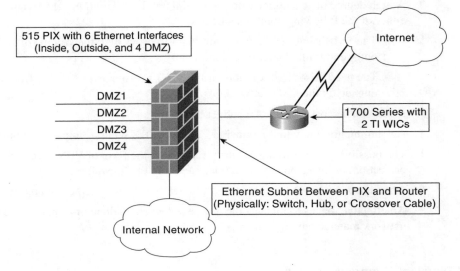

Firewall Protection Capabilities

A firewall's capabilities to filter a wide variety of unauthorized traffic are definitely a key deployment consideration, but you should not construe it as the primary one. Articulating the technological prowess and the protocol support alphabet soup of a firewall or any other device to the decision makers without clearly stating how the device will advance the SMB's position in the marketplace is a formula for getting nowhere in terms of deployment.

Firewalls from several prominent security vendors, not just Cisco, meet a certain minimum of the current mainstream criteria for filtering of unauthorized traffic. Other factors must play a role in differentiation between them. Ease of configuration, solid technical support, and, of course, the cost are always important factors in the selection of any security solution by a typical SMB that is looking for ways to stretch its IT budget, especially in leaner times. And keep in mind that implementing a firewall solution often means different things to different people, especially those whose tenure in the IT security industry spans a decade or more.

Whereas the latest firewall technologies sport dedicated appliances with stateful inspection filtering, static packet filtering and application layer proxies still remain a part of the firewalling landscape. Their capabilities need to be considered and their architecture sufficiently understood if a case is to be made for a dedicated security appliance with stateful filtering ability.

Static Packet Filtering

Static packet filtering is not considered an effective firewall solution. Usually implemented on routers, it offers a degree of basic protection against the amateurs, but it alone cannot stop the more determined and sophisticated intruders.

Examining packets in isolation, and only at the network layer, against access control lists (ACLs) misses the bigger picture of analyzing the pattern of the aggregate traffic attempting to pass through a security device. Also, extensive use of ACLs degrades router performance.

Application Layer Proxies

Application layer proxies—also referred to as *circuit-level gateways, application layer gateways*, or *proxy servers*—precede the latest stateful inspection approach to firewalling that is found in the dedicated security appliances. These devices are now generally considered a former generation of firewall technology.

From an operational point of view, they can be secure if they are configured properly. From the implementation and design points of view, they are complex and cumbersome to work with because they combine the use of general-purpose hardware and OS (typically a flavor of UNIX or Windows) with specialized firewalling software.

Application layer proxies examine all of the traffic layers and use context information from the traversing packets to make decisions regarding the establishment of sessions through the firewall. In terms of traffic flow, they break the client/server model by forcing two connections: one from the client to the firewall, and one from the firewall to the desired resource or server. This approach, however, allows for a solid enforcement of user authentication and authorization policy for connections through the firewall.

A big problem with the application layer proxies is their lack of scalability because they tend to be application specific. Even though they offer strong security for inbound and outbound connections, potential security flaws in the general-purpose operating systems that they use make the entire platform vulnerable.

When compared to a dedicated security appliance, application layer proxies usually require a much higher degree of training and sophistication to set up and to configure properly, which is not readily available at many SMB sites. Operating at the application layer, they also exact a performance penalty as the amount of traffic and connections increases through the firewall.

Stateful Inspection Firewalling

Stateful inspection capability in a dedicated security appliance with a hardened, special-purpose operating system is the recommended norm when deploying a firewall solution for an SMB. *Stateful inspection*—also referred to as *dynamic packet filtering*—means that the firewall keeps track of the past and current status (or *state*) of the traffic that passes through it.

Information from packets traversing the firewall is placed into a state table, which is then used to assist in determining whether to permit or to deny incoming or outbound connections. The state table can contain information from all of the layers associated with data encapsulation (not just the IP header), from previous communications (a *communications-derived state*), and from previous applications (an *application-derived state*).

Cisco further enhances the stateful inspection process with the Adaptive Security Algorithm (ASA), which creates a hash out of a number of IP and Transmission Control Protocol (TCP) parameters. That hash acts as a unique identifier of the client initiating the inbound or outbound connection. Because Cisco also randomizes the TCP sequence numbers and they happen to be part of the hash, the ASA raises the bar for hackers attempting to penetrate the PIX firewalls.

Firewall Availability

By its nature as a guardian of the internal network, a firewall represents a single point of failure. What easily happens within a typical SMB's environment is a gradual increase in reliance on Internet access over a period of time. Some SMBs might not realize their degree of reliance on the Internet until the Internet access is cut off.

More than just e-mail and browsing rely on Internet access; other affected areas include online banking, interactions with various government agencies and entities, communication between branches, and even IP Telephony. A single firewall represents a single point of failure, but this does not need to be the case.

More sophisticated firewall solutions include the ability to perform an automatic failover to another device to ensure uninterrupted service. The SMB must decide before deployment how critical the ability to maintain uninterrupted Internet access service is to its mission and what the cost is of downtime. Cisco offers failover support beginning with its PIX 515E and higher-end models.

Firewall Scalability and Performance

It is interesting to note that in many actual deployment scenarios, the capacity of the WAN connection to the Internet is more likely to become the chokepoint than the firewall throughput. However, when large pipes to the Internet are present on the order of Optical Carrier (OC)-3 (155 Mbps) or higher, and the SMB deploys popular resources available to the public or partners on the DMZ networks, close attention needs to be paid to the aggregate firewall throughput as compared to the size of the Internet connection.

Because Cisco firewalls also support VPN services, you need to take the following into account when considering the scalability and performance of a firewall solution:

- Will VPN service on a firewall be activated?
- How many users will participate in the VPN if it is activated?
- How is a given firewall model rated for VPN throughput?

Firewall performance and scalability are closely related. Experience and common sense dictate that a solution must perform well to be effective. Extra cost of the solution might be forgiven and forgotten if the solution performs well, but poor performance lingers in the memories of many for a long time.

WARNING   In an attempt to save on cost, which is always a critical factor in proposing a given solution, you might be pressured to propose a less-capable solution than a situation requires. Steer clear from that approach in designing networking solutions of any kind.

The Cost of a Firewall Solution

The cost of a firewall solution is one of the biggest considerations in the decision-making process leading to deployment. It is critical to consider all of the aspects that contribute to the cost of the solution, not simply the cost of a single device in isolation.

To be appealing from a financial point of view, a solution needs to show low total cost of ownership (TCO) over a period of time. Factors that contribute to the TCO are as follows:

- The anticipated amount of time that needs to be spent on configuration
- The cost of any incremental equipment or software that is required for deployment of the complete and effective solution (for example, a router, or management or reporting software)
- The cost of technical support
- The cost of maintenance contracts

Poor-quality technical support can significantly increase the TCO. When a problem develops, poor technical support can tie up the usually thinly stretched internal IT resource for hours or even days in fruitless troubleshooting efforts.

Although it is not always easy to quantify in terms of actual funds, solid solution performance needs to be stressed as lowering the TCO over a period of time by improving employee productivity and morale. As an example, if 10 minutes a day is lost by 100 employees because of performance problems associated with a poorly designed firewall solution, that adds up to a thousand minutes or approximately 16 hours a day. Multiply this by a nominal 250 working days in a year (50 weeks × 5 days/week), and you've got 4000 hours. At even $12/hour, that's a $48,000 loss in productivity. Although it is not an outright expenditure from the SMB's bank account, sooner or later, productivity loss is reflected in the bottom line. Does it make sense now to spend an extra $2000 or $3000 to ensure adequate performance?

Firewall Integration with Other Security Solutions

When it comes to integrating a firewall solution with any other security implementations on an SMB's network, there is no clear-cut absolute recommendation. On one hand, it is desirable to have a single-vendor, end-to-end security implementation throughout the network. The arguments are appealing: a single source of technical support (especially if it is competent and readily available, like the Cisco Technical Assistance Center [TAC]) and, generally, a greater uniformity in configuration, which saves time and minimizes the need for additional training of the IT security staff. Cisco offers a spectrum of solutions that provide end-to-end security, and I lean in that direction in terms of recommending a comprehensive security implementation.

On the other hand, there is also the principle of "security through diversity," which relies on the fact that if a flaw is exposed in one of the vendor's systems, the same flaw might be present in others. Thus, having systems from multiple vendors prevents the network from being completely compromised. The catch here is ensuring interoperability between solutions from different vendors and trying to resolve a problem when something goes wrong.

Although troubleshooting is a step removed from the design process, a designer should be aware of the potential interoperability problems when solutions from multiple vendors are involved. If you've ever felt like a ping-pong ball bouncing between tech support teams from different vendors, you can relate to the need for solid integration and interoperability between various solutions.

The Cisco PIX line of firewalls integrates well with the Cisco VPN-capable routers, IDSes, and VPN concentrators, all of which are configurable and manageable through the VMS platform.

Additional Security Services in a Firewall

After going through the steps of a networking solution design process as discussed in Chapter 1, it might be obvious that the firewall (or the device that's sitting on the parameter of the network) should incorporate additional security services. Those services typically are virus scanning, VPN capability, and a limited degree of intrusion detection.

Virus Scanning

A regularly updated virus-scanning program within the firewall might seem sufficient for virus protection because all external traffic, including outside e-mail, must pass through it. However, this approach to virus protection applies and is effective only in environments in which viruses cannot be introduced internally; it does not guard against the introduction of viruses from storage media like floppy disks, zip drives, memory sticks, or CDs that employees bring in and use in their workstations.

Some firewall vendors incorporate virus-protection capabilities into their firewalls, but I have found that even in those situations, SMBs that deploy those firewalls still rely on server-based virus-protection programs to guard against viruses introduced from the inside.

Otherwise, the SMB must rely on the goodwill of the employees, who are told not to do certain things such as bring infected storage media into the SMB's premises. No respectable security administrator relies purely on the goodwill of the employees, given the disruption that viruses can cause on a corporate network.

If a firewall has a built-in VPN support, it is probably more appropriate to start calling it a *multipurpose security appliance*. Whereas a multipurpose appliance leverages the hardware and the CPU power of a single device for diverse although complementary capabilities, what you always need to consider is the level of performance and scalability when all of those capabilities are used to the maximum.

VPN Capability

With the exception of the lower-end PIX firewalls (501 and 506E), which support up to 5 and 25 remote VPN users, respectively, all of the remaining models support up to 2000 remote users through the VPN concentrator services (Easy VPN server) built into the firewall. If an SMB decides to leverage the VPN capability of a Cisco firewall and begins to pay a performance penalty, the good news is that the VPN 3000 series concentrator becomes a breeze to integrate into the scenario. Refer to Figure 5-1 in the VPN section for the illustration of a topology that combines the deployment of a firewall and a VPN concentrator.

VPN capabilities within a firewall offer an attractive proposition for a multisite SMB. Even if telecommuter or remote-access VPN services are not the requirement for the SMB, the ability to establish site-to-site VPNs might prove to be desirable for anyone who has multiple locations. If a private network is already in place between the multiple locations, but each location has its own access to the Internet through a VPN-capable firewall, establishing a site-to-site VPN between the locations—even initially, as a backup to the private network— might be an effective and practical way to transition from a private network to a VPN.

Establishing a site-to-site VPN between just two locations using VPN-capable firewalls allows for a gradual introduction of a VPN solution while the private network infrastructure remains in place. Rather than placing oneself into an irreversible position of scrapping the private network and becoming totally reliant on the VPN, the SMB has the luxury of trying the VPN solution between any of the desired locations and evaluating its performance. In the meantime, the private network is still there, and switching back and forth between the VPN and the private network is a matter of minimal reconfiguration.

If the VPN performance is satisfactory, and the financial calculations show savings over the ongoing use of the private network, it is only a matter of time before the entire communication between the SMB's locations becomes VPN-based. After the site-to-site VPNs are in place, the SMB will soon discover the other advantages of a VPN solution. Such benefits might include secure remote access to the network for a range of employees, including top executive management.

Intrusion Detection

Intrusion detection is another security service that Cisco has incorporated into its series of firewalls that are effectively turning into integrated security appliances. As was the case with VPN support, decisions need to be made that take into consideration the degree of intrusion detection capability required and the impact that it will have on the device performance.

It is important to understand that the IDS support in routers and firewalls does not compare to that of dedicated IDS. As opposed to the dedicated units, perhaps less than 10% of the recognizable signatures are supported on a firewall. A rough analogy to the difference might be to compare static packet filtering to that of stateful inspection.

But if funds don't permit and performance allows, activation of IDS on a firewall represents another level of security protection. And although no matter how much security you have, it seems there is never enough, the flip side is that some security is better than none.

Firewall Configuration and Management

GUI configuration capability is desirable for a firewall (or any networking device, for that matter) because it typically requires less training and experience on the part of an administrator to configure a device. Firewalls from some vendors come with GUI configuration capability only.

It also has been my experience with certain networking devices—those that support both GUI and a more cryptic form of configuration from a command line—that a GUI interface might lack the necessary granularity and is only valid for a minimal initial configuration. That is not the case with the Cisco PIX Device Manager (PDM), which allows for complete firewall configuration and which represents one of three methods for configuring a PIX firewall. The other two methods are an integrated management solution in the form of CiscoWorks VMS and, of course, CLI. Figure 5-4 illustrates the initial home screen for PDM.

Whereas PDM is a single device configuration and management tool, the CiscoWorks Management Center for Firewalls, which is the VMS component for firewall configuration, scales up to 1000 firewalls.

The fundamental issue with firewall configuration and management is similar to that of the VPNs: determining the exact point where a device-management solution is no longer a value proposition, and an integrated platform needs to be installed. Many SMBs do not perceive the absence of an integrated-network management system as a problem. Only when an SMB faces the consequences of misconfiguration or operational disruptions resulting from the lack of an effective systemwide monitoring capability does the value proposition of an integrated-management system begin to make sense.

An integrated-management platform such as VMS offers many advantages over the one-device-at-a-time management approach. VMS offers device inventory, software distribution capability, and integrated network monitoring in addition to facilitating larger-scale configurations. One feature of the Management Center for Firewalls is the Smart Rules. When large numbers of firewalls are involved, a rule that is defined once on a single unit is consequently inherited by a group or all of the firewalls in a deployment scenario. To put this in perspective yourself, compare scenarios in which 2 and 200 firewalls are being deployed.

Figure 5-4 *PDM Home Screen*

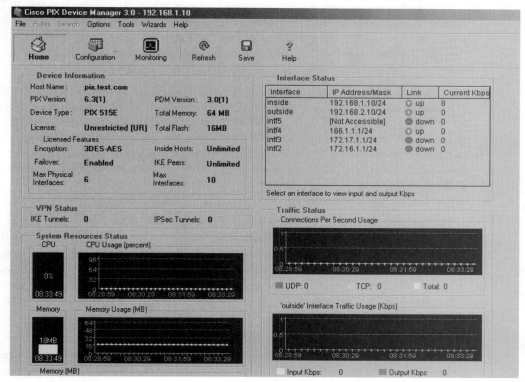

The Cisco PIX Product Line and the IOS Firewall

Collectively, the Cisco PIX product line addresses all of the firewall deployment considerations discussed in the preceding sections. The networks for PIX deployment range from SOHOs to those of carrier-class service providers. It is your responsibility to appropriately position each model as a function of the SMB's current size, growth potential, and desired capabilities.

Overview of the PIX Line Capabilities

The entry-level PIX 501 is an integrated security appliance meant for the SOHO networks. It supports an integrated four-port 10/100 Ethernet switch for the inside network while at the same time delivering VPN concentrator service for up to 10 users with up to 3 Mbps

3DES throughput. Without the VPN service with 3DES, the 501 PIX is capable of throughput of up to 10 Mbps. A typical SOHO is likely to have a broadband service in the range of 256 Kbps to 1.5 Mbps, which is anywhere from only 2.5 percent to 15 percent of the firewall's 10-Mbps throughput. In addition to being able to act as an Easy VPN server, the PIX 501 can act as the hardware VPN client.

The 506E, which is the next model in the PIX product line, increases the firewall throughput to 20 Mbps but does not provide an integrated four-port switch. It offers two 10BASE-T interfaces, inside and outside. The 506E also scales up to 25 users for the VPN concentrator service. Neither the 501 nor the 506E supports DMZ interfaces, but the 506E offers dynamic Open Shortest Path First (OSPF) support, which implies a dynamic routing capability. Both products deploy well at SOHOs and small branch offices.

The firewall throughput increases drastically in the midrange and high-end PIX models. The 515E model supports firewall throughput of up to 188 Mbps, whereas the throughput on the PIX 535 scales up to 1.7 Gbps and 500,000 simultaneous connections. If perhaps these specifications seem outside the typical SMB requirements, consider that a relatively small enterprise could run a successful e-commerce operation that would require these kinds of capabilities. All PIX models beginning with the 515E support multiple DMZ interfaces, VPN concentrator service of up to 2000 remote users, and an active/standby failover support for increased redundancy.

In addition, PIX firewalls support protocols associated with VoIP deployments that allow SMBs to leverage their data networks for telephony. Those protocols include the International Telecommunications Union Telecommunications Standardization Sector (ITU-T) recommendation H.323; Session Initiation Protocol (SIP), which is an effective H.323 competitor in the enterprise arena and the Media Gateway Control Protocol (MGCP), which operates between media gateways and softswitches, typically in carrier-class deployments.

As a function of the user requirements, a PIX Security Appliance can be deployed either as an integrated security solution offering firewall, VPN, and IDS services or as a firewall only, with the VPN and IDS functions offloaded to dedicated devices optimized for those purposes.

Effective Firewall Positioning Within the Network

With multiple connections to the Internet, a single firewall is not going to solve an SMB's security problems. And it is easy to provision broadband Internet service these days or to connect a notebook equipped with a modem to the internal network and to dial out, bypassing a firewall.

Moreover, if a vulnerable dual-homed host is connected to the inside and the outside networks, the entire firewall solution can be easily defeated because the vulnerabilities of the operating system on the host can be potentially exploited to gain access to the internal resources. Designing a firewall solution on paper is one thing, but integrating it effectively into a real-life scenario is an entirely different ball game.

Human behavior and adherence to the internal security rules might ultimately be what determines whether or not the sophisticated level of protection that Cisco firewalls provide will be successful. Firewalls must be properly positioned at every opening from the inside to the outside networks.

With the exception of a VPN concentrator, as shown in Figure 5-1, a firewall should be the only device that connects to the inside and the outside networks. What this also implies is that the physical location of the firewall must be physically secured with restricted access. Otherwise, the most sophisticated firewall solution could be easily bypassed. After an internal network is compromised, fixing the damage is not just a matter of ensuring that the firewall is properly positioned and secure; you must verify that no trojans or logic bombs have been planted anywhere on the network, which can be a costly process.

The IOS Firewall Feature Set on Cisco Routers

If a full-featured firewall is not affordable or desirable, an alternative is to use the IOS firewall on a Cisco router. This solution, however, needs to be kept in perspective, for the simple reason that the primary purpose of routers is to route or switch packets.

If the routing configuration on a router is simple—for example, a couple of static routes—it might make perfect sense to use the IOS firewall features. Given that this solution scales all the way from the 800 series through the Cisco 7500 series and the Catalyst 6000, it provides another way you can leverage existing equipment if cost is a big consideration.

Needless to say, even as integrated solutions offer more and more flexibility, they also challenge you to position products appropriately. Adhering to the design process, and knowing which devices are optimized for what purpose, should help you make these choices.

Intrusion Detection Systems

When considering network security, deploying intrusion detection might not be the first thing on the mind of a security administrator at the site of a typical SMB. And even if it is, Cisco probably does not top the list of IDS vendors that comes to mind because of the many freeware IDS products available and a certain well-ingrained perception of Cisco as a networking company.

In the final analysis, however, the truism stands: You get what you pay for! With its wide range of IDS solutions—from dedicated devices to focused (partial) and full-blown IDS services integrated into routers, switches, and firewalls—Cisco should top the list of vendors for IDS solutions. This holds true especially if an SMB has already deployed, or is considering deploying, other Cisco security solutions. When making a value proposition to an SMB, you should always be thinking about how to leverage the deployed equipment and seamlessly integrate a new solution (IDS—or any other, for that matter) into the existing security infrastructure.

With the increasing number and sophistication of potential attacks, both from the inside and the outside, firewalling an SMB's network might not be sufficient to protect it against disruptions or theft of confidential information. Effective use of IDSes represents a key component of an integrated end-to-end security solution.

Effective intrusion detection relies first and foremost on the accurate identification of all potential threats. Those intrusion threats can include the following:

- Reconnaissance activity, which is usually intended to identify points of vulnerability within a network. Port and ping sweeps are forms of reconnaissance.

- Denial-of-service (DoS) activity, in which bandwidth is consumed by frivolous traffic. DoS attacks can be directed against common TCP/IP application services like Simple Mail Transfer Protocol (SMTP) (e-mail) or Hypertext Transfer Protocol (HTTP) (web). SYN floods are a form of DoS attack. Because the SYN flag in the TCP header is at the core of setting up TCP connections, perhaps there is not an absolutely foolproof method of protection against SYN floods. But SYN floods can be detected and mitigated through IDSes.

- Misuses of corporate security policies, where employees might be attempting to gain access to information that they are not authorized to see or to transmit confidential information outside of the corporate network.

- Exploits indicative of attempts to compromise the system, including multiple failed logins, unusual login times, unusual traffic patterns indicative of large file transfers, attempts at installation of unauthorized malicious software like remote access trojans (RATs), or TCP session hijacking.

Multiple detection techniques are required for an IDS to recognize such a wide variety of potential threats. When you consider that those threats do not remain static, you can see that securing a computer network is a never-ending battle. Even as attack signatures become understood and subject to mitigation, new ones emerge that must be considered and dealt with.

IDS Deployment Considerations

The Cisco IDS solution is an integral component of the end-to-end security implementation for an SMB, and, as such, its deployment considerations both overlap with and differ somewhat from those of VPNs or firewalls.

The overlaps are in the following areas, which universally apply to any security solution:

- Management and configuration
- Performance
- Reliability
- Resilience
- Scalability

However, given the nature of IDS, there are also some key differences in the deployment considerations. For example, the failure of a VPN or a firewall can result in an immediate disruption to the network. Failure of a dedicated IDS sensor might not have such an immediate impact, but a prolonged absence of IDS from a security implementation might result in far more damaging activities going undetected than the effects of a temporary firewall or VPN failure. Thus, even the value proposition of an IDS solution is somewhat different.

Consider the following IDS solution design considerations:

- Understanding the value of an IDS solution
- Understanding network traffic patterns
- Placing an IDS within the network
- Keeping an IDS solution current

Understanding the Value of an IDS Solution

Using an imperfect analogy, an IDS is an intelligence-gathering solution that leads to more effective network security. Consider the range of threats, as outlined in the previous section, that an IDS can detect.

But unlike firewalls or VPNs, IDSes are still making their way into the mainstream vernacular, even in IT departments, perhaps because the absence of an IDS from a security implementation does not seem to trigger a sense of immediate danger in the minds of network administrators or SMB executives. However, the absence of immediate danger is not the equivalent of long-term security, which is what an IDS can facilitate. An IDS solution designer needs to articulate the value proposition so that an SMB can make an informed decision about whether or not it is worthwhile to pay to obtain knowledge of how the network is being utilized and what threats against it are being mitigated.

As with any deployment, an SMB must have a clear sense of value that an IDS delivers if the deployment is to be successful. Because of the growing number and the increasing level of sophistication of attacks against computer networks, the IDS-related budget discussion might boil down to whether or not to deploy a dedicated system or to use a focused subset of IDS capabilities within an integrated security appliance.

Understanding Network Traffic Patterns

Cisco IDS solutions use multiple detection methods to identify and to analyze potential threats. Similar to stateful firewalling, an IDS uses stateful pattern recognition while keeping track of the state of communications across the network. Traffic and protocol anomaly detection, along with extensive protocol monitoring, are also used.

An IDS is capable of monitoring and analyzing all of the major protocols from the TCP/IP suite, including application layer services like FTP for file transfers, SMPT for e-mail,

Domain Name System (DNS) for domain resolution, Telnet for terminal access across the network, HTTP for web access, and more. Moreover, an IDS can monitor and analyze the transport layer protocols like UDP and TCP, and the lower-layer protocols like ICMP and IP, for any unusual patterns or malformations.

But malicious exploitation of TCP/IP weaknesses of the incoming traffic is not the only potential threat to an SMB. As discussed in Chapter 4, internal security breaches can be as damaging, if not more so, than external ones. Internal and outgoing traffic patterns are consequently of equal significance to the incoming traffic. Every SMB is going to have certain internal operational resources—for example, accounting, customer relationship management (CRM), or human resources (HR)—that are normally available only to authorized employees.

An IDS solution, whether it is dedicated or on a router or a supported switch, can be configured to detect unauthorized attempts to access confidential information, whether by guests, curious employees, or perhaps even corporate spies.

Placing an IDS Within the Network

The effective integration of IDS-capable devices into the network topology is critical if an SMB expects to take full advantage of IDS capabilities. In shared media networks (remember coax and hubs?), monitoring network traffic was easier because all of the traffic passed by every device attached to the shared media. In switched internetworks, the collision domains have shrunk so that they are now effectively single devices plugged into switched ports. But a switch port can be mirrored to allow traffic from a network segment or a virtual local-area network (VLAN) to be observed by an IDS sensor.

It is a common strategy to deploy an IDS on the outside network to see what is hitting against it. But to have a perspective of what is pressing against the network from the outside versus what is happening behind the firewall (and what the firewall is filtering), an IDS should also be deployed on the inside. Because some IDSes have only two interfaces—one for command and control, and one for sensing the network—it is important to decide which network segments are going to be monitored because it might require multiple units. However, Cisco also offers an IDS solution with multiple sensors in a single box.

Keeping an IDS Solution Current

The number of different signatures that a dedicated Cisco IDS can detect is around 900. This number is likely to grow because of the misdirected creativity of many individuals, who have taken upon themselves the task of trying to compromise other peoples' networks, either for thrill or for profit. Updates to IDS signatures might not be as frequent as those to virus scanners, but an IDS solution should include a subscription service to leverage the investment in IDS hardware and to stay as current as possible against emerging threats.

In addition to staying current with IDS signatures, it is important to keep up with any operating system upgrades, especially if a security flaw has been discovered in an OS. Keeping the OS up to date applies universally to all security and network products as well as to host operating systems.

Cisco IDS Product Lines

The Cisco IDS product lines, which span equipment categories and scale in the degree of detection and protection that they offer, include the following:

- Dedicated IDS sensors
- Integrated security appliances with IDS
- Modular units

4200 Series Dedicated IDS Sensors

The 4200 series dedicated IDS sensors scale from the 4210 to the 4250-XL models, with scanning performance ranging from 45 Mbps to 1 Gbps, respectively.

The 4215 model is particularly noteworthy because it supports multiple NICs and is capable of monitoring up to five network segments. This model is a major improvement when compared to a dedicated IDS sensor that typically comes with one network (sensor) interface and one command and control interface.

You should always verify the up-to-date operating system requirements for any unit that provides a premium capability (for example, multi-NIC support) or that accepts a specific IDS module, as in the modular IDS approach that is discussed later in this chapter.

All of the 4200 series models can be managed via the Management Center for IDS Sensors, which is a component of the integrated management platform VMS. They can also be managed and configured from CLI or via a web-based device manager. They all implement a comprehensive database of attack signatures and IDS antievasion techniques, allow for user-defined signatures, and facilitate automatic signature updates.

Integrated Security Appliances with IDS

Most of the Cisco devices that fall into the category of integrated security appliances support a degree of IDS detection and mitigation. These devices include the entire line of Cisco PIX firewalls as well as select models of the 1700 series routers, with the appropriate software feature pack.

The PIX IDS support is a focused subset of the dedicated IDS solution. It represents signatures of the most common information-gathering scans and the DoS attacks with the greatest potential for severe network disruption.

At the time of this writing, the number of IDS signatures supported on the PIX ranges from 60 to 70, as compared to about 900 for a dedicated solution. However, the value of an integrated security appliance, even with a small subset of total IDS signatures, should not be underestimated.

PIX can be configured to take action when it detects packets that meet an IDS signature. Malicious packets can be dropped, an offending TCP connection can be reset, or a network administrator can be notified about the suspect traffic. Figure 5-5 displays a configuration screen for enabling and disabling IDS signatures on a PIX 515.

Figure 5-5 *Configuration Screen for IDS Signatures on a PIX*

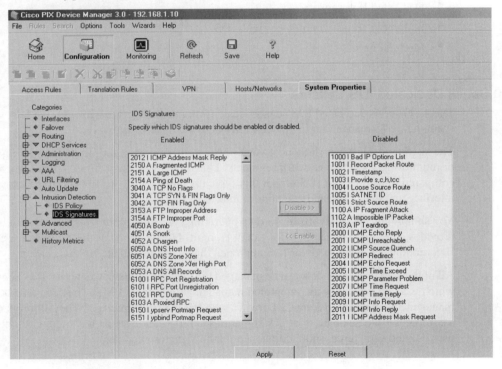

Modular IDS Solutions

In certain deployment scenarios, the use of a modular IDS solution might be more appropriate than using a dedicated or an integrated security appliance. You might be steered toward a modular approach because of performance requirements or the desire to leverage the existing equipment or space. Modular IDS can be deployed on routers or in integrated routing and switching environments.

Specifically, the IDS Network Module is designed for the 2600, 3600, and 3700 series platforms. It offers performance ranging from 10 Mbps on the 2600XM up to 45 Mbps on the 3700 series. Given the VPN, firewall, and multiservice capability of these router platforms, the addition of the IDS Network Module turns them into a midrange, fully integrated modular security appliance that can satisfy the routing and security needs of many SMBs. Of course, the performance also has to be adequate when all of the security and multiservice services are combined and activated in a single platform.

For the 6500 Catalyst switches, Cisco offers the Intrusion Detection System (IDSM-2) Service Module. The IDSM-2 sports up to 600-Mbps IDS inspection performance and allows for the monitoring of the switched traffic across the Catalyst through the use of the Switch Port Analyzer (SPAN) feature. In SMB environments where a Catalyst 6500 series switch is already deployed, the IDSM-2 leverages that deployment and, given its performance characteristics, becomes a natural choice for an IDS solution.

Router Security Features

SMB's routers and network switches, just like network hosts (servers and workstations), are a potential target for hackers and inside intruders. A router is not a direct repository of an SMB's confidential information in the form of financial statements, minutes from board meetings, memos outlining a business strategy, or e-mail databases, but, potentially, all of that information could pass through a router while being accessed or transferred across the network. This is another case for VPN deployment.

By manipulating a router's routing tables, packets carrying confidential data could be redirected to a compromised subnet and captured for future decoding. If the information in the packets is not encrypted, it is almost as easy as lifting the files off a server or a workstation.

In addition, by their nature, routers must understand the topology of the internetwork in which they operate. The routing tables on a single router in a multirouter environment might not reveal the entire network topology, unless of course the network is small. However, addresses of the neighboring routers and devices on subnets interconnected by a compromised router can be easily gleaned by examining a router's routing tables.

After a single router is compromised on the network, the neighboring routers might potentially become victims as well, eventually leading an attacker to the discovery of the entire network topology. An understanding of the network topology, in turn, can easily reveal any other weak spots in the network that could be further exploited. As mentioned in Chapter 4, the goal of the outside hacker is to become an insider. An IDS solution can be of assistance in blocking such access by detecting traffic anomalies.

A compromised router can also become a source of an all-out DoS attack or intermittent performance problems on an SMB's network. Although routers have emerged from obscurity into the mainstream during the past decade, there might be a growing tendency to treat them as just a box that directs traffic to appropriate destinations; however, although a security solution should concentrate on the more glamorous aspects of network security—like firewalls, IDSes, or even VPNs—it is critical that all of the router security features be fully utilized as well, especially if some of those other solutions have not been implemented.

Router Security Deployment Considerations

Because routers represent a fundamental building block of the global Internet as well as of corporate networks, router security features should be well understood and deployed to the maximum. Routers typically represent the first line of defense for an SMB's internal network, and there is no excuse for leaving them vulnerable to attack by not configuring them to be as secure as possible.

Cisco routers come with a variety of security features. When such features are properly configured, they offer a significant barrier to anyone trying to hack a router. The following are the minimum elements of router security:

- Use of strong passwords and privilege levels

- Configuration of effective access control lists (ACLs)

- Use of the new Authentication, Authorization and Accounting features (**aaa new-model** commands)

Password Protection and Privilege Levels

Passwords represent the first line of defense on a Cisco router. Unfortunately, unauthorized users can frequently discover a user/password combination for line access (console, Telnet via one of the VTY lines, or modem via the AUX port) through means of social engineering or outright bad security practices, such as writing passwords down. It thus becomes critical that a router's configuration be protected through the strongest available technique, which is the use of the **enable secret** IOS command. **Enable secret** uses the Message Digest 5 (MD5) hash that, given the current state of technology, is supposedly not reversible.

The reason for encrypting the enable mode password is to ensure that if the configuration file that is stored externally or printed out is somehow compromised by falling into the wrong hands, at least the privileged access to the router will still be protected despite the fact that the attacker might understand how the router is configured. However, using the MD5 hash for enable password encryption is effective against a determined hacker only if the password that has been chosen is a strong, random one.

Common passwords, even if encrypted with MD5, can be reversed through the use of brute force *dictionary* attacks, in which the hash of the password from the compromised configuration file is compared against those for all of the words that can be found in a dictionary of a given language or multiple languages. The **enable password** and the **service password-encryption** IOS commands are weaker implementations of password security than **enable secret**.

Cisco routers offer privilege access levels ranging from 0 (lowest) to 15 (highest). Only privilege Levels 0, 1, and 15 are configured by default. The **enable secret** command, by default, is intended to protect access to Level 15. All configuration and **show** commands are available from Level 15, thus allowing full control over a router. Levels 0 and 1 offer only a limited set of commands.

Privilege levels facilitate distribution of router configuration and administration between multiple individuals with varied levels of responsibility and capability. By configuring the privilege levels, certain nondisruptive commands (a group of **show** commands, for example) that are available at Level 15 might be permitted at lower levels for the purpose of allowing router administration to be shared by more than one person.

Whether or not the implementation of privilege levels is even desirable needs to be determined as a function of the SMB's network administration and security policies. If only a single individual manages the SMB's network, and this individual requires access to Level 15, the configuration of privilege levels is perhaps superfluous. But when multiple individuals performing different functions are involved in legitimate router access and management, use of the privilege levels is highly recommended. Before implementing privilege levels, a designer who is familiar with router capabilities should determine which individuals need which level of access to the SMB's routers.

Access Control Lists

The subject of ACLs on Cisco routers could be the subject of an entire publication. ACLs are available for different protocol suites, including TCP/IP, IPX, AppleTalk, DECnet, as well as Layer 2 bridging. In TCP/IP networks, the commonly used IP standard and extended ACLs are only a small subset of all of the ACLs available on a Cisco router. The IP extended ACLs allow for inbound and outbound filtering based on the parameters in the IP and TCP headers, which allow for the creation of complex filters. However, even the most sophisticated extended static ACLs cannot match the stateful filtering that takes place on a firewall.

Static ACLs examine packets in isolation and do not detect aggregate traffic patterns. However, ACLs can still be deployed as a security measure on a Cisco router. Network and security administrators need to remember that malicious hackers are not the only threats to the SMB networks; ACLs can be quite effective against curiosity seekers and amateur hackers who do not have the necessary technical expertise to get past them.

Several categories of ACLs are available that add incremental degrees of effectiveness to the ACL approach of securing network access:

- **Dynamic ACLs**—Create a temporary entry as a result of a valid user authentication. When the session initiated by the authenticated user is finished, the temporary entry is removed from the list.

- **Reflexive ACLs**—Create an entry that permits inbound traffic in response to an outside connection.

- **Context-based ACLs**—Support applications that rely on the use of multiple ports— typically multimedia applications—including VoIP.

New Model AAA Features

The new model AAA features on a Cisco router allow the use of external servers like TACACS+, RADIUS, or Kerberos for user authentication, authorization, and accounting functions. The advantage of an external server is the centralization of AAA services.

As the number of routers in an internetwork increases, local password administration simply does not scale and is prone to errors, thus posing a greater security risk. TACACS+ is a Cisco proprietary protocol. TACACS+ is often preferred in Cisco environments and is generally considered to be more mature and robust than the open standard RADIUS that is specified in RFC 2865.

In addition to facilitating user authentication and authorization, a useful security feature that can be configured using TACACS+ is the logging of all of the keystrokes typed into a router. Thus, when any configuration or **show** commands are executed on a router—even if legitimately so—they can be logged for future reference should there be a need to reconstruct events leading to a security or misconfiguration incident. Naturally, if a router is hacked for a malicious purpose, the attacker could disable the keystroke logging. But even so, the logs preceding the hack could offer clues about who was responsible for the hack. The new model AAA is another router security element that raises the bar for potential hackers or internal intruders.

Implementing Routing Protocols Security

Routing updates that are exchanged between neighboring routers carry information pertaining to the network topology. They allow routers to maintain accurate routing tables, choose optimal paths for sending packets to their destinations, and respond quickly (converge) to any changes in the network topology, like a failure of other routers in the network. Someone who understands the network topology even without having configuration access to the routers can potentially cause a great deal of damage to the network or gain access to unauthorized information passing through a router.

If router access is protected so there is minimal or no possibility of an attacker being able to alter the routing protocol configuration or to configure static routes, one way to manipulate the routing updates (and, consequently, other routers' routing tables) is through the introduction of a new router into the network. This obviously might require physical access to the network, but if such access is gained, a new router in the internetwork configured with a malicious intent can corrupt routing tables for the entire internetwork.

This is where the security feature that allows for the authentication of routing updates comes in. If the authentication is configured for whatever routing protocol is used in the network (OSPF, Routing Information Protocol [RIP], Interior Gateway Routing Protocol [IGRP] or Enhanced IGRP [EIGRP]), routers will exchange updates only with their trusted neighbors, and the introduction of a new router that could introduce malicious routes to divert the traffic elsewhere is not going to have the desired effect.

Summary

Cisco offers a wide range of security solutions that span the layers of the OSI model and security threat categories. They include perimeter security (firewalling), secure connectivity (VPNs), intrusion detection and mitigation (IDS), security management platform (VMS), and identity services (AAA). A comprehensive approach to network security is referred to as an end-to-end security solution.

Cisco is commonly thought of as a networking company, but it is a security company as well, given the range and sophistication of security products that it offers. Although product lines like routers or firewalls retain their dominant purpose of offering routing or firewall services, they also have become multipurpose integrated security appliances that offer VPN, IDS, firewall, and routing capability in a single unit.

The flexibility in design that this cross-pollination of functionality offers is unprecedented, but it also makes your job more challenging because of the large number of choices. Adherence to the design principles as outlined in Chapter 1 and understanding the primary purpose of each device, as well as its performance characteristics, should facilitate the process of positioning appropriate products for any given deployment scenario and budget that might arise in SMB environments.

CHAPTER **6**

The Wireless LAN Solution

The modern world is full of wireless communication systems. To mention a few, there are broadcast radio and TV, dispatch radio, cellular phones, walkie-talkies, and, of course, cordless phones within households. Consider the flexibility, mobility, and convenience that these communication systems offer. There is no need to be stationary or physically connected to a particular communication system to use it. You can listen to a radio while traveling in a car, speak on a mobile phone while navigating crowded sidewalks of a major city, or freely move around your kitchen making dinner while chatting with a friend on a cordless phone.

Yet, like all wire-based communication systems, wireless communications have their inherent and unique limitations. To gain a practical understanding of some of these limitations, try using your cellular phone outside the coverage area, walk too far away from the base unit antenna in the middle of a conversation on a cordless phone, or have your nerve endings frayed by static and interference while trying to tune into a radio station that is being jammed or that is a bit out of range. Also, if your credit card bill shows strange charges after you've given a merchant your credit card information using a mobile phone, you will gain a greater appreciation of how easy it is to intercept cellular communications and to take advantage of information that is transmitted through the air.

Notwithstanding any of these limitations, the growing popularity and widespread use of wireless technologies prove not only their marketplace appeal but also their commercial viability. The same holds true for wireless local-area networks (WLANs). WLANs began to emerge in the networking arena (initially with limited success) in the mid-1990s, spurred by the work of IEEE that led to the publication in 1997 of the 802.11 standard. However, the 1 to 2 Mbps data rates as specified in the 1997 802.11 standard were at that time significantly below the rates of the mainstream 10/100 and the emerging Gigabit Ethernet. Thus, the limited initial acceptance of WLANs! That's not so anymore, but it's a winding road.

In 1999, the 802.11 standard was updated and further supplemented by two additional WLAN standards (802.11a and 802.11b) offering higher data rates but lacking compatibility with each other. 802.11b specified the continued use of 2.4-GHz frequency bands, as in the original 802.11. It also specified data rates of up to 11 Mbps thanks to a more efficient modulation scheme known as the *complementary code keying (CCK)*. 802.11a specified the use of the 5-GHz bands with data rates up to 54-MHz using the multicarrier system of orthogonal frequency division multiplexing (OFDM) and several relevant modulation techniques to support the higher data rates. From the perspective of the network end user and the designer, WLAN performance improved and choices increased, but confusion mounted.

There is hope! The promise of reconciliation between 802.11a and 802.11b now lies in the 802.11g standard, which incorporates the 802.11a OFDM system to achieve data rates of 54 Mbps, uses the 2.4-GHz bands, and also requires the implementation of 802.11b modulation techniques. This makes 802.11g backward compatible with 802.11b and potentially avoids regulatory issues in some countries that are associated with the use of the higher frequencies in the 5-GHz bands.

Needless to say, WLANs come to the networking world with their share of capabilities, limitations, and a measure of confusion. The confusion stems not only from the 802.11a/b incompatibilities but also from the availability of a relatively large number of different security-related protocols that have been implemented to compensate for the initial WLAN shortcomings in the area of security. Such is the price of progress.

However, any of the perceived WLAN limitations should not be cause for avoiding WLAN deployment. They can be readily overcome when, in the course of a WLAN design, proper consideration is given to the issues of standards, performance, topology, and the desired level of security.

When deployed judiciously, WLANs introduce into data networking and telecommunications the same degree of convenience, flexibility, and mobility that some of the other wireless technologies bring into other aspects of our lives. This chapter addresses the design and deployment of an SMB WLAN solution in the context of the following major topics:

- WLAN-specific security considerations
- WLAN performance and topology considerations
- WLAN components
- The Cisco WLAN (Aironet) products family
- WLAN deployment scenarios

WLAN-Specific Security Considerations

Compared to wire-based LANs, WLANs introduce into the design and deployment of data networks additional and unique security considerations, which are used as communication platforms for passing sensitive business information. Generally, any effective communication process represents an interaction and a relationship among five elements:

- A transmitter
- A receiver
- A message

- A transmission medium
- Rules or protocols that govern the message transmission between the transmitter and the receiver

Transmitters and receivers exchange messages using a transmission medium and are subject to the rules or protocols that govern the timing, the structure, and the representation of the messages, thus making the communication process possible, practical, and effective.

The biggest (but not the only) difference between wireless and wired LANs is the nature of the transmission medium. Air is considered an unbounded and leaky transmission medium (a new security threat here!) as compared to bounded media like coax, copper, or fiber. In bounded media, the signals representing the message are confined to a specified pathway, and physical access to the media is required to tap into the network. This is not the case with unbounded media. The signals easily propagate past their intended target, and they can be readily intercepted, interfered with, or used to gain access to the network.

Anyone standing in a crowd and carrying on a full-voice conversation with another person is painfully aware that their voice messages propagate over the airwaves in multiple directions past the intended recipient. The continuance of such a conversation depends on whether the individuals involved in it (who alternate as the transmitter and the receiver) care if there are unintended recipients of what is being said. What are the consequences of the conversation being heard by other people? Does it still matter if anyone hears the conversation if it is conducted in a language that is known and understood only by the individuals involved in it? Would it take long for an unintended listener to learn the unknown language in which the conversation is being carried on?

As discussed in Chapter 4, "Overview of the Network Security Issues," any aspect of network security is best considered in the context of a security policy that identifies the threats. WLAN security is no different. The following subsections outline WLAN security threats, mechanisms, and sound practices that counter some of the threats. However, it's up to you as the designer—based on the user requirements and an SMB's network security policy—to determine the potential impact of the threats, the relevance of the available protection mechanisms, and the implementation of sound security practices that apply to WLANs. Otherwise, they all remain abstractions devoid of practical meaning.

WLAN Security Threats

Security threats unique to WLANs stem from the unbounded nature of air as the transmission medium for network communications. Consider an SMB that occupies a building with a wired private network. The connection to the Internet is considered to be secure thanks to the deployment of a firewall, an intrusion detection system (IDS) on the inside and outside networks, and the maximum implementation of available router security features. The building has reasonable physical security.

All visitors to the SMB's facility must first sign in with a security officer in the lobby. Visitors are allowed to bring notebook computers into the building for the purpose of making presentations or taking notes during meetings, but the SMB security policy does not allow visitors to connect to any portion of the internal network using their notebooks. While on the premises, visitors are to be escorted at all times, with the exception of restroom breaks. SMB employee escorts are responsible for enforcing the policy of preventing visitors from making physical connections to the internal network.

Penetrating this SMB's network from the outside is not going to be easy without collaboration with someone on the inside. But this challenge might be a lure for intruders, if you want to factor the psychology of hacking and cracking into the security equation.

Now, imagine that the same network is wireless. Eavesdropping on the wireless signals and the potential introduction of a rogue access point (AP) can lead to the compromise of that network more easily than if it remained wire-based. Yet, put those threats in perspective. There is a certain irony here that makes WLANs less desirable targets for intruders than wire-based networks.

It's a well-known fact that it is easy to penetrate a poorly secured wireless network. But gaining access to a WLAN through almost an open door makes it a pretty blah experience for those hackers who are after a real challenge. That is not necessarily the attitude of those who are engaged in industrial espionage, if the information transmitted over the WLAN warrants their attention.

The perception of the ease of wireless hacking is mostly thanks to the lack of implementation of the available security features at WLAN installations. In some ways, a WLAN can be more secure than its wire-based counterpart, especially in scenarios in which a wire-based network is poorly managed and the network administrator does not know how many ports are available on the network and where they are located. With a WLAN, you normally secure all or none of your ports.

Thus, it's vital that you create a network security policy, do a risk assessment analysis, and comply with sound network management practices. Dangers to WLANs are real, but so are the means of protecting them from those dangers.

Wireless Eavesdropping

Often, and without detection on the network, unauthorized individuals can readily "listen" or eavesdrop on the WLAN transmissions that propagate outside of an office building where a WLAN is installed. But what does "listening" really mean? It means, for example, that a listening device in the form of a notebook PC with a wireless network interface card (NIC) or a handheld PC with an antenna must be physically present within the range of the wireless signals.

Assuming that the listening device is also equipped with software to identify the presence of an 802.11 WLAN or to collect and decode the wireless data stream, an act of wireless eavesdropping takes place. However, such an act, if sustained over a long period of time, might force a potential intruder to be physically too close for comfort to the actual WLAN location.

NOTE   Wireless products vendors (AirMagnet, for example) offer tools for detecting the presence of wireless intruders on the network.

It's one thing to drive around with a wireless listening device and to attempt to identify WLAN locations and service set identifiers (SSIDs). (It's referred to as *wardriving*. *Warchalking* further pinpoints these locations and SSIDs through markings on buildings or sidewalks.) It's another matter, however, to spend hours in the WLAN proximity collecting a sufficient amount of data to be able to crack wired equivalent privacy (WEP) or to even join a completely unsecured WLAN and start using it.

Ironically, wireless hacking requires a greater degree of physical exposure of the perpetrator than hacking a wired network from the privacy of one's own surroundings. If an SMB is sufficiently conscious about physical security, the act of eavesdropping on WLAN transmissions might be quite detectable because of the uncharacteristic level of physical activity in the proximity of the WLAN location.

Other Forms of WLAN Intrusion

What about WLAN intruders who just want to connect and scrounge off some bandwidth, possibly for free Internet access? If there is no malice on their part, they could, in a worst-case scenario, degrade the WLAN performance. A potentially more devastating way to penetrate WLAN defenses than just eavesdropping or scrounging off bandwidth involves placing an unauthorized wireless access device where it should not be. That method usually requires assistance from the inside, be it deliberate or through nonmalicious ignorance of network security policies.

Rogue Access Points

The introduction of rogue APs into a WLAN means that an AP that is outside of the administrative control of an SMB is masquerading as a legitimate entry point into the SMB's network. A rogue AP does not always mean that someone has placed an additional physical unit on the SMB's premises without the knowledge of SMB's IT personnel. That, however, is a distinct possibility, whether the perpetrator is an outsider or, most likely, an employee.

A rogue AP could be a legitimately installed AP that has been accidentally or deliberately reset or reconfigured so that it no longer complies with the SMB's network security policy.

Effectively, that AP is outside of SMB's administrative control and becomes a potential open door for penetrating the WLAN and then using it to launch attacks against the rest of the network. Consider now the practicality of rogue APs.

An AP normally connects to the rest of the network via a wire uplink. For an outsider who is attempting to penetrate a network, it might be difficult to gain the kind of physical access to an SMB's facilities that would allow the installation of a rogue AP with an uplink to the rest of the LAN. And placing a rogue AP on the SMB's premises (or off the premises) without an uplink might be of limited value to a potential perpetrator.

Cisco supports repeater APs that do not physically uplink to the rest of the network; instead, they form an association with another AP that might or might not have a physical uplink. The use of APs in the repeater mode requires configuration and the activation of the Aironet extensions, which actually offer a measure of deterrence. Also, not all vendors support repeater APs.

In all likelihood, a rogue AP will prove to be an inside job. If it is deliberate and perpetrated by a skilled IT employee, the SMB has a more serious problem on its hands than just WLAN hacking. Physical security and sound WLAN management practices can prevent or, in the worst case, detect the presence of unauthorized APs that result from accidental resets or benign reconfiguration.

WLAN Security Mechanisms

When it comes to WLAN security mechanisms, the intention is always good (that is, to provide solid security), the execution involves compromises (because we live in a real world), the outcome is debatable (because you can't make everyone happy), and the debate will continue for some time to come (that's what makes the standards process so valuable and exciting). But how effective are the various WLAN security mechanisms?

To start at the beginning, there is the use of the spread spectrum (SS) technology (in 802.11a/g) that dates back to the days of World War II. SS modulations employ wide-frequency bands to transmit comparatively narrow-bandwidth information signals. This makes SS transmissions hard to intercept and more resistant to jamming. SS technology has long been a favorite in military communications, which attests to its inherent security value. However, there is definitely a problem in WLAN deployments with reliance on the inherent security qualities of SS.

If the SS transmitters and receivers (APs and clients, for example) are to be commercially successful, which is what all WLAN vendors want them to be, they need to talk to each other and be widely available to all (including potential intruders) who want to purchase them. Thus, any reliance on the properties of the spread spectrum for security in the context of WLAN deployment is misplaced.

WARNING   The 802.11 standards clearly spell out the frequencies, the modulation/demodulation techniques, and the sequence codes that vendors need to implement to bring to market compatible wireless products. Open commercial environments negate the inherent security value of the SS technology. It is quite a different scenario from secret military communications.

Next come the SSIDs, which are necessary to establish an association between a wireless client and an AP. At best, SSIDs are a weak form of passwords, and free tools exist for detecting them. In addition, if an administrator does not change them from the default values during WLAN deployment, it's not just leaving the door unlocked—it's leaving it wide open.

WARNING   SSIDs are useless as a security mechanism. The exception, perhaps, is an instance where the most benign of hackers who, upon detecting a default SSID with no other security measures implemented, would warn the WLAN administrator of the danger to his or her WLAN. Use of SSIDs to connect to a WLAN is referred to as *open authentication*.

Now it is time for encryption (to protect the transmitted data) along with an overlay of security enhancements to facilitate robust authentication. Authentication and encryption are widely deployed and well understood in wire-based networks. They represent the areas of WLAN security that warrant a designer's serious attention. Any of the issues regarding the early WEP should be cleared up and replaced with an understanding of the scope of strong security measures that are now available to designers in deploying WLANs.

The Promise and Shortcomings of WEP

The early version of WEP was known to be weak. In 2001, a free program (Airsnort) became available on the Internet to crack WEP, provided that a sufficient amount of data could be accumulated for the program to analyze. Time estimates for WEP cracking range from hours to days, depending on the network's utilization. For a heavily utilized WLAN with a lot of packets radiating through the air, the time to WEP crack is shorter. All that's needed is a Linux-based PC, a wireless 802.11-compliant NIC, and a sufficient amount of time in the vicinity of the victim WLAN.

Yet, what needs to be emphasized here is that the readily crackable WEP is the earlier generation WEP, which relies on the use of static keys that are shared among multiple users. By having dynamically generated keys and implementing measures to guard against replay attacks, WEP acquires more teeth and credibility.

The enhancement that Cisco made to WEP includes the Temporal Key Integrity Protocol (TKIP), which has also been standardized via the 802.11i specification. TKIP relies on per-packet keying (PPK), which involves the use of a different key per packet (or per relatively small group of packets) to prevent cracking the key due to WEP's weak initialization vector of 24 bits. In addition, TKIP implements the message integrity check (MIC), which is a stronger mechanism to prevent message tampering through replay attacks than is the cyclic redundancy check (CRC)-32, which is part of the earlier version of WEP. Cisco supports its own version of TKIP as well as the standards-based one. Whereas WEP provides data encryption, 802.1x facilitates strong authentication.

IEEE's 802.1x Standard in WLANs

The premise of the 802.1x standard is simple. It's sometimes impossible to prevent unauthorized devices from physically attaching to the LAN infrastructure, either through LAN switches (think of all those RJ-45 data jacks accessible to visitors in SMB office environments) or through wireless APs (you don't even have to get inside a building to exploit these). Consequently, 802.1x offers the means (but not the algorithms themselves) to authenticate and to authorize a device that physically attaches to a LAN switch port or that establishes an association with an 802.11 AP. 802.1x defines the concepts of a supplicant, an authenticator, and an authentication server.

Mapping these concepts to the typical WLAN components, a WLAN client becomes the supplicant, an AP is the authenticator, and the presence of an authentication server—Remote Access Dial-In User Service (RADIUS), for example—which is already so common in wire-based LANs, is introduced. By incorporating an authentication server into WLAN security, 802.1x facilitates the implementation by vendors of per-port mutual authentication techniques.

Mutual authentication allows for the authentication server to verify the client credentials (user ID, password, digital certificate), and it allows the client to issue a challenge to the server to authenticate the AP. Mutual authentication that involves the authentication by a client of the AP prevents rogue APs from being used to mount man-in-the-middle (MITM) attacks. The exchanges between the client, the AP, and the server take place via a variant of the Extensible Authentication Protocol (EAP). 802.1x and EAPs are closely coupled.

The Adoption of EAPs in WLANs

EAP was originally developed to extend the rather limited authentication options of the Point-to-Point Protocol (PPP). Prior to EAP, PPP could use Password Authentication Protocol (PAP) or the Challenge Handshake Authentication Protocol (CHAP). RFC 2284 specifies PPP EAP.

EAP, however, has been popularized through its adaptation into the 802.1x standard. From the WLAN design perspective, 802.1x/EAP combinations offer you several authentication-related options to enhance SMB WLAN security. The following EAP variants have been defined:

- Cisco Light EAP (LEAP)
- EAP with Transport Layer Security (EAP-TLS)
- EAP with Tunneled TLS (EAP-TTLS)
- Protected EAP (PEAP)
- EAP Subscriber Identity Module (EAP-SIM)

Each of the EAP variants has its own unique characteristics, which affect WLAN security design decisions.

LEAP

LEAP, which is commonly referred to as the Cisco Wireless EAP, is popular and widely deployed in Cisco wireless products. LEAP supports mutual authentication via a shared secret or a password.

EAP-TLS

EAP-TLS relies on the use of the TLS protocol (standards track RFC 2246) to enhance the security of the authentication process itself. TLS is composed of the TLS Record Protocol and the TLS Handshake Protocol. The TLS Record Protocol ensures the privacy and reliability of the connection between the communicating entities (the client and an authentication server), and it is used to encapsulate the TLS Handshake Protocol.

The TLS Handshake Protocol allows a server and a client to authenticate each other and to negotiate an encryption algorithm and crypto keys before any application-level data is transmitted. Effectively, the TLS Handshake Protocol makes the authentication negotiation secure. It makes the negotiated secret unavailable to eavesdroppers and prevents MITM attacks by denying the secret to those who would place themselves in the middle of an authenticated connection. The negotiation is also reliable because it does not allow an attacker to modify the negotiation without being detected by the communicating parties. EAP-TLS uses digital certificates for mutual authentication and is generally considered more secure than LEAP.

EAP-TTLS

EAP-TTLS extends the TLS Handshake Protocol authentication negotiation process and allows for the exchange of more information over the secure connection than EAP-TLS does. EAP-TTLS also allows the client to use legacy password-based authentication protocols like PAP, CHAP, or the Microsoft versions of CHAP while protecting the use of these protocols against eavesdropping and MITM attacks.

PEAP

PEAP relies on TLS as well. PEAP further extends the security of the EAP framework by incorporating device identity protection, which all of the preceding EAP variants lack.

EAP-SIM

EAP-SIM extends the EAP framework even further to enhance the security of authentication and key distribution in Global System for Mobile Communications (GSM).

Summary of the Functionalities of EAPs

As the "extensible" in EAP implies, there will likely be more EAP variants as a function of time, new security exploits, overall maturing, and a greater level of deployment of the WLAN technologies. Keep in mind, as a general perspective, that collectively the combination of 802.1x/EAP facilitates the following:

- Mutual per-port authentication, which minimizes or eliminates MITM attacks through the use of rogue access points

- Use of dynamic keys for encryption following authentication, which minimizes or (if intruders are not able or willing to exert considerable effort) eliminates the potential for data decryption

- Configuration of security policy parameters relating to reauthentication and the timing of the dynamic key regeneration, which gives an SMB a considerable amount of control over WLAN security

If an SMB wants to harden WLAN security, the bar can be raised high even for the most determined intruders. The question is: Is a typical SMB aware of and desirous of implementing maximum security when deploying a WLAN? That's where a designer's expertise in this area comes in.

WLAN Sound Security Practices

The following list identifies sound practices that can be used to enhance WLAN security. Consider applying these practices as appropriate depending on an SMB's security policy, the size of the WLAN installation, and the available features of the WLAN products.

- **Use the strongest authentication possible**—Alternatively, use the authentication method that is in compliance with the SMB's security policy. 802.1x/EAPs offer several choices for mutual authentication and secure key exchange. Check for availability of local authentication that might eliminate the need for a dedicated Authentication, Authorization, and Accounting (AAA) server in smaller deployments. Under no circumstances should SMBs rely on SSIDs as a security mechanism. Change SSIDs from default values and consider turning off SSID broadcasts altogether.

- **Activate WEP and any of its enhancements, such as TKIP**—Despite all of the hoopla about WEP's vulnerability, it takes time and a deliberate effort to collect enough data to crack even its early version. The principle here is that imperfect security with clearly understood limitations is better than none. The type of WEP that uses static shared keys is readily crackable; use of dynamic keys makes it significantly harder to crack WEP. Use stronger encryption—Wi-Fi Protected Access (WPA), 802.11i—if available.

- **Disable Dynamic Host Configuration Protocol (DHCP) and use static IP addresses instead**—DHCP offers convenience in administration, but it also conveniently serves an IP address to an intruder or a loafer within a WLAN range. Keep this practice in perspective, though, as a function of network administration convenience. Static address ranges (especially private) can be guessed or deciphered from e-mail headers. Consider MAC level authentication if DHCP remains enabled.

- **Ensure that the antennae do not emit too much power**—You want to ensure proper coverage for the areas from which authorized users might connect to a WLAN, but ideally you do not want strong signals to travel outside the authorized coverage areas. This process requires some experimentation.

- **Provide physical security for APs**—APs without adequate physical security can be accidentally or deliberately reconfigured or reset to factory defaults.

- **Deploy WLAN management**—WLAN management products are available to help administrators enforce compliance with the SMB's security policy (consistency of AP configuration, for example). You can also use WLAN management tools to monitor WLAN performance, check for the presence of rogue access points, and identify wireless intruders. More than a dozen companies offer products that can assist with WLAN management.

WLAN Performance and Topology Considerations

In wire-based networks, after the cabling is completed and the LAN switches are in place, the performance and topology of an individual network connection are not much of a design consideration. Performance is predetermined by the combination of the speed of the LAN switch port to which a user connects and the NIC in the user's device. And unless there are hardware failures or performance bottlenecks closer to the core of the network, the user can have a reasonable expectation of connecting to the network at the same speed (and also from the same location!).

In WLANs, the convenience of user mobility alters the individual connection performance/topology equation. The speed of the individual connection (an association between a client and an AP) can vary depending on the following:

- A user's distance from an AP
- Placement of APs in multi-AP deployments

- Sudden and unexpected interference from other wireless devices operating at the same frequency
- Type of WLAN technology in use

When considering WLAN performance, put it into perspective by considering voice communications and the attenuation rate of a voice message. Ask yourself the following questions:

- How far away can your voice be heard without some amplification?
- Are there any physical obstacles that will stop your message dead in its tracks, not allowing it to propagate further?
- What is the potential for interference with your message from other sets of vocal cords around you?

All these conditions affect the quality of voice communications between people as well as the performance of an association between an AP and a wireless client.

WLAN Performance Considerations

At this time, the throughput capacity of the electromagnetic waves in the WLAN radio frequency bands is lower than the throughput capacities of the traditional bounded media (fiber, twisted pair copper, or coax). Thus, WLAN performance limitations must be considered in the context of certain advantages: not having to install physical cabling and having considerable mobility.

Even though the voice quality in mobile phones continues to improve, it is, in general, still not on par with landline handsets. Yet, as the exploding mobile phone market seems to indicate, the degradation in performance is worth the convenience of being reachable just about anytime and anywhere. (Sometimes mobile phones might ring at inconvenient times—but that's a separate issue.)

When deploying a WLAN, consider the following factors that have an impact on the WLAN performance:

- **The type of WLAN technology**—802.11b/g products use the 2.4-GHz frequency bands with three nonoverlapping channels. Because the 802.11g maximum (and theoretical!) data rate of 54 Mbps equals that of 802.11a, the key differentiator between them becomes the number of nonoverlapping channels. Technically, 802.11a supports up to 12, but the usable number might be smaller because of regulatory requirements (11 in the United States, for example). WLAN products themselves might support fewer channels than are even permissible in a regulatory domain. The issue of nonoverlapping channels applies in multi-AP deployments. For single-AP deployments, the maximum data rate and perhaps even the field-tested data rates would be the key factors in considering performance. 802.11a and 802.11g offer higher data rates than 802.11b (which offers 11 Mbps).

- **Uplink bandwidth sharing**—Consider that every AP has a fixed amount of uplink bandwidth to be shared between all of the users accessing resources on the wired LAN. A large number of bandwidth-intensive users will overload that link and degrade performance, regardless of what the ideal association speed is between the users and an AP.

- **Use of repeater APs**—Cisco supports repeater APs, which do not connect directly to a wired LAN; instead, they form an association with another AP (root) that is connected to the wired LAN. Use of repeater APs exacts a performance penalty for users as they get further and further down the repeater chain. But topology requirements might mandate repeater AP use regardless of the performance penalty. Not all vendors support repeater AP use.

- **Impact of interference**—Interference can be in the form of other wireless devices operating at the same frequencies, causing "dead spots," or it can be in the form of permanent changes (such as addition of new furniture, especially metal) in the WLAN deployment area. Interference can result in performance degradation with a throughput far below (50% or more) the theoretical link rate for a specific WLAN technology.

- **Level of security**—Although security is a big consideration in WLAN deployments, use of an authentication mechanism (one of the EAPs) can impact WLAN performance. The trade-off between security, convenience, and performance is an inevitable design issue that can ultimately be resolved only as a function of an SMB's business priorities.

WLAN Topology Considerations

In WLANs, topology considerations are closely tied to performance considerations. In wire-based networks (LAN/WAN combinations), maintaining the same throughput capacity (an equivalent of a T3, for example) for a mile or hundreds of miles is not as much a technical issue as it is an economic one.

In WLANs, distance (and, consequently, topology) quickly translates into performance considerations. APs from different vendors are often rated on the speed of association as a function of the client's distance from the AP. The longer the distance between a client and the AP, the slower the speed of the association. Eventually, as the distance between a client and an AP increases, establishing an association and transmitting data is no longer possible.

All of the performance considerations that were addressed in the previous section apply to WLAN topology as well. The following factors, although they are more on the topology side, also affect performance:

- Choice of antenna gain
- Performing a radio frequency (RF) survey
- WLAN topology determination steps

Choice of Antenna Gain

The use of higher gain antennae translates into a larger coverage area for APs and longer distances for bridged point-to-point links. Larger coverage areas and longer point-to-point links affect the overall WLAN topology.

Performing an RF Survey

With the exception of the simplest of WLAN deployments, it's a sound WLAN design practice to perform an RF survey before proceeding with an installation. An RF survey conducted by a competent professional should help to determine a viable WLAN topology, which in turn enhances WLAN performance. An RF survey can identify the following:

- Types and sources of interference that cannot be eliminated. For example, neighboring businesses or individuals might be operating in the same frequency bands using the same technologies, which can pose security risks and performance degradation. Judicious AP placement after locating the potential sources of interference is the answer to this problem.

- Dead spots. Don't expect to establish a connection from those locations.

- General boundaries from within which users can establish connections to an AP.

As much as possible, you should use a survey tool that has a radio and NIC comparable to those that users will have in their equipment, with the understanding that the wireless clients might end up being more diverse than initially planned. An AP that is used during a survey should be what is planned for the actual deployment. In multivendor WLAN deployments, a designer should keep in mind the variations in power ratings for NIC radios.

WLAN Topology Determination Steps

The critical element in determining the WLAN topology is to have some a priori knowledge of where the wireless access is needed and what the performance requirements for that access are. WLAN topology can extend considerably for lower data rates and shrink in size as a function of demand for higher levels of performance. In addition, topology requirements change as a function of time, so the following steps apply to the initial topology mapping as well as to future adjustments:

1 Start with an idea of where the users need access and how much bandwidth they need.

2 Perform an RF site survey.

3 Create a topological map that identifies boundaries and throughput levels.

These are steps in the right direction in terms of defining a WLAN topology.

WLAN Components

The wireless network components can be roughly mapped to the OSI reference model and broken down into the following categories for the purpose of providing a degree of structure when considering various design issues:

- Radio frequencies, transmit power, and antennae (layer 1, physical)
- APs and wireless bridges (layer 2, data link)
- Wireless routers (layer 3, network)
- Wireless clients (higher layers)

Radio-wave frequencies, the transmit power levels of a wireless device, and the type and gain of antennae replace the cabling considerations at the physical layer. Similar to the LAN switches, APs aggregate wireless clients and bridges extend the reach of a wireless LAN at the data link layer. And wireless routers extend the wireless reach into the network layer.

All of this occurs in support of the wireless clients, which allow people to satisfy their incessant desire to communicate with a greater degree of flexibility, mobility, and convenience. Now, consider the generic characteristics of these WLAN component categories and the relevant issues that must be taken into account in the course of a WLAN design.

Radio Frequencies, Transmit Power, and Antennae

A design consideration with respect to WLAN devices and antennae entails regulatory compliance with the permissible radio frequencies in a deployment region. For example, not all countries permit the use of the 5-GHz spectrum, which disqualifies 802.11a products from being deployed. However, with the 802.11g standard, which allows data rates up to 54 Mbps in the 2.4-GHz bands, a designer has choices.

Another regulatory element to consider is the Effective Isotropic Radiated Power (EIRP), which is derived from the combination of the following:

- A wireless device's transmit signal power
- Antenna gain
- Antenna cable signal loss

NOTE   The European maximum values for EIRP differ from those in the United States.

These three elements are expressed in decibels (dB). A decibel represents 10 times the base 10 logarithm of the ratio between the measured power level and a reference power level, as expressed in the following formula:

$$10 \times \log_{10} \; (measured\ level/reference\ level)$$

If the measured level is 100 and the reference level is 1, then the base 10 log of that ratio is 2. When expressed in decibels, it is 20 dB (10×2). In practice, the dB symbol is combined with another symbol to represent what is being measured or what physical units are being used with a given product. When a device's transmit power is measured in milliwatts, the symbol dBm (m for milliwatts) is used to express power levels in decibels.

An easy rule to remember regarding decibels is that an increase of 3 dB represents a twofold increase in the power level, whereas a decrease of 3 dB corresponds to a halving of the power level. Assume that a device can transmit at power levels from 0 to 1000 milliwatts. Translated into decibels, the power levels for that device can be represented as follows:

1 milliwatt (mW) = 0 dBm

2mW = 3 dBm

4mW = 6 dBm

8mW = 9 dBm

32mW = 15 dBm

The maximum power of 1000mW is 30 dBm.

Through the use of the log function, decibels allow the representation of larger numbers in smaller increments. Power level configuration parameters for wireless devices are often expressed in decibels rather than in milliwatts or watts.

Antennae are critical elements of the wireless infrastructure because their characteristics determine the coverage range and performance of a wireless installation. For some WLAN products, you do not have a choice regarding an antenna because it comes integrated with a device. However, understanding antenna characteristics can help with the design of the WLAN topology. Consider next the antenna gain in the context of calculating EIRP. In addition to the gain, other key characteristics of antennae are the frequencies at which they operate, their direction, and their polarization.

EIRP and Antenna Gain

In contrast to transmit power levels, antenna gain is expressed in two ways:

- **dBi**—In reference to an isotropic antenna. An isotropic antenna is the purely mathematical concept of a nondirectional antenna that radiates equally in all directions. When compared to itself, it has a 0-dB power loss/gain, making it easy to be used as a reference. The simple rule regarding antennae is that the greater the dBi, the higher the antenna gain, which can translate into a greater and more accurate coverage area for a WLAN. An antenna gain of 20 dBi represents 100 times more signal strength than the ideal isotropic reference. A gain of 30 dBi represents 1000 times more than the reference.

- **dBd**—In reference to a dipole antenna. Dipole antennae are practically possible, and their gain is expressed in decibels as dBd (the second "d" is for dipole). A dipole antenna also has a 2.14-dB gain (which is often rounded up to 2.2) over an isotropic antenna. To convert a dBd antenna rating to a dBi rating, add 2.14 (or 2.2) to the dBd rating.

To calculate the EIRP, consider a hypothetical device with a maximum of 24 dBm (256mW maximum power), an antenna with a 28-dBi gain, and a cable from the device to the antenna with a 5-dB loss. EIRP is the sum of the decibels for all of those components, or 47 dB (24 + 28 $\angle$ 5). To derive the final EIRP value, loss means subtraction rather than addition because loss represents a negative value.

Always review the maximum permissible EIRP levels in a deployment region before proceeding with a more complex or large-scale WLAN implementation.

Antenna Radio Frequencies

For WLAN applications, the radio frequencies are either in the 2.4- or 5-GHz bands, which are broken into multiple channels. The 802.11b standard defines in the 2.4-GHz range 14 direct sequence (DS) channels that are 22 MHz wide, with 11 of these channels approved for use by the Federal Communications Commission (FCC) in the United States. In other countries or regulatory domains, the approved channel use might coincide or vary from that in the United States.

Due to the 5-MHz separation between the center of frequencies in the 802.11b channels, they overlap and interfere with each other if adjacent channels are used at an installation. Four successive channels are required between any two nonoverlapping channels, thus allowing for three nonoverlapping channels (1, 6, and 11) out of the 11 approved by the FCC.

WARNING   Use of overlapping channels in adjacent AP installations can lead to performance degradation and is not recommended. As a general rule, the 2.4-GHz antennae support all of the 802.11b-defined channels, but that's not necessarily the case with the 5-GHz antennae.

The 802.11a standard defines 12 nonoverlapping channels in the three Unlicensed National Information Infrastructure (UNII) 5.4-GHz bands for use in the United States. From the regulatory perspective, design considerations that apply to the 2.4-GHz frequencies are similar to those that apply to the 5-GHz bands.

NOTE   As a WLAN designer, you should always remember the frequency spectrum regulatory issues when planning multinational wireless deployments. Always check the spectrum regulatory requirements at the regulatory domain or the country of WLAN deployment.

Antenna Polarization

Antenna polarization refers to the orientation of the electric field component (with respect to the Earth's surface) of the transmitted electromagnetic waves (horizontal or vertical) and whether the electromagnetic radiation remains in a single plane (linear) or multiple planes (circular or elliptic). Most WLAN equipment antennae are linear and vertically polarized, with some exceptions that offer either horizontal or vertical polarization for the same model. Horizontally polarized antennae are used in broadcast TV in the United States.

The critical design issue regarding polarization is that the communicating antennae should have the same polarization. Although in practice there might be some performance-impacting exceptions to this guideline, don't make the mistake of using antennae with different polarization for longer line-of-sight (LOS) point-to-point communications between wireless bridges.

Antenna Direction

An antenna's type and style determine the direction of the radiation of the radio waves. Table 6-1 explores the characteristics of the two antenna categories—omnidirectional and directional—with respect to their direction of radiation.

Table 6-1 *Antenna Direction Category Characteristics*

Antenna Direction Category	Style	Action	Deployment Scenarios
Omnidirectional	Typically shaped as a circular rod. The standard dipole antenna (the classic rubber duck) is an example.	Radiates in all directions or in a 360-degree pattern.	"Base stations" or APs in an office building where clients want to connect from any direction.*
Directional	Yagi, patch, sector, and parabolic dish.	Radiation is focused in a specific direction	Longer outdoor point-to-point bridge links.* Should work for a short-distance indoor bridge link. When mounted in a ceiling corner, it might be a perfect choice for a group of stationary wireless clients residing within its pattern of radiation.

*These are typical deployment scenarios. An actual deployment scenario is always a function of user requirements and might depend on the applications and location of the communicating devices.

Because an antenna does not amplify the received signal from a wireless device but rather retransmits it in a different form, a directional antenna of comparable gain as an omnidirectional one will have a longer range. That is a result of all of the radiated energy being confined to a smaller angle of radiation.

Additional Antenna Considerations

Certain WLAN deployment environments are prone to multipath distortion or interference that occurs when a radio signal takes multiple paths while traveling between a source and a destination (a client and an AP, for example).

Multiple paths for an RF signal can result in a portion of the signal taking a longer path and experiencing a longer delay than the rest of the signal. This situation can lead to bit errors that eventually result in packet retransmissions and degraded performance. Environments with a lot of metal structures are most prone to multipath distortion. Consider the use of diversity antennae in those kinds of environments, which should be identified for the potential of multipath distortion via an RF site survey.

Diversity antennae are intended to overcome multipath distortion (or at least to minimize it) by utilizing two antennae to cover the same area. The antennae should not be so far apart that they cover distinctly different areas or be so close together that diversity does not occur. The separation between antennae in a diversity scenario should be in the range of 1 to 8 feet or approximately 0.3 to 2.4 meters.

A wireless device, such as an AP equipped with a diversity antenna, automatically switches between the two antennae to establish the best possible connection to a client without any intervention on the part of a user. Support for diversity antennae in an AP might be a design consideration if the user needs robust coverage in areas prone to diversity interference.

Access Points and Wireless Bridges

From the network infrastructure perspective, a wireless AP is effectively equivalent to a LAN access switch that is aggregating a variety of wireless clients. LAN switch characteristics, as they relate to network design, are considered primarily at the data link layer and are addressed in Chapter 3, "Network Infrastructure Requirements for Effective Solutions Implementation." But similar to a switch, an AP also functions at the physical layer. In the case of an AP, the antenna characteristics, as presented in the preceding section, must be considered instead of cabling-related issues.

Another big difference between a typical AP and a LAN switch is that an AP is going to have a single 10/100 Mbps uplink to a LAN switch. That link must be shared by all of the wireless clients attached to an AP if they are accessing resources on the wire-based LAN. At first glance, the uplink capacity might seem to be a performance bottleneck. But consider that 802.11a and 802.11g specify maximum data rates of 54 Mbps, with 802.11b being lower. With the availability of dedicated Gigabit Ethernet to the desktop, a 54-Mbps data rate for a single client (or a group of clients sharing the total AP bandwidth) and a 10/100 uplink might seem archaic and slow. However, keep in mind that 10 Mbps Ethernet was the norm nearly a decade ago, and even 10 Mbps dedicated bandwidth is a screamer for many SMB applications.

Typically, servers might not be considered candidates for connecting to an AP, but nothing prevents a wireless notebook computer or a desktop from being configured as a server, even for temporary use. Naturally, large file transfers going on all day long, heavy-duty video editing, or graphic design work demanding high bandwidth would not be the ideal applications to be deployed over a wireless LAN with a limited bandwidth capacity. But as I've stated many times before, well-defined user requirements drive deployment.

As a function of the user requirements, an AP might have to support VLANs, VLAN trunking over the uplink, mobile IP if multiple subnets are in use in a larger WLAN deployment, quality of service (QoS) for prioritizing voice or other time-sensitive applications, and a variety of security protocols to ensure the security of the communications. APs must of necessity offer good support for authentication and data encryption. And if there is one place where you should be looking at security features, it is on APs.

In the early days of networking, bridges were either local or remote. Remote bridges operated in pairs to create a point-to-point link extending the LAN into a WAN or a metropolitan-area network (MAN), whereas a single local bridge could be deployed to improve network performance through segmentation of shared LAN segments. Wireless bridges also come in two flavors. Wireless bridges without additional attributes are a form of what used to be (and in some SMB installations still are) remote bridges. Wireless workgroup bridges, on the other hand, allow a small wire-based workgroup to connect to the workgroup bridge, which in turn can form an association with an AP. Figure 6-1 illustrates the two types of wireless bridges.

Figure 6-1 *Types of Wireless Bridges*

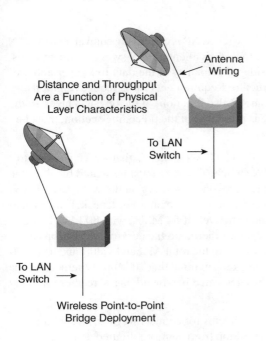

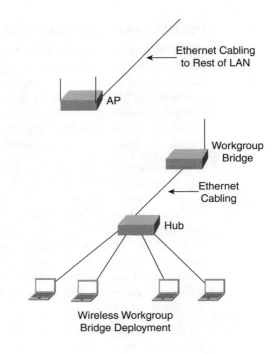

Unlike APs, bridges do not directly aggregate wireless clients. Instead, they extend a wireless or a wire-based LAN topology as a function of their physical layer characteristics and user requirements.

The physical layer characteristics that determine the ability of bridges to extend the size of a LAN include the following:

- Radio frequency at which they operate
- Transmit power settings
- Antenna gain, direction, and style

In addition, bridges might need to support the following features, which are normally supported on the nonworkgroup bridges:

- VLANs
- VLAN trunking
- Spanning Tree Protocol (STP)
- Quality of service (QoS)
- Authentication

Wireless Routers

Think for a moment about the fundamental appeal of a wireless router—integration that is aimed at a specific market segment. A router that combines a WAN interface (cable/digital subscriber line [DSL]) and a standards-compatible AP to aggregate wireless clients has its place in networking, but most likely at the SOHO or SMB workgroup level.

Given the significant performance differences between maximum throughput capabilities of a wire-based versus a wireless link, a core switch/router that is installed in a highly secure data center and supporting Gigabit Ethernet and/or OC-192 interfaces is not likely to be incorporating an AP for aggregating wireless clients. You never know, though, what the future might bring! On the other hand, an access router incorporating a small switch (for a server or another wire-based device), an AP, a WAN interface for Internet access, and perhaps even a firewall might be a perfect wireless solution for a small branch office, an SMB workgroup, or a SOHO-type business.

Several companies offer wireless routers aimed at the home networking and SOHO markets. In mid-2003, Cisco Systems acquired the privately held Linksys Group, Inc., which specializes in home networking equipment. Wireless products from Linksys include several router models, client NICs, and even a wireless camera.

Wireless Clients

Wireless clients include notebook computers with built-in wireless adapters, Peripheral Component Interconnect (PCI) NICs that can be installed in servers or desktop workstations with a PCI slot, PC cards that nicely complement a notebook with PC slots but without a built-in wireless adapter, handheld personal digital assistants (PDAs), phones, cameras, universal serial bus (USB)-based wireless clients for ad hoc or AP-based communications, and more.

Given the availability of varying WLAN standards, the number of security protocols, and the number of vendors in the wireless networking field, the biggest challenge that you will probably face when considering wireless clients' deployment will have to do with compatibility and interoperability between the WLAN infrastructure and the potential clients.

The issues of compatibility and interoperability come into play even more when certain proprietary techniques are implemented in the wireless products to improve their performance or security. There is, however, no cause for alarm because the networking field, in general, is full of gear from numerous vendors. It is almost impossible to find an SMB installation without some kind of a multivendor network solution. The key is to be aware of the protocol implementations in the clients and the infrastructure devices (APs, routers) with which they will associate.

If compatibility problems persist for the same protocol implementations from different vendors, consider a single-vendor solution or be prepared for some lengthy discussions with technical support personnel of multiple vendors.

The Cisco WLAN (Aironet) Products Family

The wireless product line that Cisco offers provides considerable flexibility in designing a wireless solution for a wide range of SMB requirements. The 1400 series bridges extend the reach of wire-based LANs or WLANs for distances in excess of 20 miles (32 kilometers) and throughput rates of multiple T1/E1s.

Dual-mode APs from the 1200 series support both 802.11a and 802.11b standards, which makes them an effective integration tool in wireless scenarios that already deploy or desire to deploy clients that comply with either standard. The 1200 series APs are also available in the 802.11g standard, and the 802.11a/b units are field upgradeable to 802.11g. Client NICs are available in all three standards: 802.11a, 802.11b, and 802.11g. A wide range of antennae allow for the fine-tuning of transmission power and distance requirements.

All products incorporate extensive security support. Consider these wireless products and their characteristics in more detail in the context of creating an effective wireless infrastructure and client environment.

The 1400 Series Bridges

The 1400 series bridges are an element of the network infrastructure whose purpose is to create wireless high-capacity point-to-point or point-to-multipoint links that extend the boundaries of a LAN in areas where wired infrastructure is not feasible. The 1400 bridge complies with the 802.11a standard, which means that data rates up to 54 Mbps are possible.

Configuration of the bridge radio settings allows for the selection of data rates ranging from 6 Mbps through 54 Mbps, with the intervening options being 9, 12, 18, 24, 36, and 48 Mbps. Bridge configuration also allows for the optimization of throughput so that the bridge transmits at the highest rate possible as a function of changes in the transmission path environment.

In practice, lower data rates are selected for longer distances between the bridges, and data rates are likely to vary from the product specification as a function of obstacles in the transmission path. The 1400 series bridges operate in pairs for point-to-point configurations and in larger groups for point-to-multipoint scenarios. For point-to-point transmissions, the 1400 is specified for 12 miles (approximately 19.2 kilometers) at 54 Mbps and for 23 miles (approximately 36.8 kilometers) at 9 Mbps using the 28-dBi dish antennae. Other antenna options for the 1400 include the 9.0-dBi vertically polarized omni antenna and the 9.5-dBi sector antenna, which supports vertical or horizontal linear polarization.

The 1400 series bridges are well suited as an alternative to outdoor leased lines, but nothing prevents them from being deployed indoors as well. A data rate of 54 Mbps is roughly equivalent to the capacity of 35 T1s, or 1 T3 + 7 T1s.

TIP

Given that the 1400 series bridges are LOS devices with a maximum transmission distance of about 23 miles, they qualify for extending a LAN or creating a MAN rather than being a key building component in a long-haul WAN. Ultimately, however, how the 1400 bridges will be deployed boils down to the user requirements and the availability of wired infrastructure and WAN services.

If you contemplate a LAN extension, the link between the 1400s can be configured as a VLAN trunk (802.1q encapsulation) if traffic from multiple VLANs must transit through it. Considering the outdoor nature of the 1400 bridge, power is supplied via a power injector that can be housed indoors closer to a power source. The injector is equipped with a 100BASE-T port for connection to a LAN and a pair of RG-6 coaxial cables that extend to the bridge. Both sets of cables (Cat 5 and the two coaxial) extend to up to 100 meters, allowing a bridge unit to be up to 200 meters from the connection to a LAN switch.

The 1400 series bridges implement the Wireless Security Suite from Cisco. Authentication is supported via 802.1x with LEAP, which provides for mutual authentication and dynamic per-user and per-session encryption keys. Data encryption is supported via WEP with 40- and 128-bit keys. Also supported is TKIP WEP, which offers PPK and MIC. In addition to the 1400 series bridges, Cisco offers the 350 series bridges, which include a workgroup bridge.

The 1200 Series Access Points

The Aironet 1200 series APs offer maximum design flexibility due to the following characteristics:

- They support 802.11a/b/g standards.

- They are modular and can be configured in single or dual mode, meaning that radios supporting either the 802.11b/g or 802.11a can be installed in a single unit. Single-mode 1200s support up to 16 VLANs, whereas dual-mode 1200s support twice that.

- They support mobile IP and QoS for wireless clients, such as 802.11b mobile phones, which might require subnet hopping.

- They support varying transmit power and receive sensitivity settings that allow for customization of these settings as a function of topology. For example, lower settings might be most appropriate near areas such as parking lots or front lobbies, where visitors could more readily intercept the signals.

- They offer extensive security support:
  - Similar to the 1400 series bridges, security in the 1200s is implemented via the Cisco Wireless Security Suite.

  - Authentication support is more extensive than in the 1400 series bridges and includes 802.1x and the associated EAPs (LEAP, PEAP, EAP-TLS, EAP-TTLS, and EAP-SIM).

  - Local (directly on the AP) LEAP authentication support is available for up to 50 users, which means there is no need for a dedicated AAA server. You should verify IOS versions for which local LEAP or RADIUS support is available.

  - Encryption is offered via WEP, with 40- and 128-bit keys and the TKIP enhancements to WEP that facilitate PPK and MIC.

  - The 1200s also support the WPA security, which offers stronger encryption than WEP.

Perspective on WPA

WPA is the result of efforts to enhance WEP security by the Wi-Fi Alliance. WPA is a result of the rather lengthy nature of the standards development process through standards bodies like IEEE. Consider WPA as a precursor to the 802.11i WLAN security supplement. WPA is likely to be around for a long time to come (along with 802.11i), giving a designer still more choices in WLAN security.

From the administrative perspective, the 1200s allow for the simultaneous configuration of up to 16 SSIDs. Various AP settings can be associated with each SSID, including the client authentication method, the VLAN number, the maximum number of clients for the SSID, and even the repeater mode. Being able to map the repeater mode to an SSID allows, for example, one SSID on a root AP to be allocated for an association with a repeater AP. The repeater mode mapping to an SSID also includes username and password, which can minimize the potential for a rogue repeater AP to gain an association with a legitimately installed AP.

The 802.11a AP comes with an integrated diversity patch and diversity omnidirectional antennae that provide two distinct coverage patterns. The coverage for the patch antenna extends up to 70 feet (approximately 21 meters) at 54 Mbps and up to 200 feet (approximately 61 meters) at 6 Mbps. The omnidirectional antenna coverage is a bit shorter (60 feet at 54 Mbps and 170 feet at 6 Mbps), but it is uniform in all directions.

The integrated diversity antennae address the issue of multipath distortion. For the 802.11b/g AP options, you have a choice in antenna selection depending on the coverage requirements. The 1200 series APs come with a 10/100BASE-T autosensing uplink and are manageable via CiscoWorks.

NOTE   In addition to the 1200 series, Cisco offers the 1100 and 350 series APs. Review the specifications for each series to see which one best meets a customer's WLAN requirements.

The Aironet Antennae

Cisco offers a variety of antennae for its Aironet series products in support of all of the 802.11 physical layer standards. If an antenna is not already integrated with a product, the choice of antenna should be driven by the following criteria:

- Application environment
- Gain
- Direction
- Style
- Physical size
- Mounting method
- Appearance

Table 6-2 summarizes the key characteristics of the Cisco Aironet antennae. Remember that you should always consult data sheets for all of the specific antenna characteristics.

Table 6-2   *Summary of Key Characteristics for Cisco Aironet Antennae*

Antenna Characteristic	Antenna Characteristic Values
Gain	2.2–21 dBi for 2.4-GHz bands, and 5–28 dBi for 5-GHz bands
Direction	Directional, omnidirectional, diversity omnidirectional
Polarization	Linear vertical, linear horizontal
Style	Dipole, patch, sector, yagi, dish
Frequencies	2.4–2.484 GHz for 802.11b and 802.11g UNII-1 (5.15–5.25 GHz) UNII-2 (5.25–5.35 GHz) UNII-3 (5.725–5.825 GHz) for 802.11a in the United States

The Aironet Clients

Cisco Aironet clients include the 5-GHz LAN client adapter and the 350 series 802.11b compliant adapter. The 5-GHz adapter features a CardBus Type II form factor and operates in the two lower UNII bands. Security support on the authentication side includes 802.1x with LEAP, PEAP, EAP-TLS, and EAP-SIM. Encryption support includes static and dynamic WEP with 40- and 128-bit keys as well as WEP with TKIP. The 5-GHz adapters are well suited for any deployment in which the 1200 series 802.11a APs are installed.

The 350 series client adapters feature PC Card and PCI form factors and support the same security features as their 5-GHz siblings. Both types of adapters support drivers for many of the common operating systems, including versions of Windows, Mac OS, disk operating system (DOS), and Linux.

Other wireless clients from Cisco besides the Aironet series include the 7920 mobile IP phone, which works well with the Aironet 802.11b infrastructure, as well as clients available through the Linksys product line.

WLAN Deployment Scenarios

Given the growing popularity of wireless technologies, opportunity abounds for IT staff and SMB users to come up with creative WLAN deployment scenarios. Health care, education, retail, manufacturing, and general administrative office environments are only a few of the SMB types for which WLANs are prime candidates.

Consider the following generic scenarios that approach WLAN design based on the size of the WLAN infrastructure and the anticipated number of users and their activities, rather than the size or type of the business itself:

- A small office or a workgroup deployment

- An enterprise deployment
- A telecommuters deployment

A Small Office or Workgroup Deployment

In a small office or a workgroup deployment, one or at most two APs are installed. The coverage area is limited, and the number of clients is relatively small. The deployment could involve a single conference room at a large enterprise, a high-school classroom, a small warehouse housing an SMB's inventory, or a small administrative office where there is considerable mobility among the employees.

The topology criterion is to provide coverage for one of the following:

- A group of users with notebook computers coming together temporarily in a relatively small area (for a meeting or for instruction)
- One or more users being able to move freely throughout the entire coverage area:
  - A forklift driver receiving requests for inventory deliveries in a warehouse of a manufacturing facility
  - An employee visiting others in an administrative environment

Conference Room or Classroom Scenario

Let's consider the conference room or classroom scenario. Those present need Internet access for browsing and document downloading. They might need to exchange files and use e-mail during the meeting. High performance is naturally preferable, given the nature of the anticipated traffic. Security is of reasonable but not paramount concern given that the WLAN will be used mostly for Internet and web-based e-mail. Clients are limited to notebook computers. No mobile IP phones or wireless cameras are in use. What is the solution?

An Aironet 1200 series AP that is placed directly in the conference room or the classroom and equipped with the 802.11a radio and an integrated omnidirectional antenna providing data rates of 54 Mbps at up to 60 feet addresses the performance criterion. Depending on the size of the room, consider placing two APs to maximize performance. If you are using 802.11g with two APs, be sure to configure them with nonoverlapping channels. Given the reasonable but not paramount security concerns, connect the APs to the rest of network outside of the firewall, and don't perform 802.1x mutual authentication.

If the users need to get onto the corporate network, they can do so by using the VPN through the firewall. Use DHCP to maximize convenience for the users, but don't use default SSIDs, which would allow casual bystanders or passersby to easily connect. Turn off power to the APs when the conference room or the classroom is not in use to prevent unauthorized users from forming an association to gain access to the network. Verify the coverage area and lower the AP transmit power settings if the coverage extends too far outside the room. The requirement is to have coverage in the room and not anywhere else.

Warehouse or Mobile Office Scenario

Let's now look at a warehouse or mobile office scenario. In a warehouse, the volume of transmitted information is relatively small, so the design driver here is proper coverage throughout the warehouse, even if it is at lower data rates. 802.11b/g technology might be better suited for this scenario than 802.11a. In general, lower frequencies provide a larger coverage area, but at lower data rates. An RF survey should definitely be conducted to map out the coverage topology. In the classroom/conference room scenario, you might be able to avoid an RF survey, although performing one is a recommended WLAN deployment practice, especially if the WLAN were to expand beyond the single room. In a warehouse, you don't have the option of turning off power to the AP(s) because operations are ongoing 24 × 7. What is the solution? Consider the following:

- Equipment might be similar to the conference room/classroom scenario, but the design/deployment approach varies.

- Greater care is needed in mapping out the coverage area via a detailed RF survey.

- Multiple APs might be needed to ensure that all of the required locations are covered.

- Security is of paramount concern because the APs connect to the inside network, and the interception or alteration of transmitted information might compromise SMB operations. The strongest mutual authentication available between the client and the AP should be configured (PEAP, for example, if supported on the client), with the encryption relying on the 128-bit WEP key, WPA, or the 802.11i standard.

An Enterprise Deployment

A generic enterprise scenario combines as follows all of the wireless infrastructure components and a wider range of clients than small office or workgroup deployments:

- The coverage topology is larger.

- Dozens of APs might be involved.

- Wireless links between locations via bridges have been identified as a requirement.

- Security is to be maximized.

- A wider range of clients from multiple vendors needs to be supported.

Which SMBs are potential candidates for enterprise deployments? Again, the total size of the business might be far less relevant than the group of users within the business being served by the deployment or the convenience that is offered by not having to rely on a wire-based WAN infrastructure like Frame Relay or leased lines.

A candidate for multi-AP deployment might be a university library that wants to offer both Internet and internal network access for students who combine more traditional forms of research and learning with online access. A candidate for wireless bridge deployment might be a small city government with LOS between the buildings of the various agencies.

The branches of car rental agencies or manufacturing facilities using robotics are candidates for enterprise deployments. Another example where enterprise deployment would be appropriate is hospitals, where doctors or nurses need access to applications and patient data right at the patient's bed, and the data might need to be moved quickly, depending on the patient's needs. Is there a single enterprise solution? No, but there are numerous choices to meet a wide range of enterprise deployment requirements.

University Library Wireless Deployment

Assume that the requirements have been identified through the recommended design process. The need for a larger coverage area at a university library to support different standards within a wide spectrum of clients is met through one or a combination of the following:

- Multiple dual-mode APs
- The designation of certain areas of the library to support only a specific standard

The 1200 series APs support 802.11a/b/g in dual or single mode. Use of diversity antennae with the APs minimizes the potential for multipath distortion. Repeater APs can be set up to extend the coverage topology as needed, even if performance might suffer as a result. Multiple VLANs can be configured to facilitate user differentiation through varying authentication mechanisms that afford different access levels to the internal network. Some APs that are configured for specific VLANs might connect to the wired infrastructure in front of the firewall to allow Internet access with minimal security considerations. Those APs connecting to the inside network should use the strongest 802.1x/EAP authentication method available.

Wireless WAN Link Deployment

How about a wireless deployment, without wireless clients, which addresses only the WAN link requirements? Be it a city government linking various buildings, a financial institution that needs a link between two high rises, or a university campus that wants to interconnect a group of departments, Cisco 1400 series bridges or even the earlier 350 series models can extend the wired network topology in scenarios in which the wire-based WAN is either too expensive or is simply impractical to deploy. The wireless WAN topology can, of course, be extended with wireless client workgroups or full-scale wireless coverage for the enterprise.

TIP   In an enterprise scenario in which mobile IP phones need to be supported and the WLAN spans multiple IP subnets, the proxy mobile IP support in the 1200 series APs provides seamless roaming.

Key Design Considerations for Wireless Enterprise Deployments

The following points summarize the key design considerations for wireless enterprise deployments:

- Identify the coverage areas, number of users, and performance requirements. Remember the tight coupling between performance and topology in wireless deployments. Higher AP density can improve performance, but remember to have only three nonoverlapping channels for adjacent APs using the 802.11b/g radios.

- Perform an RF survey for the required coverage areas and decide what WLAN management tools to deploy.

- Identify the client connection requirements and provide a mix of 802.11/a/b/g if necessary to accommodate clients complying with varying standards.

- Determine if any wireless point-to-point links are required. Choose antennae with the highest gain for longer distances.

- Identify the required level of security. Wireless security mechanisms boil down to the method of authentication and the type of encryption. Multiple authentication mechanisms allow for client differentiation. Use the strongest encryption available (WEP with 128-bit key, WPA, or 802.11i), depending on availability and need.

Unless the performance and topology requirements for network deployment are simply outside the scope of wireless standards, there is hardly a WLAN deployment scenario that cannot be accommodated with wireless WLAN products from Cisco.

A Telecommuters Deployment

For wireless telecommuters, the most significant design consideration is probably security, because, in all likelihood, the telecommuter is connecting to a corporate network via a public infrastructure while using a wireless client. Consider a telecommuter in a SOHO environment with an AP that is interfaced to a broadband router and a wireless client in the form of a telecommuter's notebook computer. If the telecommuter's notebook is equipped with a personal firewall and an IPSec-capable VPN software client, VPN security extends from the client to the corporate network, and the wireless security options and/or configuration are less, if at all, relevant.

On the other hand, if the VPN is implemented via hardware that sits between the AP and the router, or the VPN capability is incorporated into the router, the portion of the overall connection between the client and the AP remains vulnerable to attack, and it ought to be protected via the available means for securing wireless networks. Assuming that the AP supports any or all of the EAP variants for authentication, and that it also supports encryption via WEP, WEP with TKIP, WPA, or 802.11i, use any one of these methods to implement both the authentication and the encryption that are in compliance with the SMB's security policy.

NOTE	IPSec-based VPNs can be deployed over the internal WLAN infrastructure within a large enterprise because WLANs and VPNs are not mutually exclusive. However, using VPNs internally over a WLAN might be cumbersome for the WLAN users.

Summary

This chapter looked at WLAN solution(s) from Cisco in the context of security, topology, performance, the generic WLAN components, the specifics of the Cisco Aironet wireless product line, and, finally, several generic WLAN deployment scenarios. Security and performance in WLANs have been significantly enhanced since the approval of the 802.11 standard in 1997. In addition, since then, IEEE revised the 802.11 standard and approved a number of supplemental standards (802.11a/b/g/i and others), expanding the choices in WLAN deployment. Physical layer considerations associated with the transmit power of a wireless device, the antenna characteristics (gain, direction), and the type of radio technology (2.4-GHz spread spectrum or 5-GHz OFDM) all have an impact on the WLAN topology and performance.

Performance and topology considerations are closely coupled in WLAN deployments. The Cisco Aironet series offers a comprehensive suite of WLAN products—which includes APs, client adapters, wireless bridges, and antennae—all of which are in compliance with the IEEE standards and which implement additional proprietary and industry-accepted protocols that have not been standardized by IEEE. Deployments of Cisco wireless products scale from a single AP or a wireless router in a workgroup or a SOHO environment to enterprise deployments with dozens of APs, bridged point-to-point links, and a large number of clients compliant with the numerous physical layer and security standards.

CHAPTER 7

Customer Relationship Management Solutions

Any successful SMB knows that customer acquisition without proper service and the resulting retention translates into a continuous and, at best, costly customer turnover. Although it might be hard to find business missions that advocate poor customer service or high turnover, in some cases, lack of customer retention could be part of an overall SMB strategy.

In a health care–related industry, perhaps no customer retention is the ideal model. That is, if an SMB is truly dedicated to the customers' well-being by healing the patients so that they never need to come back, that SMB might eventually go out of business. While the patients are being treated, however, excellent customer service is vital for the health care SMBs, especially given the emotional nature of their business. On the other hand, a retail store, a bank, a manufacturing company, or an accounting or legal firm might consider a different approach from the hypothetical health care SMB. Serve the customers so well that they never want to leave or even consider looking for another supplier of the goods and services that the SMB offers.

All of the solutions discussed in the other chapters of this book represent either the elements of the network infrastructure (routing, switching, security, wireless) or enabling applications (IP Telephony, unified communications, IP/TV) that ultimately lead or should lead to the following principle: Acquire customers with ease, provide them excellent service with minimum effort, keep them satisfied and inspired, and retain them for the long haul. Without diverging into unrelated topics of philosophy and psychology, suffice it to say that customers are complex creatures that the SMB is trying to acquire, service, satisfy, and retain.

At a minimum, SMBs that find value in the preceding principle should make an effort to understand their customer base. The best way to do so is through a customer relationship management (CRM) solution that uniquely fits the SMB's business model and which, aside from being a set of software applications and enabling platforms, is also a form of business strategy and philosophy for creating long-term, mutually beneficial relationships with customers.

CRM Deployment Considerations

Any effective CRM solution offers an SMB the opportunity to provide excellent customer service 100% of the time or, at least, close to it. In the information age, it means that no matter which employee is interacting with a customer, he or she has access to the relevant information (directly or through other employees) to meet the customer's needs effectively, in a timely manner, and without confusion. Whether it's taking an order, resolving a technical support issue, accepting a reservation, or offering information about a new service or product, a CRM solution should facilitate the interaction and the decision-making process on the part of the SMB's employees. In the eyes of the customer, a successful transaction might mean any of the following:

- No need to make follow-up phone calls after the initial contact (a reduced level of interaction with the SMB, thus saving the customer time)

- Receiving a confirmation e-mail about an order (an increased customer comfort level about a transaction in process)

- Being able to track the status of a transaction online

- Having access to the SMB's staff or self-help 24×7

From the SMB's perspective, successful transactions might translate, in aggregate, into any of the following:

- Additional and faster sales

- The ability to develop new and needed products and services to meet changing customer demand (effective response to new market opportunities)

- Reduction of marketing expenses due to a better understanding of a typical customer profile

- The ability to optimize services

Ultimately, ongoing successful transactions should increase customer loyalty. Because customer satisfaction and loyalty are generally harder to win and retain than to lose, consider how negative (rather than successful and positive) customer interactions could affect an SMB's reputation and ultimately its bottom line.

CRM deployment considerations differ from all of the networking solutions considerations in the sense that, as discussed in Chapters 2 ("SMB Networking Environments and Solutions Design Considerations") and 3 ("Network Infrastructure Requirements for Effective Solutions Implementation"), it is a given that an SMB will have a network infrastructure. The issue is what elements of that infrastructure to deploy and how to do so in a way that best supports the SMB's business mission. It is not a given that an SMB will deploy a CRM solution, although I believe that all SMBs have CRM in one form or another, whether they call it a CRM or not, and whether or not it deserves to be called a CRM.

A CRM solution designer can be reasonably certain that, with the possible exception of the smallest of businesses, all CRM solutions will require a well-functioning networking infrastructure. A well-functioning network will facilitate speedy access to relevant customer information across physically diverse business topology, whether it involves offices in the same building, a campus, or multiple buildings on different continents.

Actual CRM deployment considerations focus more on why and when a CRM solution should be deployed and what operational conditions create a ripe deployment environment rather than centering on the elements of the infrastructure that must be present for CRM implementation.

CRM vendors offer data sheets that address the processing power and storage requirements for their applications. In addition, as a network designer, you must always be mindful of the bandwidth requirements for movement of large volumes of data, especially across a WAN, and all the security issues that must be addressed when planning a CRM deployment. Bandwidth calculations are performed as a function of the traffic load that individual transactions (user interactions with the CRM software) place on the network.

Don't expect to find this kind of information on the CRM vendors' websites. If the CRM vendors' developers cannot supply traffic load figures for their software, the design document should reflect this fact. You can then make reasonable estimates, and you can leave open the possibility of having to provision extra bandwidth in the future, mostly for WAN links.

Any concerns regarding the security of CRM data should be incorporated into a security policy (see Chapter 4, "Overview of the Network Security Issues") and acted upon, either with networking security tools or at the level of the applications themselves.

CRM deployment considerations should take the following into account:

- Modes of the SMB's interactions with customers
- Customer information accessibility
- The SMB's customer categorization capability
- Levels of commitment to CRM on the part of the SMB and its employees
- Analytics tools and metrics within CRM solutions

Modes of the SMB's Interactions with Customers

Ask the following questions to determine how an SMB interacts with customers:

- What are the prevalent modes of communications through which the SMB interacts with its customers (phone, e-mail, fax, in person, and so on)?
- Is the SMB able to quantify the customer interactions (both inbound and outbound) in terms of their numbers, average duration, types, and results?

If the answers to these questions are "Don't know" and "No," the SMB is more than likely in need of a CRM solution.

Customer Information Accessibility

Ask the following questions with respect to customer information accessibility:

- How accessible is the customer information to any of the SMB employees who interact with customers?

- Is the customer information scattered across multiple (and incompatible) corporate databases or, worse yet, stored on unshared numerous local hard drives?

- Does an SMB employee taking an order have access to order history, correspondence, or any support issues that transpired in the past?

- Does an SMB employee resolving a technical issue have access to previous case histories?

- Is an SMB employee responding to inquiries fully aware of the latest promotions?

If the answers to the preceding questions are "Hardly accessible," "Scattered all over," "No," "No," and "No," the SMB is definitely in need of a CRM solution.

SMB's Customer Categorization Capability

Statistically speaking, a small number of customers tends to consume a disproportionate amount of an SMB's resources without a corresponding payback. At the same time, a similarly small number of customers (20% or less, as a rule of thumb) is responsible for about 80% of the business. (This is another instance of the "80/20" rule I referred to in Chapter 1, "Effective Networking Solution Design Process"; it applies equally to CRM in addition to applying to some aspects of the operation of the networking infrastructure.)

Ask the following question: Is an SMB able to categorize its customer base according to a quantifiable value (monetary, for example) that the customers contribute to the SMB's operations?

If the answer is "No," the SMB is in need of a CRM solution to understand its customer base.

Levels of Commitment to CRM

With respect to an SMB's commitment to CRM, the designer ought to clearly identify and/ or define the following:

- The level of across-the-board commitment on the part of the SMB and its employees to proceed with CRM

- What constitutes commitment to CRM

- What are the down-the-line, everyday implications (and attendant responsibilities) on the part of the SMB and its employees of making a commitment to CRM

To help determine the preceding, consider the following specific elements of commitment to CRM:

- **Clarity of purpose from the start**—A clear definition up front of measurable CRM goals is vital. The goals can be simple: increasing the revenue by a certain percentage, increasing the number of customers, or reducing customer turnover. The goals can also be far more complex. But defining clear goals and deciding on a mechanism to measure progress toward their achievement are elements of an effective design process, which takes time and a level of commitment on the part of the SMB and its employees. An SMB that thinks that deploying a CRM solution is somehow equivalent to just installing a piece of software on the network to acquire, satisfy, and retain customers is likely to be disappointed with the outcome.

- **Communication during the design and deployment**—Effective communication between employees from different departments is often a challenge in SMB environments. However, communication must exist during the design and deployment of a CRM solution, meaning that an SMB might need to eradicate turf warfare from its culture if CRM is to succeed as a philosophy.

- **Capture of relevant customer data**—SMB employees who interact with customers have to take the time to capture all of the possible (not just the basic) customer data. Complete data capture is often a challenge for understaffed SMBs. A CRM solution without a readily accessible and integrated database composed of complete data from multiple contact channels might prove to be quite useless for two reasons. First, employees interacting with the customer might not have a full view of the customer, which can lead to inadequate service, with all of the attendant consequences of customer dissatisfaction. Second, insufficient or incomplete customer data will, in the long run, minimize the value of any output from the analytics tools regarding strategic trends.

Before proceeding further with CRM design considerations, ask this question: Is there an across-the-board commitment to a CRM philosophy on the part of an SMB and its employees? If the answers is "No" or a lukewarm "Yes," chances are that even if the best CRM software is deployed, the overall effort will be a failure.

Analytics Tools and Metrics

Assuming a decision to proceed with CRM deployment based on an SMB's needs and commitment, consider that a CRM solution is not only about having access to information that allows an SMB to offer excellent customer service. The solution must also include analytics functions that allow an SMB to translate the voluminous customer information into real business intelligence (BI). BI comes about when customer-related data is translated into information that can be acted upon.

As a CRM element, analytics tools might need to be capable of performing simulations (rather than providing only static reports) that will answer some of the simplest yet most fundamental questions that an SMB might raise regarding its business operations:

- What happens if I raise prices by 8 percent versus 15 percent?
- What happens if I reduce my marketing budget?
- What is the net effect of discounts on my bottom line?

Answers to these questions facilitate more incisive financial decision making on the part of an SMB's management. But try getting accurate answers to these questions—first, without a network that actually works; second, without a CRM solution that actually captures all of the required data; and third, with relatively primitive static reporting tools. Good luck! Analytics are a vital CRM component.

A CRM solution should also track metrics about the employees' interaction with the customers. Those metrics might relate to the duration, the number of, and the results of call/interaction(s) per employee with the existing or potential customers. These metrics can help SMBs evaluate the quality of customer interactions and take steps to upgrade it. This is why you often hear the following message when you make a call to many types of businesses: "This call might be recorded for the training and development of our associates, or for quality assurance purposes."

Figure 7-1 illustrates an SMB environment that is ripe for a CRM solution.

Figure 7-1   *SMB Environment in Need of a CRM Solution*

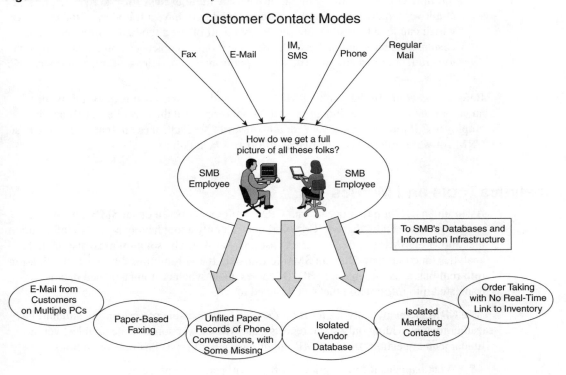

Popular CRMs' Relationship to Cisco Products

CRM solutions are multifaceted. They span not only the typical spectrum of touch points or channels through which an SMB interacts with a customer (marketing, sales, service, and support) but can extend these channels of interaction to include contract management, file and document management, and analytics tools.

Analytics are a vital CRM component. They can include a variety of standard periodic reports as well as real-time snapshots of the various aspects of business operations. For a CRM solution to be most effective, all aspects of the CRM should be integrated to provide a uniform view of the customer from any point of interaction. Ideally, every interaction with a customer should result in the strengthening of the relationship and an opportunity to sell the SMB's product and/or service or to resolve the customer's problem. When the components of CRM are integrated into a cohesive whole (either as part of the initial package or through various integration techniques), the next step toward a seamless applications environment is to integrate them with the back office applications, which is discussed in Chapter 10, "Front and Back Office Integration Solutions."

The relationship of Cisco products to CRMs is twofold:

- First, via the networking solutions (layers 1 through 4 infrastructure, wireless, security), which facilitate CRM deployments on the networks

- Second, via the IP communications solutions that include elements of IP Telephony, IP Contact Center (IPCC), and Intelligent Contact Management (ICM) software

Cisco IP communications solutions create strategic customer contact platforms that integrate with CRMs at the level of call routing and accessing the CRM database for selecting the most appropriate skills group to handle a particular contact. For the detailed specifics of each company's CRM features, I encourage you to contact that company's sales and technical support channels. Assuming that each company uses its own CRM solution, it might give you the perfect opportunity to experience that solution firsthand. Consider next some of the popular CRMs and their vendors' relationship to Cisco and its products.

E.piphany CRM

The E.piphany CRM solution encompasses marketing, sales, and service. Each of these customer contact channels, or E.piphany product lines, consists of a number of components. The interaction advisor is a component common to each of the three channels. Each product line is also equipped with customer analytics tools.

The unification of the customer data and processes across the contact channels takes place via the E.piphany Customer Relationship Backbone (CRB), which offers a set of services based on Sun Microsystems' Java 2 platform Enterprise Edition (J2EE). Based on open standards and supporting Web services, CRB also facilitates integration of the E.piphany CRM product lines with any existing legacy applications.

E.piphany has entered into different categories of partnership with different vendors. The partnership categories include platform, consulting, and business. Both Cisco and Sun Microsystems are E.piphany's platform partners. They both supply enabling technologies that enhance the capabilities of E.piphany's applications. The joint Cisco and E.piphany CRM solution integrates E.piphany's applications with the Cisco IPCC and its underlying capabilities of call routing and distribution.

SAP mySAP

mySAP CRM represents one of many elements in the mySAP Business Suite of solutions from the German software maker Systeme, Anwendungen, Produkte in der Datenverarbeitung— or Systems, Applications, and Products in Data Processing (SAP). SAP's mySAP solutions are designed to meet the operational needs of more than 20 industries. In addition to CRM, SAP's solutions include applications related to human resources, financials, supplier relationship management (SRM), supply chain management (SCM), product life cycle management, and the marketplace. Each solution can be deployed individually or in conjunction with others.

The viability of SAP's CRM solution hinges on three key activities and their enabling technologies:

- The capture of customer information (often via customer call centers)

- The warehousing of customer-related information (data warehousing relies on a viable network infrastructure and storage technologies such as storage-area network (SAN) or network-attached storage (NAS), as discussed in Chapter 3)

- The use of the Internet to enhance customer interactions via a high degree of self-help or self-serve capabilities

SAP integrates with IPCC and ICM from Cisco via the SAP adapter for ICM, which leads to data capture by providing routing capability and simultaneously enhances the customer contact support via the Internet.

PeopleSoft CRM

PeopleSoft's CRM solution is a component of its Enterprise and EnterpriseOne product lines. The underlying philosophy of PeopleSoft's CRM is to offer SMBs and major enterprises alike a product that makes customers continue to want to buy from them in the presence of competitive alternatives. It's a philosophy worth pondering for any SMB contemplating a CRM deployment, whether or not the PeopleSoft solution is used.

The PeopleSoft-specific CRM modules relate to field service, customer self-service, marketing, sales, mobile sales, and support. The CRM solution integrates through numerous points with other PeopleSoft applications, including the enterprise resource planning (ERP) and SCM suites. In that context, PeopleSoft refers to its expanded CRM solution as Customer Lifecycle Management (CLM).

The integration of Cisco products with PeopleSoft's CRM is at the Computer Telephony Integration (CTI) platform level, which means integration with the IPCC and ICM product families. PeopleSoft also works with contact platform and telephony vendors such as Avaya, Concertro Software, Apropos, Genesys, and Interactive Intelligences, Inc.

Pegasystems Customer Process Manager

Pegasystems refers to its customer contact solution as the Customer Process Manager. Whereas the required networking infrastructure to support this application and its integration with IP communications are routine, the application uses a unique enabling technology to service customers.

Underlying the Pegasystems business solutions is the enabling technology of business process management (BPM), which relies on a business rules engine to automate the process of decision making as a function of organizational best practices and customer requirements. The effective use of the business rules engine through customization and addition of new processes (even by managers, rather than IT staff) facilitates one of the fundamental goals of any CRM solution: one-call or one-contact resolution of any customer issue. Pegasystems solutions span the spectrum of industries, including health care, financial services, retail, and insurance.

Not unlike other CRM and business software providers, Pegasystems partners with multiple vendors in categories of services, solutions, and technology. Partnership with Cisco falls into the category of technology because Cisco IP Communications solutions provide robust customer response platforms over which CRM applications operate.

Microsoft CRM

Although Microsoft CRM is a more recent addition to the CRM offerings than its aforementioned competitors, the product has been designed specifically for the SMB market, and it integrates well with Microsoft's e-mail, web browser, and OS platforms, which are already prevalent in SMB environments. The two major modules of the Microsoft CRM are Sales and Customer Service. Each module includes numerous components that are collectively designed to meet the SMB CRM objectives related to sales and customer service:

- Sales module components: management of leads, opportunities (qualified leads), orders, territories, and sales literature; competitor tracking; correspondence and mail merges; product catalog; workflow; and reporting
- Customer Service module components: case, e-mail, and contract management; service request association with cases; case queuing for future processing; routing and workflow; product catalog; searchable knowledge base; and reporting

Both modules integrate with Microsoft Business Solutions applications.

Cisco partnership with Microsoft is aimed at integrating several of its IP Telephony solutions with Microsoft CRM. The Cisco CRM Communications Connector (a middleware application) allows for Microsoft CRM to interoperate with the following:

- The Cisco CallManager Express (see Chapter 8, "IP Telephony Solutions")
- The Cisco CallManager bundled with the Cisco IPCC or IPCC Express
- The Cisco CallManager standalone installation without IPCC

From the CRM user perspective, which you must always take into account, the specifics of the Microsoft CRM and Cisco IP Telephony solution integration include the following:

- Screen popups with customer information upon call arrival
- Click-to dial feature from within Microsoft Outlook or the CRM application based on a customer record
- Call timing and tracking for the purpose of internal management and performance evaluation
- Voice mail notification (planned as of the time of writing)

The support for IP phones in the combined preceding solution is extensive but remains a function of the call processing agent (CallManager Express or CallManager) and its version and/or model. Always check with the vendors on the latest specifications of any solution.

Cisco Solutions for CRM Integration

As mentioned earlier in this chapter, Cisco integrates with popular CRMs via elements of the Cisco IP Communications suite, which includes the Cisco IPCC Express and the Cisco ICM and IPCC product families.

The two product families include core and optional components that offer SMBs and large enterprises alike the ability to scale and adopt a customer contact solution that is most suitable to their unique needs. Both families are closely coupled and share several of the same optional components. However, the ICM family represents somewhat of a subset of the IPCC family because the IPCC family encompasses the core component of the ICM family and combines it with Cisco IP Telephony products to create a fully IP-based contact management solution. The IPCC Express is a scaled-down version of IPCC aimed for contact centers of up to 150 users.

Cisco ICM Product Family

The core component of the ICM product family is the Cisco ICM Enterprise Edition, formerly known as the Cisco Intelligent Contact Management. Additional family components include the Web Collaboration Option (formerly called the Cisco Collaboration Server), the E-Mail Manager Option (formerly known as the Cisco E-mail Manager), the Enterprise Reporting, and the ICM Hosted Edition.

The ICM Enterprise Edition (ICM EE) software provides a customer contact platform that transcends the concept of a more traditional contact or call center, which typically offers a single mode of customer interaction by phone. ICM EE creates a dynamic and varied customer contact environment that Cisco calls the Customer Interaction Network.

SMBs that deploy ICM EE can communicate with their customers via both synchronous and asynchronous communications channels—including phone, web, text chat, e-mail, or Voice over IP (VoIP)—all during the same session. ICM EE is not a CRM solution in and of itself. It integrates with CRMs and can use data from a CRM database to facilitate even more incisive and precise call routing than is possible based only on the initial customer input (dialed number, number called from, customer responses to voice prompts). ICM EE's core capabilities are skill-based call routing, queuing, and monitoring, coupled with extensive fault tolerance features in the event of a component failure.

The ICM EE is available with many different hardware configurations that scale in capacity to service one or more call centers, with a varying number of agents per call center. The ICM EE operates on Intel-based hardware platforms, with storage requirements varying as a function of the final configuration, but typically in dozens of gigabytes. The software components of the ICM Enterprise Edition include the following:

- The Central Controller
- The Peripheral Gateway (PG)
- The Network Interface Controller (NIC)
- The Administrative Workstation(s) (AWs)

Central Controller

The Central Controller component of the ICM EE software uses one or more computers and is responsible for making the call routing decisions. The Central Controller is composed of several software processes, which include the CallRouter, Database Manager, Logger, Synchronizer, and Agent. Each of these processes has unique functions, and when an ICM deployment is viewed through a hardware (as opposed to a software) lens, some of the individual computers on which the Central Controller is installed might be referred to by the process name.

It's common to have a call router and database server computers in an ICM deployment. The Logger, Synchronizer, and Agent processes offer interface functions within the Central Controller as well as between it and other elements of the ICM architecture.

The database server relies for its operations on the Database Manager and Logger processes, which are always installed on the same computer. Typically, the CallRouter is installed on a separate computer, except for the smaller deployments, which actually apply in most SMB environments. The database server (SQL Server) stores the central portion of the ICM database, with the local elements of the database residing on the AWs. The composite database (central and local) is composed of approximately 200 tables in a dozen categories.

A portion of the ICM database is designed to facilitate a proper ICM integration with a wide variety of on-the-premises phone systems and provider networks. Collectively, the tables that comprise the information about the ICM's interfaces to local and public phone systems are referred to as *device data*. Cisco offers a detailed schema of the ICM database (all the tables and the fields in each table) as part of the ICM product documentation.

ICM integrates with the Cisco CallManager (see Chapter 8), as well as with phone equipment (ACDs/PBXes) from Avaya, Ericsson, Nortel Network, Siemens, and others. ICM also integrates with Interactive Voice Responses (IVRs) and Voice Response Units (VRUs) from at least a dozen vendors. The provider networks include major phone companies like AT&T, British Telecom (BT), Sprint, France Telecom, and others.

NOTE	In the case of only ICM/CallManager integration without the presence of the traditional hardware-based ACDs, the scenario becomes that of IPCC, which is considered in the section "Cisco IP Contact Center" later in this chapter.

Similar to how the heart of the ICM software is the Central Controller, the heart of the ICM database is the collection of tables that facilitates the selection of the most suitable resources to address a customer's needs. The resource selection is based on the following:

- Required type of service (What does the customer need?)
- Agent skills (What is the knowledge level of agents to address the customer needs?)
- Agent availability (Is anybody around? How long is the wait?)
- Current service levels (How busy overall is the system?)

The best destination for each call is chosen as a function of these variables. To select the best route, the Central Controller must interact with the PGs (located on the SMB's premises) and a provider's public telephone network. The Central Controller's interface with the PG(s) takes place over the LAN/WAN infrastructure where ICM is deployed. The interface to the provider's network occurs via the Network Interface Controller (NIC). (Note that this is not the other NIC — which stands for network interface card — with a MAC address that connects a PC to a LAN!)

Peripheral Gateway

The PG acts as the interface between the site's phone system (PBX, CallManager, or a hardware-based ACD) and the Central Controller software. The site's phone system is referred to as the peripheral in the context of ICM deployment.

The PG accepts input from the peripheral that relates to the status of the system (agent availability, call wait times) and forwards it to the Central Controller following a conversion into the ICM-database compatible format. The Central Controller, in turn, uses the information from the PG to make call routing decisions.

The ICM software has features referred to as prerouting and postrouting. *Prerouting* applies during the Central Controller's interaction with the NIC (see the next section), whereas *postrouting* applies to exchanges between the Central Controller and the PG. With postrouting enabled, the PG can receive routing instructions from the Central Controller, which effectively turns the phone system (peripheral) into a routing client to the ICM. The practical impact of the postrouting feature is the ability for intelligent call transfers either between agents or VRUs, which further enhances the ability of the ICM software to service the customer.

Network Interface Controller

The NIC interfaces the Central Controller with the public signaling network, typically SS7. The signaling network assumes the role of a client with respect to the Central Controller, with the NIC acting as an intermediary between them. Through the NIC, the signaling network delivers instructions about an incoming call to the Central Controller and expects to receive instructions before the call is forwarded to its final destination. The instruction that the Central Controller receives is the routing request from the caller, which includes all digits that have been entered by the caller (the dialed number and any caller-entered digits [CEDs] in response to prompts) as well as the caller's billing number (typically, the calling line ID).

Based on the status of the site's phone system that the Central Controller obtains from the PG, the Central Controller might decide to accept the call into a particular call center or pass routing instructions through the NIC into the signaling network for additional call routing to the best destination. *Prerouting* is the feature of the ICM software that allows the Central Controller to interact with the signaling network through the NIC before the call is delivered to its final destination. The NIC as a software process might run on separate hardware, with the appropriate interface into the provider's network, or it might run on the same hardware as the CallRouter process.

Administrative Workstation(s)

The purpose of an AW is to allow real-time monitoring of call center activities and to provide tools for managing the ICM software configuration. The configuration tools include the Configuration Manager and the Script Editor. The Configuration Manager is used to update the ICM database with information regarding skill groups, agent assignment to skill groups, data for devices with which the ICM interfaces, and all of the other relevant configuration information that is stored in the approximately 200-table ICM database. The Script Editor is used to create routing scripts that match a contact with a particular route and queue, which translates into the assignment of an agent to handle a particular contact.

At least one AW is required per ICM deployment. Multiple AWs offer redundancy and facilitate a greater degree of distributed configuration management. There are two types of AWs in the ICM architecture: distributor and client. The distributor AW maintains a direct connection to the Central Controller element of the ICM software and receives from it real-time and historical data about the call center activities. That data, in turn, is passed on to the client AWs that do not communicate directly with the Central Controller. In a multi-AW scenario, with a distributor and client AWs present, the distributor AW offloads the Central Controller from having to communicate with and transfer data to all of the AWs, thus allowing the Central Controller more CPU cycles to perform its core function of routing calls and communicating with the NIC and PGs.

Factors That Affect ICM Deployment Design

Deploying the ICM Enterprise Edition, with or without any of the options, is a serious design decision. You and the potential SMB need to take multiple variables into account while proceeding through the design process. These variables will affect the final configuration and the cost of the system. Assuming the decision is made to proceed, consider the following:

- **Size and number of call or contact centers**—ICM scales to multiple sites, but it can be deployed at a single site as well. For multiple sites, a WAN or Internet connectivity is assumed. The size of individual call centers affects the hardware requirements. ICM uses highly distributed hardware architecture and, as a function of the number of agents servicing a call center, it becomes possible to combine software processes on fewer or even a single hardware platform, which is a major benefit for SMBs.

- **Location of the contact center(s)**—Are all of the contact centers in a region serviced by the same phone provider, or is the SMB global in nature, with multiple locations serviced by different providers? The location of the contact centers will affect the number of NICs and their interfaces to the public telephone network(s).

- **Existing phone equipment**—Is the existing phone equipment compatible with ICM? Check the latest ICM documentation to verify the compatible PBX/ACD/IVR equipment vendors. Existing equipment will affect the selection of interfaces for the PGs.

- **Differentiation in the agent skill levels**—Are all of the personnel at a similar skill level, or is there a significant differentiation between them? Does the nature of customer support require a significant skill level differentiation? Determining the different skill levels before implementation will be extremely helpful during ICM configuration.

- **Server hardware**—Does the selected and/or available server hardware meet the minimum specifications for installing ICM? Consider selecting equipment with performance and storage capacities that are higher than the recommended minimums for better scalability in the event of growth. Cisco provides a Bill of Materials (BOM) that identifies the hardware processing and storage requirements for installing ICM in varying configurations. As a function of the size and/or topology of the ICM deployment, consider what processes can be combined on the same hardware platforms and which require separate units. Two key variables that affect hardware requirements are the number of agents and the maximum busy hour call attempts (BHCA). BHCA represents the number of calls coming in at the busiest time. Ideally, all calls should be answered properly.

- **Operating systems (OSes)**—Are the OSes for the selected hardware compatible with ICM? Make no assumptions; verify compatibility by checking the latest Cisco documentation or by consulting an account representative who has access to knowledgeable system engineers.

- **Database design**—Have you familiarized yourself with the ICM database and decided on the values for the various categories of tables? It's advisable to develop the ICM database before implementation as part of the design process.

- **Documentation of the current network**—What is the state of the current network documentation? If the current network is poorly or not at all documented, the implementation stage of ICM might suffer. One reason that the current network should be documented is to fit ICM components into the existing IP addressing scheme.

- **Fault tolerance**—What is the desired level of fault tolerance in the ICM system? What are the business goals behind building fault tolerance into the system? ICM uses hot standby and synchronized execution approaches to implement fault tolerance. In hot standby, critical processes are duplicated, with the primary performing the active tasks while the secondary remains idle. In the event of the primary task's failure, the secondary process takes over. In a synchronized execution approach, critical processes are duplicated on separate computers and run concurrently in synchronized fashion. In the event of failure of one of the synchronized processes, the other one continues to run. A Node Manager process within ICM is responsible for restarting any failed processes.

Cisco IP Contact Center

The IPCC platform combines the ICM software with Cisco IP Telephony products to create an IP-based contact management solution. CRMs integrate with the IPCC through the ICM software. The IP Telephony products that are part of the IPCC include the Cisco CallManager and the IP IVR application. CallManager is a VoIP PBX and is a core component of the numerous IP Telephony solutions from Cisco, including the MCS 7800 series and the retiring ICS 7750. IP IVR is a software application that is used in the IPCC environment for call queuing and the playing of announcements to callers, in addition to prompting callers for input regarding their accounts or menu options.

Although IPCC is an entirely IP-based contact solution, given the extensive Time Division Multiplexing (TDM) integration options of its components (the ICM software and CallManager), it readily integrates with TDM-based legacy telephony platforms. This means that SMBs considering migrating from a legacy to a fully IP-based contact platform can do so in increments, especially when multiple call center locations and a considerable amount of legacy equipment are involved.

The IPCC deployment topology follows the models that are applicable to the CallManager and, consequently, the CallManager-based solutions, as discussed in Chapter 8. Architecturally, when comparing the deployments of IPCC to that of ICM with the traditional ACDs, the IPCC deployment simplifies routing, decreases system load, and even allows for the combining of optional software components on the same servers, thus reducing the hardware requirements. From the overall design perspective, it follows that all of the design considerations that are applicable to CallManager and the ICM software (see the previous section) also apply to IPCC. Table 7-1 summarizes the design considerations that apply to the IPCC solution.

Table 7-1 *Design Issues Applicable to IPCC*

Design Issue	Relevant Characteristics
Topology	As applicable to CallManager (CM), the ICS 7750, or the Media Convergence Server (MCS) 7800 series solutions: single site, distributed multisite, centralized multisite
CM hardware	As applicable to CM, ICS, or MCS
ICM minimum hardware	Pentium III or Xeon based servers with 1 to 4 CPUs, 1 to 4 GB RAM, CPU processing speed of 733 MHz and up (typically, 1 GHz+)
Servers OS	Windows 2000; always check latest data sheets
Site phone equipment	Interfaces with ACDs, PBXes, IVRs, and VRUs from major vendors
Carrier interfaces	Major carriers: AT&T, Sprint, BT, France Telecom, and others
Fault tolerance	Extensive fault tolerance via CM, ICS, and MCS; ICM hot standby and synchronized execution
BHCA	From 7000 to 250,000
Agents supported	From 200 to 5000+

In addition, when considering IPCC, you need to think about the implications of CallManager being an IP-based telephony solution. IP Telephony offers flexibility in the deployment topology of call agents (folks taking customers calls, not software processes)— a flexibility that is not found in TDM-only scenarios.

It follows that IP connectivity between all of the physical locations where the agents are located is a must. But if you consider how readily IP broadband connectivity is available between most locations over the Internet, then even a SOHO, an employee's home, or a small branch office suddenly becomes a viable element of a distributed IP call center. A key element in the decision to proceed with an ICM product family versus IPCC might boil down to what telephony equipment the SMB already has in place and how distributed geographically the skill resources are.

IP Interactive Voice Response Application

IP IVR from Cisco is an application that integrates with both the ICM and the IPCC product families. The IP IVR includes the following:

- **Application engine**—Manages the IVR applications in response to the incoming calls.
- **Administration web interface**—Configures the application engine itself.
- **Editor**—Develops the actual IVR applications that fit the unique needs of each installation.

In the IPCC environment, IP IVR can be installed either on the same server as the CallManager (smaller deployments) or on a separate server as a function of need for a greater overall system capacity.

The IP IVR differs from the traditional IVRs because it does not have physical telephony trunks or interfaces. In IP Telephony environments, physical trunks terminate at voice gateways rather than at IVR servers or ACDs. The IP IVR supports up to 150 logical ports, whereas a single CallManager supports up to 4 IP IVR servers. These numbers translate into a total support of up to 600 IVR ports available in a single CallManager installation, which accommodates call center needs from the smallest of SMBs to large enterprises. From the system availability perspective, in an IPCC IVR deployment, CallManager supports redundant configuration of the IP IVR servers.

NOTE	As a networking solutions designer, it's important that you view IVRs (IP IVR from Cisco and IVRs from other vendors) as applications capable of more than simply digit collection. If a call requires additional processing, an IVR can act as a routing client by communicating with the call routing process and receiving from it further routing instructions for the call.

IVRs can support call queuing if the required skilled resource is temporarily unavailable and the call cannot be routed anywhere else. While the call is in the queue, an IVR application can perform its more routine functions of making announcements, playing music, or collecting additional input from the callers. In addition, when IVRs are integrated with a contact platform like ICM or IPCC, the information that is collected through them becomes part of the comprehensive reporting that is required for the effective functioning of customer contact platforms.

IVR applications can be deployed in numerous SMB scenarios (technical support, insurance claims processing, delivery services, and transportation), but they are particularly popular in the financial services industry. Most banks and financial institutions now have online account access and an IVR application that interfaces with the core banking software. The IVR allows customers to perform many of the same account maintenance functions that are available online. The convenience of IVR in the banking industry is that in situations where online access is not feasible, customers have the option of inquiring about their account status by phone. This availability still tends to be more common than Internet access.

Which CRM Solution Is Right for My SMB?

Assume that an SMB has made a decision to consider the deployment of a CRM solution. The next step is to determine which solution or aspect thereof is the right one for the SMB. If a CRM solution is to be further integrated with the Cisco ICM or IPCC product families, all of the design considerations that apply to the deployment of those product families or even their individual components apply here as well.

When determining which solution to deploy, begin by creating a CRM solutions shortlist and follow with a systematic approach to reviewing CRM features:

- **CRM shortlist**—There are plenty of CRM vendors, most of whom are not even mentioned in this chapter. At some point, you need to come up with a shortlist of the potential candidates. Zero in on two or three vendors and review the CRM offering of each for your particular industry. In the process, consider the following:
  - A company such as SAP services more than 20 industries, which is a reflection of a high degree of expertise across many types of businesses.
  - Some companies service only one vertical market, which might happen to be yours.
  - A comparison of offerings from a smaller and more vertically focused software maker with those of vendors that possess vast capabilities across numerous industries might reveal software features and even bring to the surface aspects of business operations requiring attention that the SMB might not have considered before.
  - A vertically focused vendor might have a wider range of features for a particular industry that might alter an SMB's perception as to how to conduct business.
- **CRM's scalability**—Get answers to the following questions:
  - How does the CRM solution scale as a function of the number of users?
  - What is the relationship between the number of users and the required hardware platforms for the solution?

- **CRM's contact channels**—Get answers to the following questions:
    - Does the solution cover the typical contact channels (marketing, sales, service)?
    - Does the SMB require all of these contact channels initially?
    - Is the software sufficiently modular to provide only the desired channels at a reduced cost?
    - Is the addition of modules possible over time without a major integration project?
- **Analytics**—Get answers to the following questions:
    - What are the analytics capabilities of the software?
    - Does the solution possess business intelligence capabilities or mostly static historical reporting?
    - Is the solution capable of simulations?
- **Effectiveness measurement**—Get answers to the following questions:
    - Does the solution have a mechanism to measure its effectiveness (following implementation) as a function of the initially established goals for CRM deployment?
    - Does the measurement mechanism match with how the SMB envisions effectiveness measurement?
- **Customer contact platform**—Get answers to the following questions:
    - Is one of the Cisco contact platforms (ICM with traditional ACDs or IPCC) applicable to support the selected CRM solution?
    - Is there an integration interface or an adapter between the CRM solution and one of the Cisco platforms?
    - Could the SMB still benefit from a Cisco contact platform without a direct integration with the CRM solution? Consider that calls can still be routed based on the customer input and the caller ID without a direct integration with the CRM database.

Now, put yourself in the position of different categories of SMBs and consider the uniqueness and similarities of the CRM design process. Doing so might, in some cases, lead you to conclude that a formal CRM solution is not necessary. Given the diversity of the SMB market, there is no one-size-fits-all formula for a successful CRM deployment, even within the same industry.

I Am a Retail Outlet

What kind of retail outlet am I? Am I a mom-and-pop shop, a small geographically localized grocery chain, or a regional furniture store?

Generic Mom-and-Pop Shop

Consider a mom-and-pop shop with a single outlet in a small town. Inventory levels are checked visually, and product bar coding is still on the drawing board. Chances are that no extensive CRM solution or customer contact platforms are necessary here because the store operators probably know most of their customers on a first-name basis.

But what happens if some of the products sold at this mom-and-pop shop are so culturally or otherwise unique that they could attract worldwide demand, given the proper marketing and the ability to service a wider market? Would a CRM solution and even a robust IP-based contact platform have their place in such a scenario? Apply the criteria outlined in the earlier section "CRM Deployment Considerations" to determine the need for a CRM solution for this mom-and-pop shop suddenly being thrust into the global marketplace.

Small Grocery Chain

Consider a well-established local grocery chain with several outlets in a small geographical area. The biggest challenge the chain faces is warding off competition from larger supermarkets. A CRM solution would certainly be desired to allow this still successful chain to service its customer base more and more effectively to keep them away from the competition. A key element to consider in this kind of CRM software is the integration with the back office application that relates to inventory control and supply chain management (SCM).

Assume that this SMB implements some sort of a very important person (VIP) frequent shopper program, which collects at sign-up time the typical minimum information from the customers, including name, address, and phone number. This information is then linked to a customer ID that is put on a bar code on a plastic keychain card and issued to a customer. This simple system allows that customers' collective buying habits — including types of goods, volume, monetary value, and date of purchase — be captured and subjected to analysis.

If the SMB wants to try a more creative approach to get a leg up on the competition, consider the capture of other customer-related information that often gets lost in the grocery business. For example, suppose that this SMB allows customers to specify items that they would have purchased but which were out of stock at the time of visit to their store. Not too many retail grocers are concerned about back orders, at least not in a concerted fashion. If a customer is issued a handheld scanner that allows the capture of unavailable items, it can readily assist the SMB with SCM.

For this process to be successful, the store must implement certain procedures. A bar-code label must be readily accessible on the shelf for the unavailable item(s). And ways to ensure quality control must also be in place. For instance, if a customer scanned an item that was in the inventory, the software would recognize it as an invalid event. If the customer entered unreasonable quantities for certain items, the software would also have to recognize these as invalid events. But an element of business intelligence would begin to emerge over time from the capture of that information. Wouldn't a typical grocery shopper be surprised to receive a personalized note in the mail acknowledging the request for the unavailable item and letting the customer know that the item was expected to be back in stock on a certain date? Wouldn't that increase customer loyalty? And isn't customer loyalty what CRM is all about?

Consider for a moment the underlying networking technologies at work here. Naturally, a customer is not going to walk around the store with a cable snaking hundreds of feet, so the scanners have to be wireless. If the data about unavailable items is captured and processed in real time, it's possible that a small back-order printout could be waiting for the customer upon checkout, which would be a good reminder for the next shopping trip. An IP-based contact platform might not be necessary in this scenario, but certainly a LAN/ WAN networking infrastructure (there are multiple branches) is a must, along with the ability to integrate customer input with the marketing effort in terms of mailings to frequent shoppers, advertisements in local papers about popularity of certain items, price comparisons with competitors, and more.

Regional Furniture Store

Besides the goods that they sell, the fundamental differences between grocery and furniture stores are the frequency of visit by the same customer and the value of an average item. Buying furniture is a drastically different process than going grocery shopping. A furniture salesperson spends a lot more time with a prospective buyer than a clerk does with a grocery store customer. What unique CRM features would an SMB operating a furniture store look for?

As a general rule, in the furniture business, customers do not buy major items on their first visit to the store. They are also accustomed to waiting for furniture that they want if it is out of stock. The customers are also likely to do some comparison shopping if there are multiple furniture stores in the area, and Internet-savvy shoppers might decide to try online auction sites or outlets. Because of all these factors, the marketing aspect of CRM that is deployed by a furniture store should be strong. Elements of the overall success of such an SMB will include capturing customers' demographic information without intruding upon their privacy, understanding the current trends and styles in different geographical areas, and being able to launch multichannel advertising campaigns.

A call center platform might not be necessary for a furniture store. However, an SMB could beat its competition by such strategies as having a network with Internet access so that customers can compare the SMB's items to those of competitors, having digitized catalogs that lend themselves to viewing of unavailable items in full color and via simulations, and providing customers with color printouts or even CDs of the items that they are considering. If product and catalog management application can fit under the CRM umbrella, it's likely to prove itself useful in the furniture store environment.

I Am a Bank

What kind of bank am I? Am I a single-site community bank, a multisite bank or credit union, or a branch of a national or even an international bank?

Single-Site Community Bank

For a local community bank where customers conduct most of their business in person, a financial CRM solution is a must, but an IP or even a traditional ACD-based contact center is likely overkill. Instead of having customers who call the bank navigate a series of voice prompts before being directed to the best available financial specialist, an attendant answering the phone with a smile and manually transferring the call to an appropriate extension might be more in line with the image that a community bank wants to project.

A traditional rather than an IP-based IVR system that allows customers to check their account status or perform funds transfers should be sufficient to meet the needs of such an institution. However, because of competitive pressures, a small bank might not be able to continue in this mode into the distant future.

PBX-based phone systems, if not upgraded, eventually become dated, and their maintenance costs begin to soar. Internal users, more than customers, might find the system less and less responsive to changing business demands or internal communications requirements. Under these conditions, even if an IP-contact platform like IPCC is viewed as overkill, an IP Telephony solution by itself might well bring such an institution to a new and higher level of customer service and internal efficiency. The alternative might be a buyout by a larger financial institution, in which case an IP-based telephony solution will probably be implemented anyway.

Multisite Bank or Credit Union

For a multisite financial institution to function with any degree of efficiency, it needs to possess an IP-based WAN that interconnects all of its branches. Assuming the institution is geographically localized but nonetheless offers services to nonlocal customers who might want to call in via a toll-free number, the institution can easily benefit from an IP Telephony solution that supports a customer contact platform and that possibly integrates with the CRM applications.

Considering the level of competition in the financial services industry, customer acquisition and retention are critical. In the event that the IPCC contact platform is deemed unnecessary (at least initially), an IP Telephony solution that incorporates the CallManager and IP IVR is a logical choice for that type of institution.

Branch of a Major National or International Bank

An SMB networking solution for a major bank stretches thin the definition of an SMB because major banks are likely to have thousands of employees. However, the idea of modularity means that a branch of a major bank can be treated as an SMB, with interfaces and connectivity to the headquarters and other branches.

The concept of modularity also applies to a major bank's call center as a discrete component of the financial mammoth. A major bank probably has a call center operation, which means that an effective customer contact platform is desirable. In fact, if the call center is going to be distributed between multiple locations, given the IPCC's scalability and potential for integration with CRMs, IPCC becomes a serious contender for a customer contact platform for any major financial institution.

I Am a Manufacturer

Consider that a manufacturer is going to need an outlet for its products. From the CRM perspective, the size of the manufacturing operation is going to be less critical in making the decision to deploy CRM than the nature of the goods and the manner in which they are being distributed. Are the goods of such a nature that customer service might be required following their sale? Software products, computers, and all kinds of appliances and technical gadgetry fall into that category. Screws, nails, and all other plumbing supplies likely do not. If customer service is a requirement following the sale, then a CRM solution should be considered. But where exactly the CRM solution is required in the chain of distribution depends on how the goods are distributed.

How is the manufacturer distributing its products? Is the manufacturer acting as its own retail outlet or relying on distributors? If it relies on distributors, how many are involved? If a manufacturer is working with one or two major distributors, the distributors rather than the manufacturer are most likely going to require an effective CRM solution and a customer contact platform. If the manufacturer is working with a much larger number of distributors but still not retailing to the end users, then a CRM solution for managing the distributors as clients might be desirable. If the manufacturer does its own retail distribution, apply the procedures and CRM selection criteria, as outlined earlier in this section.

From the overall business perspective, any manufacturing SMB should consider an effective ERP application that satisfies the manufacturing operations, quality control, human resources, and supply chain management (SCM). In addition, if the SMB meets the criteria for deploying a CRM solution, it might be desirable for the ERP to be integrated with the CRM in one package. The issues related to CRM and ERP integration are considered in Chapter 10.

I Am a Hospital or a Health Clinic

Unlike some of the manufacturing SMBs that work through distributors and never interface or interact with the retail end users of their products, hospitals and health clinics of any size do much interfacing and interacting, either with individuals or their family members.

Such interfaces and interactions are complex, and deep emotions are frequently involved as a result of difficult health issues with which individuals must cope. Add the financial pressures that individuals face due to high health care costs. And, at a time when individuals are already finding themselves in life-altering crisis situations, sprinkle into the equation last-minute discoveries of the meaning of what is in the fine print in health insurance policies and the subsequent haggling with insurance companies that do not want to cover certain conditions. Any credible CRM solution should seek to alleviate as much as possible all these stress factors in the SMB health care environment.

For SMBs engaged in health care, the case for a CRM solution is clear and compelling. But what are the critical specifics of a health care CRM solution? A hospital or a clinic might not engage in a lot of sales or marketing of its products and services, but the capabilities of the service aspect of the solution it deploys need to be able to compensate for the possible absence of the other two customer contact channels.

SMBs in the health care industry need to collect a great deal of personal and health history information for each patient. The complexity of financial arrangements for treatment requires a CRM application that can accommodate a variety of personal financial information. Financial arrangements can be complex, given the number of health care plans and government programs that are available. At a clinic that is subsidized by government grants, the same service is priced differently depending on patients' income levels and ability to pay. Aside from the vertical medical software related to patients' care, any CRM solution in the health care industry should have a solid integration with the billing and collection processes.

Summary

CRM solutions apply across a spectrum of SMB industries. CRM is not only a technology—it's a business strategy and philosophy that must be practiced at all levels of SMB operations to be effective. Customer loyalty is the prize. Typical CRM contact channels are sales, marketing, and service.

You need to determine how robust each contact channel has to be and whether or not all channels are required based on the unique nature of each business. The analytics aspect of CRM is increasing in importance as the detection of trends and simulations of business scenarios enhance strategic decision making. An SMB contemplating a CRM solution should consider modes of customer interaction, accessibility of customer information, ability to categorize customers, and the level of commitment required to proceed with a solution.

The integration of Cisco with the CRMs takes place via CallManager Express, the ICM, and the IPCC product families. Numerous factors affect the deployment of these products: size and number of call centers, location of centers, exiting phone equipment, agent skills, server hardware and OSes, level of documentation of the current network, and the desired level of fault tolerance. If a customer contact platform turns out not to be a requirement for a particular SMB, the Cisco IP Telephony solution might be appropriate. SMBs in retail, healthcare, manufacturing, and finance can all benefit from either an IP-based contact platform or an IP Telephony solution subject to the SMB requirements.

CHAPTER 8

IP Telephony Solutions

IP Telephony represents the convergence of two distinct and dominant communications technologies: circuit-switched telephony and packet-switched, IP-based data networks. The impact of this convergence has been staggering in terms of the proliferation and development of new protocols, products, and communications solutions.

In November 1996, the International Telecommunication Union Telecommunication Standardization Sector (ITU-T) approved the first version of H.323 recommendation, titled "Packet-Based Multimedia Communications Systems." In March 1999, the Internet community followed with the publication of RFC 2543, which specifies the Session Initiation Protocol (SIP), considered by some a competitor to H.323. Since then, H.323 and SIP have been revised and updated multiple times. H.323 version 4 was approved in November 2000, and the SIP specification has been updated via RFCs 3261 and 3265. In addition, numerous SIP-related RFCs have been published, and increasingly, the use of packet-based networks for multimedia communications (voice included) has completely obliterated any of the traditional distinctions between circuit-switched voice and packet-switched data networks.

Given the worldwide installed base of the traditional circuit-switched telephony infrastructure at the SMB, enterprise, and carrier levels, legacy telephony will be around for quite a while. However, given the capabilities of IP Telephony and the many business drivers that make its deployment appealing, new telephony installations are likely to be dominated by IP Telephony in the SMB, enterprise, and carrier markets.

This chapter considers the design of IP Telephony solutions in the context of the following:

- IP Telephony deployment considerations
- IP Telephony components and protocols
- Cisco IP Telephony solutions for SMBs (or enterprise branches) and Internet service provider (ISP)/carrier environments

IP Telephony Deployment Considerations

Two factors make telephony successful: high speech quality and high service availability. Take away the speech quality and make the service unpredictable, and telephony falls apart as an effective business communications tool. Speech quality tends to be subjective, whereas service availability is more readily subject to measurement. International standards in the form of ITU-T recommendations define methods to quantify the voice quality of a telephone call because service availability without speech quality is not enough for any telephony solution to be successful.

ITU-T recommendations P.800 (Methods for subjective determination of transmission quality) and P.800.1 (Mean Opinion Score [MOS] terminology) include a definition of the concept of *toll quality* speech, which is represented numerically via an MOS value of 4 or higher on the scale from 1 to 5. Given the almost built-in expectation on the part of most telephony users for immediate (effectively, on-demand) availability of toll quality phone service in business environments, addressing the issues of high voice quality and service availability is of paramount importance when designing IP Telephony solutions for SMBs.

Choice of coders-decoders (codecs) and a judicious deployment of quality of service (QoS) techniques can assist you in creating a toll quality telephony solution over an IP network. Note, however, that delivering voice quality is more likely to be an issue in the long-distance (carrier/ISP) deployments than in the LAN-based SMB and enterprise branch deployments.

With bandwidth at a premium on a WAN, codecs that facilitate greater compression (G.723r53 or G.723ar53) might be required. Higher compression codecs usually require additional digital signal processing (DSP) resources, the lack of which can lead to voice quality degradation and longer delays associated with a complete call. In the LAN-based SMB networks, bandwidth is not an issue (at least, it should not be!), and voice can be transmitted without compression using G.711 codec.

To ensure the desired level of phone service availability on a packet-switched network, you have to consider all of the tools associated with building robust networks, including the following:

- Power protection for critical system components
- Use of redundant systems
- Level of hardware and software reliability
- Reliability of any links within the system provided by third parties and outside of an SMB's direct control
- Operational procedures related to system use and system failures

If the issues of voice quality and network availability can be addressed effectively through design, procedures, and user training, there are plenty of sound operational reasons (which translate into economic reasons) for IP Telephony deployments to proceed.

Consider the following when designing any kind of an IP Telephony solution:

- QoS factors
- Use of a single communications infrastructure for voice and data
- Open standards protocols
- Common operating system (OS) hardware platforms

QoS Factors

The concept of a high QoS invites almost an intuitive understanding on the part of telephony users and designers alike. A service that is readily available and that allows users to hear the other person without delay, echo, or jitter is generally expected and taken for granted in business telephone communications.

Many technologies and techniques are deployed within Public Switched Telephone Networks (PSTNs) and the traditional circuit-switched SMBs and enterprises to accommodate these seemingly simple requirements because when these requirements are not met, telephony users can react negatively. The challenge for you as an IP Telephony solutions designer is to match the circuit-switched toll quality and system availability to an equal or better quality and availability, but on a packet-switched IP network. Doing so is getting easier by the day!

Traditional circuit-switched telephony relies on the establishment of a dedicated circuit between the communicating parties. Voice traffic flows over the established path until the circuit is torn down through a normal termination (hanging up) or an abnormal condition (equipment failure or a cut wire). With a dedicated circuit between the communicating endpoints, there is no overhead associated with the addressing of those points during the data (voice) transmission phase. A dedicated circuit also implies a predictable level of performance and delay.

In IP Telephony, the voice traffic is encapsulated into IP packets, each carrying a data payload (elements of your conversation) and a header with the IP source/destination addressing and additional parameters. As a protocol, IP is considered "unreliable" in the sense that it is connectionless and does not offer guaranteed delivery. It sounds like a communications nightmare when you consider the potential problems: voice carrying packets arriving out of order (words transposed!), some packets never arriving (words missing!), experiencing unpredictable transmission delays (waiting, waiting, waiting for that sentence to finish!), or being subjected to variable packet delays that result in hearing the other party in slow motion or on fast forward. In fact, with all of their theoretical potential for being a nightmarish platform for voice, IP networks are currently the platform of choice for telephony solutions. What is it that in practice makes IP networks so reliable and desirable for telephony?

The ever-increasing robustness of IP networks to support telephony solutions is derived from multiple sources:

- The availability of dedicated high bandwidth (as opposed to shared), which is now the norm in LANs thanks to the ongoing work of the 802 IEEE committees and industry forums, coupled with product implementations by networking companies.
    - A primary example of high-capacity bandwidth capability in LANs is the deployment of 10 Gbps Ethernet products.
    - 10 Gbps Ethernet is also extending its reach into metropolitan-area networks (MANs) and WANs.

— A single IP phone is not likely to require a dedicated 10 Gbps or even 1 Gbps connection, but a 10/1 Gbps capacity might be required for an uplink between IP Telephony LAN switches or to connect a hardware platform with a call processing agent to a LAN switch.

- The improving reliability of the transmission media (fiber, Cat 5e, Cat 6, Cat 7) and lower equipment failure rates, which have steadily increased the overall network availability

- The availability of high-performance multiservice routers, voice gateways, gatekeepers, and dedicated communication platforms for LAN-based SMB and enterprise telephony solutions

Combine these factors with the proper design, especially in the areas of redundancy and QoS, and any theoretical shortcomings of the "unreliable" IP networks vanish.

In IP networks, QoS is used as a generic expression that maps to specific mechanisms that facilitate different streams of traffic to be conditioned according to their needs. Elements of QoS include queuing techniques and link efficiency management, such as link fragmentation and interleaving (LFI). Note that QoS is most useful when transient congestion occurs. No QoS is required in an overprovisioned network. If the design allows for greater bandwidth capacity than any anticipated maximum call volume, QoS becomes a moot point. On the other hand, in a mixed traffic environment, where it is statistically possible to maximize bandwidth usage, QoS deployment is a must for voice traffic.

With the introduction of AutoQoS for VoIP, Cisco gives you the option of deploying QoS with minimal configuration requirements. Simply put, this is a sound policy for IP Telephony installations.

Overcoming Unacceptable Round-Trip Delay

Voice is a real-time application that demands a consistent and low transmission delay between communicating endpoints. If, on the way to their final destination, e-mail packets are delayed from their normal transit time by 2 seconds, those engaging in that e-mail exchange would probably not notice any difference from the norm. On the other hand, a delay of 2 seconds along the transmission path of voice traffic (not a pause by one of the speakers) would probably lead to a quick conclusion of the conversation by one or both of the participants hanging up (preceding that act, perhaps, with some frustrated mutterings).

Opinions on the subject vary, but a round-trip delay of 250 milliseconds (ms) in a telephone conversation begins to make itself noticeable to human hearing. Longer delays might still be (and often must be) acceptable, as long as the communicating parties receive training on how to carry on a conversation with those kinds of delays. However, with round-trip delays of 600 ms or more, the average call length is likely to be extremely short because the communicating parties will perceive the quality of the call as unacceptable. In other words, one or both parties will hang up quickly.

Maintaining a consistent and low level of delay for voice traffic is critical for IP Telephony deployments. Multiple factors contribute to the composite end-to-end delay. They begin with codec processing, which can introduce delays from less than 1 ms to 10 ms or more. Lower bit-rate codecs introduce longer delays. Next comes the formation of packets that must be sent out of a gateway interface into the IP cloud. It's best if there is no congestion and the packet does not have to wait in a queue to be serialized for transmission over the physical media.

In congested environments, traffic prioritization implemented through QoS configuration can help. After a packet enters the IP WAN, each router (hop) that a packet (now carrying voice) must go through introduces queuing and serialization delays. The packet must then exit the WAN and be decoded for the communicating party to hear its contents.

You can perform a detailed analysis of the anticipated path that voice traffic will take and add up the individual delays to see if the sum is within the acceptable range. If it's not, there's not one silver bullet to fix the problem. To minimize delay, try the following where possible and appropriate:

- Reduce the number of hops that voice traffic must go through on the IP WAN.
- Change to higher bit-rate codes. (However, this might cause bandwidth to suffer.)
- Implement QoS to always give voice traffic the highest priority.
- Avoid mixing voice with applications that produce large packets.
- Introduce high-performance routers and gateways as necessary to deal with the issue of composite delay.

In LAN-based IP Telephony deployments, delay should not be a big issue unless the SMB is geographically dispersed and/or relies on the Internet or lower-capacity WAN links to transmit voice traffic between the LANs. However, proactively minimizing delay becomes a critical success factor in ISP/carrier voice deployments.

Echo and Jitter

Anyone who has traveled to a remote region that has a less-developed communications infrastructure has likely experienced a variety of challenges relating to voice communications. Extremely high attenuation might require raising one's voice to be heard at the other end, and significant delays are always a factor, especially if part of the communication path is through a satellite link. When you add to these problems hearing your own voice echoing back to you and hearing a garbled sound from the person at the other end (resulting from variable delays between the packets that compose the voice stream), the overall communication experience becomes less than pleasant.

PSTNs have implemented echo cancellers to minimize the impact of the amplification and reflection of your own voice traveling back to you. Echo is not as much of an issue in pure

IP Telephony deployments. However, wherever IP and PSTN interface, there is the potential for problems with echo.

Jitter comes about as a result of lack of synchronous end-to-end transmission on packet-based networks, meaning that there is the potential for variable (as opposed to constant) delays between the individual packets carrying voice traffic. For example, if some packets in a voice stream get stuck in a queue and others do not, jitter occurs.

The extent to which jitter is detectable by the end users depends, of course, on the level of variability itself. But just as echo is inherent in circuit-switched networks, jitter is inherent in packet-switched networks. Jitter can be minimized via QoS (traffic prioritization) and not mixing voice traffic with large packets on the same links (especially slower WAN links). The LFI feature, which breaks larger packets into smaller ones and interleaves them with real-time traffic like voice, reduces jitter on slower links.

Within an SMB or an enterprise where the entire IP Telephony solution operates over a high-speed LAN with only a single gateway for PSTN calls, jitter, echo, and delay are normally not a problem, provided that the IP network works well to begin with. Jitter and echo can become more of a problem in carrier/ISP deployments that combine multiple IP WANs, portions of different PSTNs, and equipment from multiple vendors. Numerous SMBs operate these kinds of networks around the world.

Network Availability

One aspect of voice communications that requires serious consideration during the design stage is a high service availability expectation on the part of telephony users. You need to obtain answers to the following questions:

- How high an availability expectation is reasonable?
- What price does an SMB need to pay to push the availability as close to the 100 percent mark as possible?

Most telephone companies (telcos) pride themselves on offering five 9s (99.999 percent) or six 9s (99.9999 percent) reliability for their central office (CO) switches or PBX products. That level of equipment reliability translates into approximately 5.25 minutes of downtime per year for the five 9s and 31 seconds of downtime for the six 9s reliability levels. These are statistical numbers, however. Despite their value, statistics can be deceiving.

From the end-user perspective, what is the meaning of this level of reliability for a singular piece of equipment in the context of an entire communications solution? Multiple components and pieces of equipment are involved in any telephony solution. The factors in total network availability calculations must include the following:

- Mean time between failures (MTBF) for all of the relevant equipment and/or communications links that make up the collective infrastructure to support the act of making a phone call

- Mean time to repair (MTTR) for all of the relevant equipment and/or communications links that compose the collective infrastructure to support the act of making a phone call
- Software reliability
- Required time for scheduled maintenance and upgrades
- Power availability

Assume, for example, that the probability of being functional through the course of a year has been calculated for every piece of hardware and software required for making phone calls. Equipment and software upgrades have been reduced to a component of the entire solution and assigned a level of probability as well.

The product resulting from the multiplication of all of the individual probabilities translated into time would give the end users a perspective of the level of service availability that they could expect.

Assume that the product of all of the individual probabilities is 0.995, or a 99.5 percent probability of the IP Telephony network being available for use. Conversely, this translates into 0.005 or 0.5 percent probability of the network not being available. Translating 0.5 percent unavailability into time over the course of the year (365.25 days $\times$ 24 hours/day $\times$ 0.005) results in approximately 44 hours (43.83 hours, to be exact) of downtime per year, or less than 2 days.

Two days per year of service unavailability in no way implies that any single piece of equipment would have this kind of downtime, because the individual components have not even been specifically identified in this calculation. The number serves only as an example of what an end user might expect. And when you put it in the context of a typical work schedule, it's not that drastic. Most SMB employees take vacations that are longer than 2 days per year.

Geographical location of the solution deployment might accentuate the factors that affect service availability. Not all telcos around the world offer five 9s or six 9s levels of reliability for their equipment, mobile phone users have traded a degree of service availability and quality for the convenience of mobility, and there is no way to tell what level of availability exists within individual networks that rely on a PBX-based system.

When approaching an IP Telephony design, the level of availability expectation on the part of the customer should be ascertained beforehand in the context of the existing and proposed solutions. This means that you need to identify solution components, assign to each a level of probability of being functional throughout the year, and translate the final product into time. It's not a bulletproof calculation, but it's a mechanism that can give a realistic perspective to the customer and avoid bad feelings following deployment.

Figure 8-1 summarizes and maps from the user perspective the QoS requirements in any type of telephony deployment with the tools that are available to you to implement a robust IP Telephony solution that meets those requirements.

Figure 8-1 *Telephony QoS Users' Requirements Versus Designers' Implementation Tools*

Single Communications Infrastructure for Voice and Data

The idea of a single communications infrastructure for all SMB communications needs might be appealing from the operations perspective. A single IP network implies greater installation/upgrade/maintenance uniformity over separate data, voice, and video networks. That, in turn, can lead to lower deployment costs and less diverse training requirements for support personnel.

Consider also the potential downsides of a single communications infrastructure:

- Does it make sense from the performance perspective to lump traffic from drastically different types of applications onto the same network? In the context of bandwidth and transmission delay requirements, the combined data/audio/video applications can be extremely bandwidth intensive but hardly time sensitive, and vice versa.

- How about the built-in separation between different types of application traffic that allows the telephone network to function even if there is a problem with the data network? In the presence of two separate networks for data and telephony, the outage of one normally does not affect the other.

The issue of redundancy and built-in high availability expectation on the part of voice users always needs serious consideration when making the commitment to a single IP-based network for all communication needs. Network availability and, consequently, service availability need not be adversely affected by a single infrastructure, as long as the components of the infrastructure are identified, along with their level of reliability. That allows for an approximate determination of the probability of the service being available during a certain time frame. You then need to match this level of probability with the SMB's expectation for service availability.

From the perspective of performance, a single communications infrastructure for data, voice, and video does not mean that every link within that infrastructure accommodates all categories of traffic. It means that the protocols, transmission media, and switching equipment are of a similar nature rather than representing different technologies, such as circuit and packet switching.

It is possible to have portions of an IP network that are dedicated to voice only or a network that shares all types of traffic. You can make decisions regarding traffic types based on anticipated traffic levels, bandwidth capacity, and switching equipment performance. QoS techniques can assist with ensuring an optimal level of performance for voice in scenarios where bandwidth needs to be shared among varied types of traffic.

TIP   Given the sensitivity of voice to delays and to variable delays that can cause jitter, it's best to avoid combining voice, which is encapsulated in relatively small packets, with applications that generate full-sized packets.

Open Standards Protocols

A general trend away from Time Division Multiplexing (TDM) and toward IP-based Telephony necessitates the use of open standards protocols for multivendor interoperability. Protocol standards can be categorized as follows:

- **Open**—Open standards are widely available. Open Internet standards in the form of RFCs are available for free, but some standards from bodies such as IEEE or ITU-T carry a price tag.

- **Proprietary**—Although a vendor might share details of proprietary protocols with third-party developers, those protocols are still proprietary to the vendor.

- **De facto**—De facto protocol standards are accepted by the industry but are not approved by standards organizations.

If you consider telephony in its totality (including its history), its operations are governed by all three categories of standards, whereas IP Telephony standards mostly fall into the open category from Internet Engineering Task Force (IETF) and ITU-T.

You are strongly encouraged to examine products and solutions from vendors to see if they use proprietary standards, which tend to make a product more efficient but can lock an SMB into a single-vendor environment. You need to decide on a single-vendor versus a multivendor environment for an IP Telephony solution based on user requirements and product availability from a single vendor. Single-vendor solutions are normally easier to support but might not have all of the desired features. Consequently, the ideal situation might be a mostly single-vendor solution that is open standards-based so it can be easily supplemented with products from other vendors.

Common OS Hardware Platforms

The use of common OS and hardware platforms for IP Telephony solutions is still elusive as compared to the special-purpose computers, which is what PBXes effectively are. However, the trend toward the use of common platforms for IP Telephony is growing. CallManager, which is the heart of the Media Convergence Server (MCS) 7800 series and Integrated Communications System (ICS) 7750 solutions, runs under a Windows version on hardware platforms utilizing Intel processors. Cisco's H.323 gatekeepers can operate on several router models as long as the appropriate IOS and the sufficient amount of memory are present. Given the specialized nature of the call-processing software, it's still best to go with a vendor-approved list of hardware, but the choices in this situation are certainly more diverse than they are for a single special-purpose computer.

IP Telephony Components and Protocols

IP Telephony solutions are applicable in all environments in which legacy telephony installations can be found, including home users, SOHOs, SMBs, large enterprises, and carriers. Even though the deployment environment and customer requirements for IP Telephony solutions differ, the design approach remains the same. Topology, performance, and budget considerations drive the choices of equipment and protocols following the identification of the stakeholder requirements. The key solution components, although they differ in scalability and capability, share the same characteristics and principles of operation. Viewing voice as an application implies that a viable IP infrastructure must be in place to support any successful IP Telephony solution deployment.

In developing an IP Telephony solution, you must also maintain a clear distinction between IP Telephony and Voice over IP (VoIP). Although the two expressions are frequently used as synonyms in casual technical discussions, consider VoIP as an enabler of IP Telephony in the context of design. An IP Telephony solution relies on VoIP standards, protocols, and equipment to create as complex or as simple a telephony system as has been determined by the user requirements and the available budget.

Consider the following key IP Telephony components:

- Gateways
- Gatekeepers
- Software-based PBXes
- IP phones
- VoIP protocols

Gateways

Generically, a gateway converts between the same layer protocols from different computing architectures or technologies. The H.323 recommendation identifies a number of gateway types (access, trunking, media, composite, decomposed) that reflect a high degree of gateway versatility in packet-based multimedia communications systems that include IP Telephony. Yet, this gateway versatility inevitably implies that in the course of designing IP Telephony or any other communications solution, you need a clear understanding of each gateway's functionality. In the context of H.323, gateways are also referred to as *endpoints*, meaning that they can initiate and terminate calls.

Cisco offers two categories of IP Telephony gateways:

- Universal series gateways (AS53xx/AS54xx/AS58xx). They are frequently deployed in the ISP and carrier environments.

- Several models of digital and analog voice gateways. They cater to the SMB and enterprise markets.

Both types of gateways convert voice traffic between the circuit-switched and packet-switched networks. The circuit-switched network is commonly referred to as the TDM network, the PSTN, or the plain old telephone service (POTS), regardless of whether the network is analog or digital. Packet-switched networks are now mostly IP based.

In an IP Telephony deployment without TDM, PSTN, or POTS interfaces, gateways are not needed. If an SMB's internal phone system is entirely IP-based, and the interface to the provider for local, long-distance, and international calls outside of the SMB network is also via IP, that SMB will not require gateways. To integrate legacy phone instruments into an IP-based telephone system, a voice gateway is required. The Cisco VG248 analog voice gateway allows for the integration of analog phones, faxes, and modems with the Cisco IP-based CallManager platforms, which are discussed later in this chapter.

If the SMB's internal phone system is entirely IP based, and the interface to a provider is via TDM instead of IP, a gateway is required for routing calls outside of the SMB network. That gateway is still considered a voice gateway, but it is also a PSTN gateway (integrating PSTN with an IP-based telephone system), in contrast to a voice gateway that is needed to integrate individual instruments into an IP-based phone system.

Topology and performance considerations are always factors in choosing gateways, but the choice is also driven by the technologies and protocols that need to be integrated into a cohesive IP-based communications system. It's generally hard to find a large SMB IP Telephony deployment without gateways, even if they are used only for backup service to PSTN.

In addition to dedicated voice gateways, Cisco offers modular routers (2600/3600 series, for example) that can be turned into VoIP gateways when equipped with appropriate voice and WAN interface cards, and an IOS that supports VoIP protocols. For the Catalyst 6500 series switches, Cisco offers T1/E1 service modules that turn the Catalyst into a VoIP gateway, integrating an IP-based phone system (CallManager) with a traditional PBX, PSTN, or both.

Because gateways represent the points of convergence between different communications systems, they can be deployed individually or in groups as a function of the size of the networks and the number of points (locations) where the different networks need to interconnect.

Gatekeepers

A *gatekeeper* is an optional element in a packet-switched H.323 network. Gatekeepers are effectively gateway managers. Gateways must be configured to register with a gatekeeper, just as the gatekeeper requires configuration to recognize the gateways.

In a multigateway H.323 deployment with multiple interfaces between the PSTN and IP networks, gatekeepers facilitate greater scalability by easing gateway configuration. In smaller deployments, VoIP gateways can be configured to exchange voice traffic over the IP network without having a gatekeeper as part of the network. However, as the number of gateways increases, you might quickly bump into high levels of configuration complexity of the dialing plan on the gateways if the design does not include a gatekeeper.

It follows that in complex networks, the gatekeeper becomes the repository of the dialing plan. The CallManager deployment models that are discussed later in this chapter allow for the presence of a dedicated gatekeeper or for the configuring of CallManager to perform call admission, which is one of the gatekeeper functions.

Assume the presence of a properly configured and functional gatekeeper on an H.323 network. Its functions are to manage the gateways, perform call admission into the IP network by monitoring and managing the available bandwidth for the anticipated call path, and to translate between IP addresses and E.164 numbers. E.164 is the ITU-T recommendation that specifies the international public telecommunications numbering plan or the generic structure of globally usable telephone numbers.

E.164 numbers are variable in length and consist of a country code (designation for a country), destination code (typically, a city or an area within a country) and the subscriber number (the number that is assigned to the end user by a local telco). Numerous configuration commands are available on gateways and gatekeepers to configure dial plans that include E.164 numbers.

In Cisco-based H.323 deployments, a gatekeeper is typically a router with an appropriate IOS. Even though gatekeepers can be involved in actual routing (switching packets between multiple interfaces), consider connecting the gatekeeper to the network via a single (preferably high-speed) interface and allowing it to perform the gatekeeping functions only without being burdened by other responsibilities, such as routing.

From a physical connectivity perspective, the gatekeeper becomes a "router on a stick" that is using the capabilities of the IOS and the router's processing power to perform its function as gateway manager. If the gatekeeping functionality embedded into IOS could be ported to a generic OS and hardware platform, the gatekeeper would not have to be a router.

In the gatekeeper-based H.323 networks, gatekeepers assume a critical function, and the issue of gatekeeper redundancy becomes equally critical. Alternate gatekeepers increase redundancy, whereas directory gatekeepers improve scalability. Multiple techniques exist for designing gatekeeper redundancy, including the following:

- The use of multiple gatekeepers to manage smaller groups of gateways, which translates into a partial versus full network outage in case of single gatekeeper failure
- Configuration of Hot Standby Routing Protocol (HSRP) for the pairing of gatekeepers
- Configuration of alternate and directory gatekeepers

Software-Based PBXes

Consider that telephony as a communications technology has been evolving for more than a century and that PBXes as private mini replicas of the phone companies' central switching offices represent a key element of that technology.

PBX Evolution in a Nutshell

The "private" part of *private branch exchange (PBX)* shows how a PBX differs from the CO, which used to be referred to as the public exchange. Since their inception, PBXes have undergone multiple distinct stages of evolution. They have progressed from electromechanical switches to complex feature-rich closed-architecture proprietary computers, and finally to open-standards IP-based platforms that integrate with data networks.

In designing an IP Telephony solution, it's not critical to be fully aware of either the history of PBXes or all of their proprietary features, developed over many decades by many telephony equipment vendors. It is critical, however, to be aware of the general functions of a PBX. These functions include the following and more:

- Call routing within the SMB or enterprise networks based on extensions (think dialing plan here!)
- Direct Inward Dialing (DID)
- Automatic Call Distribution (ACD) based on the Dial Number Identification Service (DNIS) or Automatic Number Identification (ANI)
- Accounting by groups and individuals
- Support for classes of service

Any SMB IP Telephony solution either replaces a PBX by a common-OS platform with call processing software or has to integrate with it via gateways. In either case, you need to map the key features of the existing PBX to those offered by the IP solution and ensure that user training is offered during the deployment stage to elucidate feature differences, new capabilities, or the absence of old, familiar features.

If a PBX is software based, it does not mean that there is no hardware involved; it means the use of call processing software on a common hardware platform running a common OS. The Cisco CallManager using an Intel-based computer with a Windows OS falls into the category of a software-based PBX. Programming via a web-based interface is easier than setting jumpers on printed circuit boards or using a cryptic command-line interface (CLI) language with the older, traditional PBXes. When the software-based PBX is further integrated with voice gateways and/or data networks and/or voice applications, it becomes an integrated communications solution, of which the Cisco MCS 7800 series and ICS 7750 are examples.

IP Phones

IP phones replace their TDM siblings in an IP Telephony solution. In choosing an IP phone, you need to consider the following:

- The protocols and even the version of the same protocol that the phone supports
- Codec support
- Number of Ethernet ports on the phone
- Phone power requirements
- Phone features (programmable buttons, number of lines, LCD screen, and so on)
- Any safety or emissions regulatory requirements

If you have an active RJ-11 jack supplied by the CO, you will get a dial tone if you plug an analog instrument into it, no matter who manufactured the phone. In addition, you don't need an external power source for your phone, and, of course, your calling features, if any, are limited. IP phones are network devices (minicomputers), and there is no guarantee of interoperability in terms of IP phones from different vendors working with a single software-based PBX or call agent.

As part of any generic IP Telephony design, consider the preceding characteristics of IP phones and verify IP phone interoperability with a specific call agent. IP phones use a protocol to communicate with the call agent for call control. A SIP phone will not work with an H.323-capable call agent that does not support SIP. A gateway function is needed to allow a SIP phone to integrate into an H.323 network. The job of avoiding interoperability problems gets easier, of course, when the entire IP Telephony solution (call agent, gateways, gatekeepers, IP phones, and voice applications) comes from a single vendor, as is the case with the Cisco IP Telephony solutions presented later in this chapter.

A simple analog phone does not require an external power source. A more complex instrument (a cordless phone with an answering machine built into it, for example) does require a source of power to function, even if batteries supply that power. IP phones require power. In all deployment scenarios, the source of power for IP phones is a design consideration. If the IP phone instrument comes with an external power adapter, consider the number of outlets and/or power strips and extension cords that might be needed to accommodate any sizable deployment. It's best if the phone accepts inline power delivered over the network cabling from a LAN switch.

The IEEE 802.3af standard defines the requirements for inline power delivery over network cabling. Inline power can be delivered via a power-enabled switch module residing directly in a LAN switch, or via an external power patch panel that resides between the switch and the wall outlet.

An additional consideration when choosing an IP phone is the number of RJ-45 ports on the phone. One port is needed to connect the phone to the network, but if two ports are present, it means that a PC or some other network device could utilize it. IP phones with two RJ-45 ports are definitely preferable because they give you more options for accommodating other network devices present in user work areas. However, in the case of an IP phone that is installed in an unrestricted guest area, having a phone with two RJ-45 ports could be an invitation for someone to try to hack into the network.

VoIP Protocols

The ITU-T H.323 recommendation and the IETF's SIP and SIP-related RFCs are the dominant sources for IP Telephony protocols. H.323 has normative references to 58 other recommendations, which means that those recommendations contain provisions that, through a reference in H.323, also become provisions of H.323. The list of normative references in SIP's RFC 3261 is 43.

For H.323 and SIP, there are thousands of pages of specifications for many aspects of multimedia communications over packet networks. Keep in mind, however, that only parts of the totality of these specifications apply to IP Telephony, which represents only one aspect of multimedia communications over packet-switched networks. When H.323 and SIP are complemented with the Media Gateway Control Protocol (MGCP), Megaco/H.248, and the Skinny Client Control Protocol (SCCP) from Cisco, it might seem like you have plenty of protocol choices when considering an IP Telephony solution deployment. But are these choices really that plentiful?

H.323 and SIP are competitors, but these two "families" (or umbrellas) of protocols are also complementary. It follows that H.323 and SIP are responsible for somewhat similar functions. Both H.323 and SIP are used to set up and to control communication sessions on packet-switched networks. Given the fact that gateways convert between same-layer or similar-function protocols from different architectures, if the functionality of a composite IP Telephony solution dictates the use of products based on both protocols, H.323/SIP gateways should save you from the painful choice between SIP and H.323.

As a general rule of thumb, H.323 is more prevalent and robust in the wide area deployments (ISP/carrier solutions), whereas SIP holds its own with H.323 in the LAN-based (SMB, enterprise) IP Telephony. With respect to H.323, you always need to be aware of the versions that a product supports if H.323 products from different vendors are to interoperate in multivendor environments. As IP Telephony matures, interoperability issues should decrease.

MGCP and Megaco/H.248 can also be viewed as competitors, but their functions are quite different from H.323 and SIP. When the call setup and control functions are removed from a gateway and incorporated into another device that possibly controls many different types of gateways, that device becomes a Media Gateway Controller (MGC), which is also referred to as a *softswitch*.

The gateway without control functions becomes a media gateway, which means that its functionality has been reduced to converting between media signals. MGCP and Megaco/H.248 operate between media gateways and MGCs. They facilitate greater scalability in complex IP Telephony deployments. The Internet community has proposed MGCP, whereas H.248/Megaco represents a joint (and rare!) effort between the Internet community and ITU-T. (Note the combined name.)

Cisco IP Telephony Solutions

Cisco offers numerous IP Telephony solutions that scale from the smallest of SMBs through large enterprises and ISP/carrier environments. Each solution is composed of the following high-level elements:

- A call processing application (CallManager or its variant, such as CallManager Express [CME], for example)
- A hardware platform that supports the call processing application, which can assume the form of one of the following:
    - A modular chassis with multiple specialized cards
    - A rack-mountable or a tower-based server
    - A router/gateway
- Voice applications that, as a function of capacity, might either require their own dedicated hardware platforms or be able to coexist on the same platform as the call processing agent
- IP phones (a wide-ranging selection is available)
- Legacy telephony integration platforms in the form of one of the following:
    - Standalone dedicated gateways
    - Cards for modular solutions

Integrated IP Telephony solutions include all or a subset of the preceding elements, with each solution straddling a spectrum of scalability in terms of features and capacity. To match a customer's IP Telephony requirements with the capabilities of a solution, it is recommended that you proceed as follows:

   1 Choose the applicable high-level elements for a candidate solution from the preceding list.

2 Drill down the high-level solution elements to come up with the specific solution components as a function of the following:

- The required level of scalability and performance
- The specific hardware platforms
- The desired topology
- The required configuration expertise to deploy the solution

For the purpose of designing an SMB IP Telephony solution using Cisco products, consider the following building blocks, which incorporate the high-level IP Telephony elements along with issues related to configuration and topology:

- Integrated IP Telephony solutions
- CallManager deployment options
- CallManager integration with legacy PBX
- CallManager dial plan configuration considerations
- IP Telephony voice applications
- Cisco IP Phones
- Cisco ISP/carrier solution

Integrated IP Telephony Solutions

Integrated IP Telephony solutions provide a foundational set of hardware, software, and features that allow a designer to tailor the solution to the specific customer requirements. In effect, Cisco does part of the design through its integrated product offering, and the detailed customization becomes the designer's responsibility. The following integrated solutions are considered:

- CME solution
- MCS 7800 series solutions
- ICS 7750 solution

CME Solution

CME is an IOS-based call processing application (formerly known as *IOS Telephony Services*) that is intended for small SMBs, with requirements for up to 120 physical phones. CME incorporates the concepts of Ephone (Ethernet phone) and Ephone-dn (Ethernet phone directory number). Ephone and Ephone-dn are software constructs (configurable in IOS) that collectively allow for a greater simultaneous number of calls to be processed than there are physical phones in the system.

The number of Ephones in a CME system corresponds to the number of physical phones, but the number of Ephone-dns can exceed the number of physical instruments by a ratio of anywhere from 2.4:1 to 5:1. In practical terms, through the use of Ephone and Ephone-dn constructs, the same phone instrument can handle more than one call at a time, or the same extension can be shared between multiple instruments. Ephones and Ephone-dn constructs represent a powerful capability for building customizable IP Telephony environments in small SMB scenarios.

Table 8-1 summarizes the characteristics of the CME solution. It should allow you to determine at a glance if the solution is appropriate for a given set of customer requirements. These characteristics are representative as of the time of this writing and should always be verified against the latest data sheets for additions or subtractions.

Table 8-1   *CME Solution Characteristics*

Characteristic	Values
Platform	IAD* 2430, 1760s, 2600s, 3600s, 3700s
IP phone capacity	Up to 120 IP phones as a function of platform
IP phone support	7902, 7910, 7912G, wireless IP 7920, conference station 7935 and 7536, 7940G and 7960G as a function of platform, IOS version, and firmware version
Ephone-dn	Up to 288 as a function of platform. Platforms that support a larger number of IP phones also support a larger number of Ephone-dns.
Compatibility and integration	CallManager, Unity, Unity Express**, Microsoft CRM
Deployment model	CME LAN or via a provider. Not intended for deployments over a WAN.
Features	Transfer, hold, distinctive ringing, on-hold pickup, intercom, paging, music on hold (MOH), night services, do not disturb, and many more

*IAD = Integrated Access Device.

**Unity Express is a scaled-down version of Cisco Unity, which is discussed in Chapter 9.

For smaller SMBs (up to 100 users), the higher-end IP Telephony solutions that scale significantly past the current number of users' requirements always remain a design option. That's especially true if an SMB anticipates significant growth, its budget accommodates the higher-end solution's cost, and the entry-level solution's features are deemed insufficient. However, the CME solution, with its numerous features and integration capabilities (including Microsoft's CRM), represent a serious contender for the smaller-size SMB market.

MCS 7800 Series Solutions

The Cisco MCS 7800 series represents a family of IP Telephony solutions that are capable of meeting the telephony requirements of SMBs and enterprise alike. Nine MCS models are available as of the time of this writing, with several more models having reached the end of the sale cycle.

CallManager remains at the core of the MCS series, whereas hardware platforms (tower-based and rack-mountable servers) that offer a wide range of performance and storage capacity options make these solutions scale from 200 to thousands of phones. The three MCS models that are most applicable for SMB environments are MCS 7815-1000, MCS 7815I-2000, and MCS 7825H-3000. Their collective characteristics are summarized in Table 8-2.

Table 8-2   *Collective Characteristics of Select 7800 Series MCS Models*

Characteristic	Values
Models	MCS 7815-1000, MCS 7815I-2000, MCS 7825H-3000.
Hardware platforms	Tower-based and rack-mountable with Celeron and Pentium 4 processors (1 GHz to 3.06 GHz).
IP phone capacity	From 200 to 1000, with up to 4000 with CallManager clustering.
IP phone support	All models of Cisco IP phones as a function of requirements. (See the "Cisco IP Phones" section later in this chapter.)
Application support	Unity, Unity Bridge, Cisco Conference Connection, Cisco IP Interactive Voice Response (IVR), Cisco IP Contact Center (IPCC) Express, Cisco Queue Manager.
Deployment models	As applicable to CallManager. (See "CallManager Deployment Options" later in this chapter.)
Features	As applicable to CallManager, which is the call processing application for all of the MCS 7800 series models. Given the CallManager's extensive features, you should refer directly to the CallManager specifications on the Cisco website. To determine the feature set for the integrated solution, combine the CallManager features with those of all of the relevant applications.
Integration with legacy telephony (PBX, PSTN)	Via gateways and multiservice routers.

For the larger-size SMB IP Telephony deployments that cannot be accommodated by CME, the offerings of the MCS 7800 series solutions (as detailed in Table 8-2) can be summed up as follows:

- The different MCS models of varying processing speed and capacity provide significant granularity in the number of supported users and voice applications

- CallManager provides the core telephony functionality and integration capabilities with legacy telephony installations

ICS 7750 Solution

The Cisco ICS 7750 is another integrated IP Telephony solution that scales the spectrum of SMB sizes and branch offices of larger enterprises. Physically, ICS 7750 is a multislot, industry-grade chassis system that accepts cards offering a wide range of voice connectivity and applications options.

NOTE   Cisco has discontinued the shipment of ICS 7750, but the product continues to be available through secondary markets, and the Cisco Technical Assistance Center (TAC) will continue ICS 7750 support through 2009. The ICS 7750 modular architecture readily lends itself to examples of design principles.

The capabilities of the ICS processor cards allow it to replace and/or integrate with an existing PBX system, integrate with PSTN or an H.323 network, and permit the continued use of analog telephony instruments within the SMB or enterprise networks. The ICS processor cards fall into the following categories:

- **Multiservice routers and voice gateways or Multiservice Route Processor (MRP) cards**—These cards facilitate ICS integration with H.323 networks, PSTN, and analog phone instruments within the SMB or enterprise networks. Physically, MRPs come with either one or two slots that accept more than a dozen different interface cards, including voice interface cards (VICs), WAN interface cards (WICs), and voice/WAN interface cards (VWICs). The VIC/WIC/VWIC support offers you a wide range of physical layer voice/WAN interface choices. ICS 7750 supports up to five MRPs. MRPs also offer the typical IOS services (VPN, VLAN routing, and firewalling) for integration with data networks.

- **Application servers or the System Processing Engine (SPE) cards**—These cards are full-blown computers that support a high-speed Pentium processor, onboard memory, hard drives, universal serial bus (USB) ports, a monitor port, and a mouse/keyboard port. They run CallManager, System Manager for web-based configuration and management, and a range of voice applications, including Cisco Unity Voice Messaging, IP IVR and Integrated Contact Distribution (ICD). The SPE310 is an example of an application server card. At least one SPE is required in an ICS 7750. Up to five SPEs are supported for redundancy, greater scalability, and processing power. SPEs are hot-swappable.

- **Ethernet switch or the System Switch Processor (SSP) card**—This is an IOS-based Ethernet switch that provides an interface between any of the other cards (MRPs, SPEs) residing within the ICS chassis and the Catalyst switches that connect to it. Catalyst switches aggregate the communication endpoints (Cisco IP phones or the IP SoftPhones) that are part of the ICS 7750 solution. ICS 7750 requires one SSP to reside in a specific slot.

- **Hardware monitor or the System Alarm Processor (SAP) card**—The function of this card is to integrate with the System Manager software (which resides on the SPE) by sending it the relevant system monitoring or fault detection information. At least one SAP card is required in an ICS chassis in a specific slot.

An absolute minimum ICS 7750 configuration includes a single SPE, an SSP, and a SAP card. The designer has the choice of complementing that configuration with additional SPEs and MRPs. However, with that minimal configuration (assuming a single site deployment model and no voice gateways present elsewhere on the network), calls cannot be made outside the SMB's network. To make the minimal solution more practical, an MRP card is required. An MRP card integrates the ICS 7750 with either an IP WAN or PSTN for calls outside of the network. Figure 8-2 graphically represents the functionalities and capabilities of the ICS 7750.

Figure 8-2   *ICS 7750 Functionalities and Capabilities*

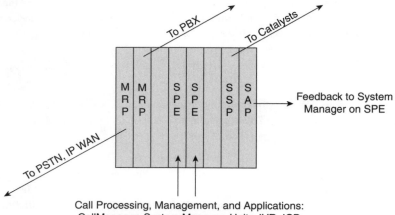

Call Processing, Management, and Applications:
CallManager, System Manager, Unity, IVR, ICD

CallManager Deployment Options

The CallManager accommodates single-site or multisite topologies, deploys standalone or in clusters, and scales for up to 10,000 users when installed in a cluster on the largest supported server platform. An IP Telephony application that supports up to 10,000 users readily exceeds the typical SMB requirements, but it also reflects that the application is scalable from SMBs through large enterprises as a function of hardware platform and configuration.

In the case of MCS 7825H-3000, a single CallManager accommodates more than the typical SMB requirement of up to 1000 users. On the ICS 7750, a single CallManager accommodates up to 500 users, but if a cluster of CallManagers is needed, it can consist either of SPEs in distinct 7750 chassis or SPEs in the same chassis.

The combined elements of topology, clustering, and PSTN/IP WAN integration on the CallManager platforms yield the following generic CallManager deployment scenarios:

- A single-site deployment with a single CallManager or a cluster
- A distributed multisite deployment with a single CallManager or a cluster at each site and PSTN between the sites
- A distributed multisite deployment with a single CallManager or a cluster at each site and an IP WAN between the sites
- A centralized multisite deployment with a single CallManager or a cluster at only one site and an IP WAN between the sites

Single-Site CallManager Deployment

A single-site deployment, with an interface to PSTN for outside calls, is the simplest of all of the deployment models and can be used as a building block for more complex designs. This model involves either a single CallManager or a cluster (for redundancy and/or greater scalability). For the MCS 7800 solutions, clustering involves multiple servers. In the case of the ICS 7750 solution, clustering can be accommodated through multiple SPEs in the same chassis.

As an example, consider the components of a typical ICS 7750 redundant configuration for a single-site deployment. These components can be mapped to corresponding hardware in any of the CallManager-based solutions:

- An MRP300 with a multiflex trunk voice/WAN interface card. The VWIC (VWIC-1MTF-T1, for example) would provide a digital interface to a PSTN of 24 DS0 channels. Other options, as a function of having to accommodate analog phone instruments or having an interface to an existing PBX, might include an MRP with Foreign Exchange Station (FXS) ports (for analog instruments), or Foreign Exchange Office (FXO) ports (for interface to a PBX).

- Two SPE310 cards, each with CallManager for redundancy and additional voice applications (IVR, ICD, Unity Voice Messaging, Unity Unified Messaging, for example). USB ports on the SPE300 would allow for the connection of external backup devices to ensure proper backups of the applications, data, and configuration files.

- The required SSP and SAP cards. The SSP provides an interface to the LAN (Catalyst switches) that is used for the IP phones. The SAP interacts with the System Manager residing on the SPE.

- An appropriate number of IP phones plugging into the Catalyst switches that are interfaced to the SSP.

A robust single-site design should include power protection for the CallManager platform via an uninterruptible power supply (UPS) and for the Catalysts (aggregating IP phones) via the Cisco Redundant Power System (RPS) 300. The Catalyst that was specifically developed for use with the CallManager-based solutions is the 3524-PWR XL, but the solutions also work with the 4000 and 6500 series switches. The 3524-PWR XL supports 24 10/100 ports with inline power, 2 GBIC-based Gigabit Ethernet ports, and a redundant power connector that can be used by the RPS 300.

Distributed Multisite CallManager Deployment with PSTN

A distributed multisite deployment, with PSTN for calls between the sites and outside the network, duplicates at multiple locations the single site with PSTN design. This deployment assumes that even if there is IP connectivity between the sites, it is not sufficient to support voice traffic. IP connectivity might be adequate to meet data transmission requirements.

Assume that the problem with IP connectivity is either too high a cost for sufficient bandwidth to support voice or poor availability of WAN services. There is still value to deploying CallManager on a corresponding platform at each site as part of a longer-term strategy to have a more fully integrated voice/data network.

For the ICS 7750, the MRP cards with their WIC support are capable of a wide range of IP connectivity options. This means that even if voice traffic is not flowing over the IP WAN, the IP WAN can be established without additional routing equipment. Given the flexibility in WAN connectivity that is afforded by the WICs, two future options for greater integration are possible:

- First, the cost of the existing WAN service would go down over time, which could allow the SMB to provide higher bandwidth and to start passing voice traffic over the WAN.

- Second, a new higher-bandwidth WAN service could become available at a reasonable cost. Assuming the availability of a compatible WIC for that service, a WIC swap and an addition of a gatekeeper might be all that is needed to support the voice/data integration on the WAN.

Naturally, there should be some economic justification for the voice/data integration over the WAN. The financial justification could come from lower costs resulting from reducing PSTN connectivity at each site (if not eliminating it completely at some sites) and from toll savings for long-distance calls between the sites.

Distributed Multisite CallManager Deployment with IP WAN

A distributed multisite CallManager deployment, with an IP WAN that interconnects all of the sites, offers you the option of using the IP WAN for voice traffic between the sites or continuing to rely on PSTN for intersite calls. The assumption here is that IP WAN will be used for intersite voice traffic.

A major design consideration in this deployment model is to determine whether the intersite bandwidth is sufficient to carry the estimated amount of voice traffic, especially if the WAN needs to be shared with data traffic. Bandwidth consumption for voice traffic is a function of the type codec that is configured on IP phones.

Cisco IP phones support G.711 and G.729a codecs, the characteristics of which are shown in Table 8-3.

Table 8-3   *Characteristics of Cisco IP Phone–Supported Codecs*

Codec	MOS	Compression Delay	Bit Rate
G.711	4.1	0.75 ms	64 Kbps (about 80 Kbps of bandwidth per call when the entire overhead associated with a call is included)
G.729a	3.92	10 ms	8 Kbps (about 14 Kbps of bandwidth usage)

The difference in MOS and compression delay between the two codecs is sufficiently small (remember that up to 250 ms round-trip delay is acceptable for voice calls). If bandwidth is at a premium, the codec that results in the smaller bandwidth consumption should be deployed. If bandwidth is not an issue, consider using the codec with the smallest compression delay and the highest MOS. Also, keep in mind that codec support is not static; it continues to evolve as a function of time and equipment enhancements.

A distributed multisite deployment implies that each site has its own CallManager (call processing agent), which is at the core of integrated solutions like the MCS 7800 series and ICS 7750. A call processing agent can also be a legacy PBX with a VoIP gateway or a Cisco IOS Telephony Services (ITS) device. A number of Cisco routers support ITS, which is meant for IP Telephony deployments of up to 48 IP phones. ITS remains viable, but it represents an older solution, which Cisco is replacing with CallManager Express.

The presence of a call processing agent at each site means that call control traffic is not carried over the WAN because it transpires between the call agent and the endpoint at each site. An additional element in this model is a dedicated gatekeeper. The gatekeeper's function is to provide call admission control. If you choose, the gatekeeper can also be used as part of the overall dial plan configuration, which would simplify the dial plan configuration on the individual CallManagers. A multisite distributed model applies in SMB environments, but it also scales for large enterprises.

A distributed multisite deployment would typically use PSTN at each site as a backup for overflow calls (insufficient WAN bandwidth availability to make a call) or in the case of the IP WAN failure. However, the use of PSTN for those functions is a design decision that depends on the user requirements. It's possible that only a single gateway at only one site will be used for all PSTN calls. That could severely limit the external call capability at various sites in the event of even a partial WAN failure.

Several options are available for designing the dial plan in this model. The most scalable option is to use the gatekeeper dial plan, which means that most of the configuration is performed on the gatekeeper, with only minimal configuration required on each CallManager. The complete opposite of the gatekeeper dial plan is the site dial plan, in which no dial plan configuration is performed on the gatekeeper, and the entire configuration is conducted on CallManagers. The site dial plan does not scale well as the number of sites increases because any change to the plan at one site requires changes at all the other sites. With the site dial plan configuration, the gatekeeper function is reduced to admission control.

A compromise dial plan, if necessary, lies in the hybrid approach in which the dial plan configuration is distributed between the gatekeeper and CallManagers. With only two or three sites, the choice of a dial plan is a lot less important than it is with a dozen or more sites. If an SMB anticipates the deployment of more than a few sites, the gatekeeper or hybrid dial plans are preferable as the initial choice. From the implementation and network administration perspective, if you change a dial plan after the initial installation and configuration, you might have to do so at some rather unusual hours.

Because a gatekeeper is of critical importance in the distributed multisite deployment model, you should consider all available redundancy techniques, including the following:

- Multiple gatekeepers (to minimize the impact of the failure of a single gatekeeper)
- Alternate gatekeepers (which are configured to take over the gatekeeping function when requests from the call processing agent to the primary gatekeeper time out)
- HSRP for the pairing of gatekeepers

Aside from any economic benefits resulting from carrying voice traffic over a WAN, the great benefit of the distributed multisite model is its high scalability. Business environments are not static; an SMB can quickly turn into a large enterprise through growth or acquisitions.

Centralized Multisite CallManager Deployment

A centralized multisite deployment assumes that an IP WAN is present between the sites but that only one site is equipped with the CallManager. In this deployment model, the IP WAN carries both the call control and the voice traffic in addition to any data traffic. Similar to the distributed multisite design, call admission control is required in this deployment model to ensure that the WAN links are not oversubscribed by the voice calls. Although the H.323 gatekeeper provides admission control in the distributed model, CallManager can be configured to provide admission control in this model.

The issues of bandwidth capacity and PSTN access in this model need to be considered in a manner similar to the distributed multisite model. The provisioning of WAN bandwidth needs to take into account the calling patterns and the type of codec that will be used for voice compression.

From the service availability perspective, each site should be equipped with a voice gateway supporting the Survivable Remote Site Telephony (SRST) feature, which allows PSTN access even in the event of a site being cut off from the call processing agent due to the WAN failure. With a voice gateway at each site, PSTN calls could also be made when the WAN link cannot carry any more voice calls due to high utilization. H.323-capable gateways afford the capability of making PSTN calls after losing connectivity with the CallManager due to WAN failure.

One of the greatest benefits of the centralized multisite deployment is the relatively simple administration and management of this model as compared to the distributed multisite model. The price, of course, is a more limited scalability in terms of the number of sites that can be supported in this model. Which model you choose depends on the user requirements. You can also view this model as a building block and combine two or more centralized multisite deployments into a distributed multisite deployment where, effectively, each centralized multisite deployment can be logically thought of as a single site component of the multisite distributed model.

CallManager Integration with Legacy PBX

Technically, the installation of CallManager integration with legacy PBX is simple. For example, if the requirement calls for PBX/ICS 7750 integration, choose an MRP card that supports a VIC (VIC-2E/M, for example) to connect the ICS 7750 to a PBX. MRP300 fulfills that requirement.

From a business perspective, however, PBX/CallManager integration has a major implication. If an SMB is wary of the proposed IP Telephony solution and is reluctant to let go of the legacy technology, the SMB does not need to scrap the existing installation before trying IP Telephony.

Integration of CallManager with an existing PBX protects the existing investment while allowing a group of users within the SMB's network to try the new solution before completely switching to IP Telephony. It's the "try before you buy" approach, which shows that IP Telephony solutions designers are not immune to dealing with budgetary constraints and/ or end-user psychology.

CallManager Dial Plan Configuration Considerations

Dial plan design is a critical component of any IP Telephony solution deployment. If an IP Telephony solution is going to replace an existing PBX (or multiple PBXes), consider that each PBX has probably been programmed and tweaked over many years. In all likelihood, there is poor documentation regarding the assigned and available internal numbers and classes of service associated with them.

An absolutely exact one-to-one mapping between the PBX programming and the new solution configuration is, perhaps, not necessary. However, it is necessary to determine the following:

- User calling patterns
- Classes of service (the ability to make international or other toll calls, for example)
- The actual E.164 numbers for all of the users (especially if DID is allowed)

Familiarity with the concepts of partitions and calling search spaces, as they are used in the CallManager configuration process, is also recommended.

Partitions and calling search spaces correspond directly to the destination numbers that an end user can dial and the class of service configuration within a PBX. Partitions aggregate destination numbers and their route patterns (a group of numbers within a certain geographical area, for example), whereas calling search spaces determine which partitions an end device (IP phone) can access to make a call. Destination numbers that are dialed by a user but that are not defined in any of the partitions, as determined by the calling search space, receive a busy signal. In other words, they are not reachable.

Use of partitions and calling spaces allows you to define the necessary level of granularity for each user (or a group of users) for all external calls via PSTN. For example, classes of service in the form of unrestricted international calls, international calls to specific countries, or even calls to specific destinations within a given country could be readily defined and associated with the users meeting the criteria for making those kinds of calls.

The dial plan complexity varies as a function of the type of CallManager deployment model. A single-site deployment is the simplest; the dial plan needs to consider only internal calls within the site and external calls through the PSTN gateway. Destination numbers within the site could be abbreviated (extensions), whereas PSTN calls would use the actual E.164 numbers that are applicable in the country where the solution is deployed or the countries that can be called.

A centralized multisite deployment dial plan has similar characteristics to the single-site model, except that voice gateways are now present at each site, and they become part of the dial plan configuration. The typical configuration allows each user at each site to make unrestricted calls within the network and to use the local PSTN gateway for outside calls. In the event of WAN failure, intersite calls are made through the PSTN gateway as well. The dial plan on each gateway should identify the CallManager for intersite calls and PSTN for external calls.

Most choices in developing a dial plan are available in the distributed multisite model, which, as mentioned previously, requires a gatekeeper. However, regardless of the ICS 7750 deployment model, the general approach to developing a dial plan is always the same: It must address how calls are made within a site, between sites, and outside the network. For the distributed multisite model, you can choose the dial plan from the following three options:

- The *site* dial plan calls for leaving the gatekeeper out of the dial plan configuration and configuring each CallManager with the destination numbers of all of the other sites and all possible routes to each site. This plan clearly lacks scalability as the number of sites grows and/or the number of redundant paths between the sites increases. Adding new sites or changing one site requires reconfiguration of all the other sites.

- The *gatekeeper* dial plan centralizes the dial plan configuration on the gatekeeper. The gatekeeper is now responsible for resolving E.164 numbers to IP addresses during the call admission process and for providing for overflow or failover to PSTN. CallManagers at each site require only a minimal configuration.

- The *hybrid* approach allows you to develop a highly customized dial plan that combines elements of the site and gatekeeper plans.

IP Telephony Voice Applications

As stated in Chapter 3, "Network Infrastructure Requirements for Effective Solutions Implementation," the applications and the value that they bring to the SMB's operations ultimately define a networking solution. It's no different with IP Telephony. If an SMB wants more than just the ability to make phone calls (plus some other basics, such as hold, transfer, speed dial, and so on), IP-enabled voice applications are a key part of CallManager-based and CME solutions.

Consider the capabilities of the following categories of select applications, which are further broken down into individual components:

- Cisco Unity Express (CUE)

  — Voice mail and Auto Attendant. Intended for CME and ITS platforms.

  — CUE is a software application residing on a hardware module that installs into a CME or an ITS platform.

- CallManager Extended Services

  — Extension mobility. It allows a user to log in to an IP phone 7960 or 7940 model and access a personal calling profile.

  — CallManager Auto Attendant. It offers entry into the company-level voice menu and leaves the caller the option of reaching an operator.

- Cisco Unity

  — Voice Messaging. It facilitates storage and retrieval of voice messages while supporting multiple personal greetings, multilingual prompts, and custom settings for call handling.

  — Unified Messaging. It provides an integrated graphic interface to e-mail, voice messages, and faxes.

  — Automated Attendant. It is functionally comparable to the CallManager Auto Attendant but is at the individual user level. It acts as a personal electronic receptionist and can manage incoming calls based on DID, DNIS, and caller ID or ANI.

  — Visual Messaging Interface. It provides a web-based interface for accessing and managing voice-mail messages.

- Customer Response Solution (CRS). The CRS applications require the CRS engine that runs on the SPE, in the case of the ICS 7750.

  — IP Interactive Voice Response (IP IVR). It incorporates the Cisco IP Auto Attendant. However, the key difference between the IVR application and the Auto Attendant is that IVR interacts with a database. After a caller enters identifying parameters (for example, password, account number, and PIN number), an IVR application allows for the performing of functions (such as funds transfers and placing of orders) and can also supply callers with information about their account status.

  — IP Integrated Contact Distribution (IP ICD). This is an IP-based equivalent of the Automatic Call Distribution feature in the traditional PBXes. It integrates with the IP IVR application and allows for the distribution and answering of calls based on several predetermined methods of real-time agent availability.

Cisco IP Phones

IP Telephony users are not as concerned with the infrastructure component of the solution as with the capabilities of the instruments that are sitting on their desks or in the conference room. Cisco offers several physical instruments, along with the IP SoftPhone, that work with numerous variants of CallManager-based solutions. Table 8-4 summarizes key characteristics and the typical use of select models of the Cisco IP Phones.

Table 8-4 *Key Characteristics and Uses for Cisco IP Phones*

Model	Key Characteristics	Typical Use
7960	Six programmable line/feature buttons and four interactive soft keys Two RJ-45 10/100 Mbps ports Relatively large LCD screen for calling information, graphics, and web-based reporting	Managers and executives
7940	Same as 7960 except that it has two instead of six programmable line/feature buttons	Low to medium traffic users
7910	One line only with four dedicated feature buttons: hold, transfer, line, settings One RJ-45 port Small LCD screen	Guest areas (lobbies, hallways, break rooms)
7914 Expansion Module	Attachment for the 7960 with 14 programmable buttons: line, speed dial, numbers	Individuals who need to monitor and manage a large number of calls
7935 IP Conference Station	Conferencing features: multiple callers, mute Three speakers One RJ-45 port Small LCD screen	Voice conferencing
IP SoftPhone	Software application running on a PC that should be equipped with a full-duplex sound card and a handset or a headset Online dialing and directories Audio conferencing of up to six participants Virtual conference room for desktop collaboration	Audio conferencing and other forms of desktop collaboration

All Cisco IP Phones support G.711 and G.729a audio compression (codec). You should refer to the data sheets for each instrument for the full description of all features, protocol support, safety requirements, and physical characteristics, such as weight and size.

Cisco ISP/Carrier Solution

The Cisco ISP/Carrier IP Telephony solution centers on the universal series gateways (AS54xx/AS58xx) and H.323 gatekeepers for creating a nationwide or worldwide IP network to carry voice traffic. Approaches to using the universal series gateways follow. Other approaches might exist or be developed as a function of the IP Telephony designers' creativity and ingenuity.

- Analog telephony end users dial in to a gateway, which ties into an IP network.
    - Voice traffic is carried over the IP network and terminates at another gateway, if possible, that has IP connectivity with the gateway receiving the call.
    - Alternatively, if the termination through another gateway is not possible, the call is terminated via PSTN.
    - The gateway operator develops the dial plan that makes this process transparent to the customer.
    - The customer's call might or might not go over the IP network, but the customer should not be aware of which way the call is routed.
- The universal series gateway is interfaced to a Class 5 switch.
    - The gateway accepts TDM traffic from the switch.
    - The gateway passes TDM traffic (following its conversion into packets) onto the IP network.

The latter approach comes about most likely because of the lower cost of routing the TDM traffic via the IP network than via the existing TDM network.

Both of the preceding approaches rely on the gateways' operator having a well-developed IP network that reaches into areas where TDM is either not available or is a lot more expensive than delivering voice traffic over IP. As of this writing, the protocol of choice for these kinds of deployments is H.323.

As a function of the number of gateways, you ought to consider deploying gatekeepers to improve the network scalability. The configuration of zones on the gatekeeper can minimize the number of dial peers (VoIP, POTS) that must be configured on the gateways, and thus can facilitate the creation of complex yet scalable dial plans.

The same gatekeeper principles that applied in the preceding scenarios apply to a LAN-based IP Telephony that is using a CallManager-based solution in a distributed multisite deployment model. You can pair gatekeepers via HSRP, configure alternate gatekeepers on each gateway, and break the network down into multiple zones to assist with gatekeeper administration and to minimize the impact of the failure of any single gatekeeper or even a group of gatekeepers. In addition, the H.323 network can further scale through the deployment of a directory gatekeeper, whose function is to manage the zone-level gatekeepers.

AS5450 scales up to 16 CT1/CE1s or a single CT3. A CT3 is equivalent to 28 T1s, resulting in 672 voice ports. AS5850 supports up to 5 CT3s or 96 T1s. The channelized ports are normally used for TDM voice traffic, whereas serial ports interface the gateways to the IP WAN.

All universal series gateways support common and scalable routing protocols, including the Cisco EIGRP, OSPF, IS-IS, Border Gateway Protocol (BGP), and more. Using a scalable routing protocol with fast convergence characteristics is important in any major H.323 deployment that involves multiple gateways and gatekeepers. It greatly improves the IP network stability. In addition to the TDM and WAN ports, each universal series gateway has 10/100 Ethernet interface(s), typically used for LAN access to Authentication, Authorization, and Accounting (AAA) servers like Remote Access Dial-In User Service (RADIUS) or Terminal Access Controller Access Control System Plus (TACACS+).

Summary

This chapter considered the design of IP Telephony solutions in the context of their deployment considerations, key components, and Cisco-specific solutions for SMBs, enterprise branches, and carrier/ISP environments. Key deployment considerations are high service availability and high voice quality. The increasing reliability of the IP-based data networks (LANs, WANs, MANs), the availability of high bandwidth—not just in LANs but across long distances—and the increase in networking equipment performance all facilitate robust IP network infrastructure to support IP Telephony.

Successful IP Telephony deployments must take into account the built-in expectation on the part of telephony users for high voice quality and service availability. Factors that can degrade voice quality (unacceptable delay, echo and jitter) can be minimized through proper design. Multiple techniques also exist to ensure high network (service) availability and voice quality. In turn, the benefit of IP Telephony lies in the streamlining of the SMB's network infrastructure and the ability to deploy voice applications that can advance an SMB's business objectives.

Cisco IP Telephony solutions for SMBs include the CallManager Express, the MCS 7800 series, and the ICS 7750. These solutions can be deployed in different models as a function of an SMB's size and topology. Collectively, they offer calling functions equivalent to and exceeding those found in many traditional PBX-based systems. In addition, they support voice applications that are critical to a successful operation of many SMB types in the Internet-driven and information services–oriented economy. Cisco IP Telephony voice applications include CallManager Extended Services, IP IVR, Cisco Unity and Unity Express, and Customer Response Solution components, among others. They facilitate effective incoming call distribution and the ability on the part of the caller to get the necessary information from the SMB without interacting with a live operator.

In the carrier/ISP market, universal series gateways from Cisco (AS54xx/AS58xx) offer performance and scalability for converting large volumes of TDM to IP traffic, and vice versa. All Cisco IP Telephony solutions allow for the creation of scalable dial plans with a high degree of granularity to accommodate complex class of service requirements. Several techniques can be used to ensure a considerable level of redundancy for gatekeeper-based deployments.

CHAPTER 9

Unified Communications Solutions

The networking and communications industries have coined multiple terms to signify differing levels of unification of the various business communication modes: *unified communications solutions, unified communications systems and services, unified messaging*, and *unified messaging systems and solutions*. Two fundamental forces are driving this trend toward unification in business communications. First is the need for high productivity and effectiveness by employees, regardless of their physical location and the communication tools that they have available to them. Second is the proliferation of communication devices.

Although each new device comes with the convenience of its own unique applications, it also comes with the inconvenience of having to remember another number or an interface to service that device. A wide range of computing platforms with Internet and internal e-mail systems, multiple types of phones (mobile, Public Switched Telephone Network [PSTN], IP), personal digital assistants (PDAs), pagers, and fax machines all vie for the attention of SMB employees. They all have their own unique and, more frequently than not, incompatible ways of receiving, sending, and storing information. When managing the multiple (often, too many) means of communication becomes a job in and of itself, it's a clear sign that diversification in communications needs to give way to a greater integration.

In the Cisco Systems vernacular, a *unified communications solution* is an element of a larger emerging trend of IP communications solutions that encompass IP Telephony, voice applications, IP video conferencing, and customer contact applications. A unified communications solution includes a unified messaging solution (UMS) and combines it with additional personal productivity tools. The Cisco Personal Assistant fills the bill of a personal productivity tool that allows users to determine and manage how and when they want to be reached. The Personal Assistant allows the user to define individual rules for call screening, routing, and forwarding. Calls can be routed based on the time of day, the calendar, or who the caller is. Calls can be forwarded to a single number or a series of numbers. The user has the option of accepting or not accepting a call in real time.

A UMS, on the other hand, integrates messages that originate from multiple sources into a single point of access with a uniform interface. A UMS does not reduce the various modes of business communication (whether real time or highly asynchronous) into one boring and monotonous mode. A UMS aggregates the typical modes of business messaging (voice mail, e-mail, fax) into a single source that is accessible via multiple types of devices in varied business settings (traditional office, while in transit, or a home office).

For example, with currently available UMS tools, a PC can be used to access and listen to voice mail over the Internet, to listen to and view e-mail messages, and to retrieve and forward faxes, in addition to performing all of the typical standard business applications. Likewise, a cellular phone can be used to access voice mail, e-mail, and faxes, although the interface for e-mail access might be abbreviated compared to that on a PC, given the size of display available on a typical cellular phone.

In SMB environments, the synergy that is created through a greater convergence in the means of communication offers a more integrated view of business information, which can readily translate into increased employee productivity and greater customer satisfaction. It is, effectively, a form of business intelligence dividend that results from having the pieces of a jigsaw puzzle (bits and pieces of relevant business information) flowing into one place in front of you, as opposed to having them scattered through multiple media types and inboxes, with varying interfaces and means of retrieval. In short, a business becomes more energy efficient.

However, the deployment of a unified communications solution is not without its pitfalls, for the simple reason that a unified communications solution will create change for just about everyone in the business. It does not matter that, in principle, the change appears beneficial. The risk-reward principle is at work here. The risk is that the larger the number of employees affected by change, the greater the potential for failure. If the changes affecting business communications are introduced in too disruptive a manner, they might be embraced in a lukewarm way, outright rejected, or, in the worst-case scenario, even sabotaged by employees following the implementation.

At the same time, the reward of sweeping changes in business communications can be enormous if those changes are introduced judiciously and are embraced by all affected parties with the aim of advancing the SMB's strategic objectives. Consequently, to minimize the potential for failure, the deployment of unified communications solutions should be subject to a design process that identifies the SMB communications requirements; considers performance, topology, and budget; maintains an ongoing executive sponsorship for the project; and, last but not least, ensures that proper user training follows the solution implementation to take maximum advantage of the available features.

The capabilities of the available unified communications solutions might not be yet at an ideal level that will handle any kind of communication, anytime, and from anywhere, using a single portable appliance; however, the industry is taking appropriate strides in that direction. This chapter focuses on the following:

- Deployment considerations for unified messaging solutions
- The Cisco Unity solution
- The Cisco IP/TV solution
- The value of an intranet in an SMB environment

Deployment Considerations for Unified Messaging Solutions

The diverse methods of business communications create not only a time-consuming communications management issue, but they also allow employees to develop a customized approach to managing (storing and acting upon) the received information. This, in turn, can lead to higher information technology (IT) support costs and that dreadful act of miscommunication between employees and/or customers due to lost, misfiled, unseen, or unheard messages. No one needs to be reminded that miscommunications can have serious business consequences.

Although unified messaging solutions vendors (including Cisco) do not claim that their solutions eliminate miscommunications, it follows that a single source for all of one's messages affords greater ease for categorizing, displaying the status of, and managing the messages than if they reside at multiple locations and in different forms. Figure 9-1 illustrates elements of the capabilities of unified messaging versus the more discontiguous approach to communications.

Figure 9-1   *Elements of Capabilities of Unified Messaging*

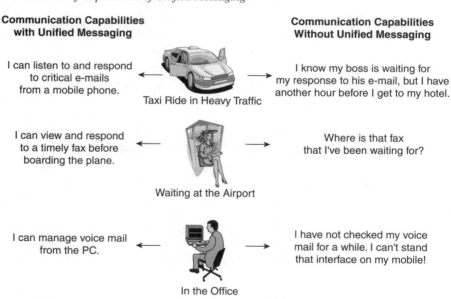

One of the biggest challenges that an SMB faces when introducing a new unified messaging solution is probably overcoming the resistance from employees and customers to the cultural change that the new solution will entail. However, because there is a trend toward integration of the communications infrastructure, integration at the end-user level is a natural outcome. And, of course, there is room within unified solutions for personalized settings. Here are some design considerations that are uniquely relevant to the deployment of a unified messaging solution:

- **The volume and diversity of messages received by SMB employees**—If the nature of the business is to communicate mostly via e-mail (with only occasional voice communications) or vice versa, the benefits of deploying a UMS might be marginal. SMBs with larger volumes of messages from multiple sources are better candidates for a UMS. Note, however, that the Cisco Unity UMS is first and foremost an intelligent voice messaging system. And given the modular nature of a UMS solution, it might be a wise strategic decision to deploy core features of a UMS (likely at a lower cost than deploying a full-blown system all at once) and continue to add additional features when the need increases. SMB's future upgrade options thus remain open and flexible.

- **State of the current IP/telephony network**—The current IP network infrastructure might require upgrades if a UMS is being implemented in conjunction with an IP Telephony or another IP communications solution, such as the Cisco IP/TV. Otherwise, a UMS by itself should not have to force infrastructure upgrades. However, the level of integration of any given UMS with the phone systems becomes a critical consideration because every UMS will not work with every phone system. As a designer, it is your responsibility to identify the phone systems that a UMS will work with and to ensure that the current and/or proposed phone system is compatible with the proposed UMS.

- **Integration with other voice mail messaging systems**—If the SMB is engaged in brand-new deployment or a forklift-style upgrade to an existing voice mail messaging system, integration is not an issue. Otherwise, you should carefully review the networking options of any UMS solution and consider whether or not they allow for the integration with other voice mail messaging systems, whether circuit switched or IP based, digital or analog.

- **Integration with the e-mail environment**—A UMS will likely have to integrate with an existing e-mail/messaging system. Various versions of Microsoft Exchange and IBM Lotus Domino, along with their respective clients (Outlook, Lotus Notes), are the dominant e-mail environments with which a UMS might have to integrate. Exchange and Domino might require other software components to be installed to facilitate integration with a UMS. The existing e-mail/messaging system will also likely facilitate fax server integration into the UMS.

- **Licensing requirements**—A unified communications solution, or even a UMS similar to the Cisco Unity, is going to have a number of components that are subject to licensing. You should identify all components of the solution that are subject to individual licensing and determine a reasonable number of licenses for each component as a function of the user requirements. The number of required licenses directly affects solution cost and might influence whether the solution is even deployed.

The Cisco Unity Solution

Being a UMS component of IP Communications solutions from Cisco, Unity is primarily aimed at environments with IP Telephony, not Time Division Multiplexing (TDM) deployments. As mentioned in Chapter 8, "IP Telephony Solutions," Unity integrates with CallManager and is part of the ICS 7750 solution. Several models from within the 7800 series of Cisco Media Convergence Server (MCS) solutions also support Unity deployment. However, because Unity does integrate with circuit-switched phone systems as well, it can be deployed in IP-only, circuit-switched–only, or mixed telephony environments.

You can also configure Unity to interchange messages with Octel voice mail systems through the use of the Bridge Networking option. In addition, Unity supports network modules that allow for integration with messaging systems conforming to the industry standard protocols: for digital messaging, Voice Profile for Internet Mail (VPIM), and for analog messaging, Audio Message Interchange Specification (AMIS).

NOTE	Octel Communications was founded in 1982 and became a leading voice messaging company. Octel's voice mail products service millions of users worldwide in a wide spectrum of business types and sizes, including SMBs. Octel Communications was acquired in 1997 by Lucent Technologies and eventually became Avaya, Inc., following the spin-off by Lucent of its Enterprise Network Group in September 2000. Currently, Octel is a registered trademark of Avaya, Inc., which produces many Octel-type products, including Octel 250/350 message servers.

At the level of e-mail/groupware messaging, Unity integrates with Microsoft Exchange and IBM Lotus Domino, and, through the use of the Personal Communications Assistant (PCA), with other groupware and e-mail environments. In addition to its core function, intelligent voice messaging, the Cisco Unity solution features the following:

- Message centralization
- Text-to-speech capability
- Multilanguage capability
- Global administration via the Cisco Unity Administrator
- Personalized administration via the Cisco Unity Assistant and Inbox

Message Centralization

A Unity administrator must create accounts for Unity users. Anyone with a Unity account is referred to as a *subscriber.* By providing a single source for e-mail, voice mail, and faxes, Unity eliminates the problem of having to navigate between communications arriving on different media (paper, voice, electronic text) and in multiple locations.

When integrated with Microsoft Exchange and the Outlook e-mail client via ViewMail, Unity affords subscribers a videocassette recorder (VCR)-style control capability for listening to voice messages. With a long message, being able to fast forward, pause, start/ stop, and rewind gives an employee the option to resume listening to the message where interrupted rather than having to start all over again.

Text-to-Speech Capability

The text-to-speech (TTS) feature of Unity allows users to listen to e-mail messages over the phone or from a PC through the telephone user interface (TUI). This capability allows users to multitask while listening to messages rather than having to devote full attention to reading or skimming a message.

TTS usage within Unity is subject to licensing and configuration of a class of service (COS), with TTS enabled via the Cisco Unity Administrator. Unity is bundled with third-party TTS products (RealSpeak or TTS3000) from SoftScan, Inc., which, toward the end of 2001, acquired the Speech and Language Technologies business of the former vendor of these products, the European-based Lernout & Hauspie (L&H). RealSpeak replaces TTS3000 as the default TTS engine with the release of Unity 4.0. Both TTS engines are available in multiple international languages, but they cannot be mixed on the same server.

Multilanguage Capability

The language support within Unity addresses different ways in which users and/or administrators interface with the product. These include via phone language for voice mail prompts, TTS language for listening to e-mail, and a graphical user interface (GUI) language for visual displays during setup and/or web-based retrieval of messages. International language support is available for each of the three categories of Unity languages, but the level of the international language support varies among three categories. For example, TTS is supported in fewer international languages than is the phone language. Phone language support is most extensive because it takes into account even the dialect of the most widely spoken languages.

Use of different languages in a Unity installation is subject to licensing. You should determine the language requirements as part of the solution design process. The language licensing does not limit the number of languages that can be installed, but it does determine how many languages can be used simultaneously. This means that, should the need arise, it is possible to reconfigure Unity to use different language(s) than those specified in the initial installation. This change can occur without necessarily changing the number of language licenses. Localized language support for international Unity customers is available in more than a dozen languages and/or dialects.

Global Administration via the Cisco Unity Administrator

The Cisco Unity Administrator facilitates the configuration of global Unity settings during and following the initial installation. Unity subscribers who are licensed to use the Unity Assistant via the PCA can assist with the ongoing management by customizing their individual accounts. The high-level categories of settings through the Unity Administrator include the following:

- Subscriber management
- Call management
- Network options management
- System settings and reports

Unity Subscriber Management Settings

Subscriber settings can be managed individually or via group templates. Subscriber settings are quite extensive, including elements of a subscriber's profile (name, display name, active schedule, COS, and so on), account status settings (unlocked or locked due to too many failed logins), call transfer options, caller input and greetings settings, messages and message notification settings, passwords, private distribution lists, and more.

As a best practice for Unity administrators, Cisco does not recommend that you use the same account to log in to the Unity Administrator as you do to log in to the individual subscriber account.

Unity Call Management Settings

Call management settings relate to the following:

- Call handlers
- Directory handlers
- Caller interview handlers
- Call routing tables
- Restriction tables

Call Handlers

Call handlers can be set up with an auto attendant and menu options that allow callers to reach a subscriber or be transferred to another menu as a result of the options chosen. A call handler can also be configured to take organizational-level messages from callers, at which time the callers hang up, and the appropriate individuals from within the organization either return the calls within a predefined period of time or follow with an appropriate action. Call handlers also provide information that is frequently requested by customers. That information might be related to hours of operations, time-limited promotions, or special events.

Directory Handlers

Directory handler settings facilitate the location of *subscribers* (called *parties*) by callers when they do not have the exact name or extension of the person to be reached. Directory handlers allow for searches and matches of the subscribers based on the caller input options.

Caller Interview Handlers

Interview handlers collect information from callers through a series of questions. If you are the financial officer of an SMB and have had to request by phone certain types of tax deposit coupons from the Internal Revenue Service, you have probably experienced an example of an interview handler, where you supplied answers to a series of questions and, upon conclusion of that interview, you were told that an action (mailing the coupons) would be taken within a specified period of time.

Call Routing Tables

Call routing tables allow for customized call processing as a function of incoming direct calls, forwarded calls, identifiable calls from subscribers, and unidentified subscriber and/ or external calls. An example of an unidentified subscriber call might be a call that originates from a phone in an SMB's lobby or a conference room that is not associated with a specific individual. Call routing tables allow unidentified external or internal calls to be routed to different greetings than the identifiable subscriber calls.

Restriction Tables

Restriction tables allow for the management of call transfers, fax deliveries, and sending of message notifications. For example, through the use of restriction tables, administrators might specify that call transfers and fax deliveries be allowed only to internal extensions.

Unity Network Management Settings

Network settings within the Unity Administrator facilitate the interoperation of Unity with other messaging environments and/or between multiple Unity servers. Within the context of Unity, a *networking option* relates to the method of message delivery from a Unity server to its intended target. Administrators can choose the most appropriate networking option(s), or none at all, as a function of the presence of other messaging systems with which Unity needs to interoperate, the need to access the Unity server(s) by subscribers over the Internet, and the need to exchange messages between multiple servers. Table 9-1 identifies the Unity networking options and their deployment scenarios.

Table 9-1   *Unity Networking Options and Deployment Scenarios*

Networking Option	Deployment Scenario
AMIS	Use to integrate with an analog AMIS-based messaging system. Messages are played by the sending system and recorded on the receiving system following a Dual Tone Multifrequency (DTMF)-based exchange between the two systems, as defined by AMIS.
Bridge	Use to integrate with Octel-based messaging systems. Communication between Unity and the Bridge, which must be installed on a separate and dedicated platform, occurs via TCP/IP. Communication between the Bridge and the Octel system is via the Octel analog networking protocol.
Digital Networking	Use to allow messaging between multiple Unity servers that are connected to a single global directory.
Internet Subscribers	Use to send voice messages over the Internet as e-mails with WAV attachments via the Simple Mail Transfer Protocol (SMTP).
SMTP	Use for messaging over a TCP/IP network between multiple Unity servers with separate voice mail directories.
VPIM	Use to integrate with VPIM-based messaging systems. VPIM uses SMTP and Multipurpose Internet Mail Extension (MIME) protocol.

Unity System Settings and Reports

Numerous system-level settings are available via the Unity Administrator. They relate to languages (phone, TTS, GUI), licensing, schedules, holidays, authentication, integration with a phone system (CallManager, Session Initiation Protocol [SIP] based, circuit switched) and more.

After Unity has been configured with the required system settings, the relevant networking options, and the subscriber and call management settings, administrators can start to generate reports related to subscriber and system activity. Reports can be used for billing purposes, to detect trends in the system usage (level of failed logins, duration of intervals between messages being left and accessed), to create a detailed listing of subscriber profiles, or to assist in actual administration by generating an audit trail of commands used during the Unity Administrator usage.

Personalized Administration via the Cisco Unity Assistant and Inbox

The PCA website that resides on the Unity server is used to access the Cisco Unity Assistant and the Unity Inbox. The Assistant represents an element of Unity administration that allows individual subscribers to personalize their settings, which include message delivery options, greetings, prompts, security codes, and more. The Assistant complements the Unity Administrator in facilitating a distributed Unity administration between the administrator(s) and the subscribers. Access to the Assistant requires an appropriate COS, and the administrator decides which features individual subscribers are able to control through the Assistant.

The Cisco Unity Inbox offers a web-based application for managing voice messages when Unity is not integrated with an e-mail system like Microsoft Exchange. If an SMB uses a messaging system like Novell's GroupWise, for example, the Inbox feature allows voice message notifications to arrive in a subscriber's e-mail inbox. An HTML link is provided from within the notification arriving in the e-mail inbox to launch the Inbox message console and to play the voice mail messages. All of the other voice mail message management functions (create, forward, reply, delete) are available from within the Inbox.

Workforce Optimization Through Unity Solution

Unity from Cisco is a powerful unified messaging solution that can enhance effective internal and external communications between employees, customers, vendors, new prospects, and any other external contacts. Effective communication is key to the successful operation of an SMB as well as optimizing its workforce.

When messages are received in a timely manner, when incoming messages can be prioritized, when an employee can view an aggregate status of all of its messages at a glance, and when employees do not have to invest precious time managing multiple types of inboxes, they have more time for selling, marketing, creating the company's product, and providing the necessary customer service.

The critical success factor in deploying the Unity solution is for the designer and the SMB to recognize the wide spectrum of its capabilities and to apply them judiciously to avoid or to solve existing communication problems. The functions available within the Cisco Unity Administrator offer a clear picture of the capabilities of the Unity solution.

The Cisco IP/TV Solution

From the perspective of market product positioning, the IP/TV solution from Cisco is an element of the Content Networking family of products. Content Networking encompasses Layers 4 through 7 switching and content delivery products, which collectively allow businesses to take advantage of the IP network infrastructure to deliver content that might otherwise require a separate network. The content that is deliverable via IP/TV includes live (streaming) video, video on demand (VoD), scheduled video broadcasts, and collaborative presentations. The Cisco IP video conferencing solution (IP/VC) complements IP/TV video content delivery with a real-time, multiway video exchange capability.

IP/TV in the Context of Unified Communications

Technically, neither the IP/TV nor the IP/VC solution is considered part of unified communications. However, IP/TV is a unified solution for content management, content delivery to the edge of the network, and content routing and switching. And given the relative novelty and the ongoing evolving nature of unified communications, it might be only a matter of time before video messaging goes mainstream and video mail becomes accessible from the same inbox as e-mail or voice mail. At this point, IP/TV and IP/VC can be viewed as part of the broader spectrum of IP communications solutions because they rely on the capabilities of the TCP/IP protocols and the underlying Layers 1 through 3 infrastructure. IP multicasting protocols figure prominently in content networking and, specifically, in the IP/TV solution to conserve network bandwidth.

Deployment Considerations for Movie-Quality Video to the Desktop

Deployment of an IP/TV solution is not a small matter for an SMB or even a large enterprise. Whether or not an SMB will consider an IP/TV solution for its operations depends to a large extent on the organizational priorities, size, geographical distribution of the SMB's facilities, the current state of the IP network infrastructure, and the resources available not only to deploy the solution but to maintain it. The broad categories of deployment considerations are as follows:

- Business motivation for IP/TV
- State of the existing network infrastructure
- Content production and maintenance

Business Motivation for IP/TV

The key factors that drive IP/TV deployment include e-communications (a live broadcast to employees by a company's CEO, for example), online learning (asynchronous, at an individual's own pace from archived content), distance learning (live training events), security-related surveillance, and monitoring of industrial processes.

Assuming the commitment and/or the need on the part of an SMB to engage in those activities, it becomes far more cost-effective to create video events via the IP network than to rely on the more traditional video communications methods via distribution of VHS/Phase

Alternating Line (PAL) tapes or the use of satellite broadcasting. Surveillance and monitoring via IP/TV might also prove to be more cost effective than reliance on the more traditional security systems. Each type of deployment should ideally be subject to return on investment (ROI) analysis before proceeding.

One thing is for sure: An SMB must have a proper IP network infrastructure in place to support IP/TV or IP videoconferencing.

State of the Existing Network Infrastructure

As part of the overall design process, you should view the IP/TV solution as an application that is going to compete for network bandwidth and CPU resources similarly to all of the other business applications on the SMB network. In the context of evaluating whether or not enhancements to the infrastructure are required to deploy an IP/TV or video conferencing application, do the following:

- Check the level of support within the application for the Moving Pictures Experts Group (MPEG) and/or other encoding (compression) standards.
- Identify the likely-to-be used compression bit rates and their impact on the available LAN/WAN bandwidth. Verify CPU requirements for decoding.
- Test the impact of anticipated audio/video streams on any exiting bandwidth-intensive applications.
- Consider the anticipated usage level of the audio/video application.

MPEG Audio/Video Compression Standards

Without compression, the combined video/audio transmission demands on the network could result in bandwidth requirements that are unrealistic for deployment. This is especially true if the transmissions must occur over the WAN, even with today's high-speed LANs and WANs. However, since the late 1980s, experts have tackled the bandwidth consumption problems that would have resulted from uncompressed audio/video streams.

Consider the standards from the MPEG, which is a nickname for a joint workgroup operating under the umbrella of the International Standards Organization (ISO) and the International Electro-technical Commission (IEC). MPEG is associated with a series of standards for audio/video coding in digital format. MPEG is a bit easier to remember than ISO/IEC JTC1 SC29 WG11, meaning workgroup 11 of subcommittee 29 of the Joint Technical Committee 1 under ISO/IEC, which is the actual full name of the group responsible for the MPEG standards.

From the network infrastructure perspective, the critical piece of information for designers is the final bit rate of the coded audio/video stream that must be transmitted over the network. Whereas multiple bit rates can be produced under the MPEG-1 and -2 standards, the MPEG-1 bit rate target is 1.5 Mbps, resulting in VHS video quality, whereas the MPEG-2 standards produce a higher, TV-like quality, but at bit rates of 4 Mbps or more.

Impact of MPEG Streams on WAN/LAN Bandwidth

A T1 line would just barely sustain an MPEG-1 stream at 1.5 Mbps and would choke with an MPEG-2 stream. The MPEG-1 standard can produce higher bit rates than 1.5 Mbps, but the 1.5 Mbps rate is common. A predominantly 100 Mbps switched LAN should not experience bandwidth problems for MPEG-1 or –2 coded transmissions, but a designer still needs to consider the CPU requirements for any software or hardware performing the decoding at the receiving end. CPU power needs to be much higher if the encoding is software based instead of hardware based.

Testing the Impact of IP/TV on Existing Applications

In addition, you need to take into account whether any other bandwidth-intensive applications are going to be running at the same time as IP/TV. Regardless of any theoretical calculations or "looks-good-on-paper" conclusions about the state of the network infrastructure, given the potential impact on the bandwidth and CPU usage through IP/TV, you should include a test plan as an element of the overall design process before you proceed with a full-fledged deployment.

During the testing phase, the solution components and the network should be subjected to maximum stress—for example, continuous scheduled broadcasting combined with all of the other SMB applications that normally operate on the network. And because network usage for SMB's applications tends to be cyclic (certain accounting or reporting functions are performed at less frequent intervals), peak network usage should be taken into consideration during any test deployment.

After the testing phase, an SMB might conclude that usage of IP/TV has no impact at all on any of the existing applications. On the other hand, the SMB might decide that some provisions need to be made to minimize the solution's usage during certain peak times.

Anticipated IP/TV Usage Level

Another element to consider in evaluating the viability of the current network infrastructure to accommodate the IP/TV solution is whether all SMB employees must be able to receive the offered content at their individual workstations. It is entirely possible that only a subset of available workstations need to be equipped for participation in IP/TV. Some of these workstations could be located in common areas (conference/meeting rooms) and be dedicated to IP/TV usage by individuals or groups of employees. Others could be in individual work areas as a function of need for access to IP/TV programming. This consideration translates into the design of the topology for the solution. Workstations participating in IP/TV might need to have higher-capacity links into the network than other workstations or network devices.

Content Production and Maintenance

Another key deployment consideration for a solution like IP/TV is the determination of the volume of content to be delivered and whether provisions have been made for ongoing content production and management. Company meetings and ongoing training events are a natural source of content, but you should recognize that they have a certain life cycle—one that will not be the same for every category of events. Information conveyed through a live broadcast of a company meeting might be of value for a week or two, even before those who missed the initial event know about its contents through other means, without resorting to viewing it on-demand from the archives.

Training events might have a longer life cycle, measured in months, but any SMB in the training business is painfully aware of how often revisions are required in course materials, even if the course titles remain the same. Specific product training is of greatest value in the earlier stages of the product life cycle, before most employees or customers have assimilated the knowledge about the product.

Video Extends Life Cycles

In the life of every business, there are certain momentous events that have ongoing value and validity, especially for new employees joining the company. When these events are captured on video, they will probably have the longest life cycle.

Overall, if the content is going to be stored following a live event for future on-demand access, you should consider as part of the solution's design the duration and location of content storage. An Archive server is the ideal answer, but some IP/TV configurations might not include it as a dedicated appliance. Removing old content according to an established policy might be as important as creating it.

IP/TV Solution Components

The heart of the IP/TV solution is the software that turns an appropriate Intel-based hardware platform with a Windows-based server operating system into a communications solution that offers live, scheduled, or on-demand video. Different IP/TV software components turn the generic hardware platforms into different types of servers.

By viewing servers as performing logical functions instead of as dedicated hardware platforms, a designer should be able to readily recognize that in scenarios with a more limited budget or a lower usage level, multiple server functionalities are possible on the same platform. The key components of the IP/TV solution include the following:

- The IP/TV Control Server
- The IP/TV Broadcast and Archive Servers
- The IP/TV Viewer

The IP/TV Control Server

The IP/TV Control Server is equipped with the IP/TV Content Manager and the IP/TV StreamWatch software. Collectively, the software is responsible for managing scheduled and on-demand programs, moving content between other servers (Broadcast and Archive), informing clients of IP/TV about program schedules (a private TV/cable guide directly to your desktop!), monitoring the Question Manager (a means for submitting questions to presenters in a scheduled broadcast), and several other functions related to preferences and network settings. The main function of Content Manager is to configure the Broadcast and Archive Servers.

The Control Server is available as a preconfigured dedicated appliance (IP/TV 3412), or the software components can be purchased separately and installed on a hardware platform that conforms to the recommended specifications. The preconfigured Starter Server IP/TV 3417 platform offers the combined, albeit limited, capabilities of a Control and a Broadcast Server. It's applicable in smaller IP/TV deployments or for SMBs that are evaluating the solution's capabilities and how it can integrate with their business operations.

The IP/TV Broadcast and Archive Servers

Cisco offers a series of Broadcast Servers that are equipped with the IP/TV Server software. The Broadcast Servers differ from one another in the capabilities and/or the number of video capture cards that are installed, as well as the processing power, memory, and storage capacities of their hardware platforms. The hardware platforms range from a single- to multi-CPU units, with the memory expandable to 1 GB, storage capacities in excess of 100 GB, and multiple network interface cards (NICs) for network connectivity.

The video capture cards differ in terms of the audio/video inputs that they accept, the encoding standards that they support (MPEG-1, -2, -4, H.261), the number of streams that they can simultaneously encode and deliver (up to eight using the 3.5 software version and select hardware platforms), and the resolution of the images that they capture. The image source for a Broadcast Server can be an analog video device or a digital file. The analog video sources include VCRs, cable or satellite feeds, and video cameras. Image resolution is defined in terms of the horizontal and vertical number of pixels, and it is often expressed numerically, together with a number of frames per second (fps) in the format *NNN* × *NNN* × *NN*, where N represents a number—for example, 704 × 480 × 30.

NOTE   Although it might seem like higher resolutions would result in higher bandwidth requirements, the encoding bit rate is actually what determines the amount of bandwidth that will be consumed during the transmission of the encoded audio/video stream (a program) over the network and/or how large the digital file will be for further scheduled or on-demand use.

D1 is a resolution standard that is used in defining the capability of a video capture card. D1 is often preceded by adjectives like *full* or *half*, or by numbers that reflect some portion of it (2/3, 1/4). Full D1 (FD1) has a specific meaning of 720 × 480 pixels (horizontal × vertical) in the context of National Television Standards Committee (NTSC) systems. FD1 means 720 × 576 pixels in the PAL systems. NTSC systems are in use throughout North America, parts of South America, and Japan. PAL is dominant in Europe.

Because the number of frames per second in NTSC and PAL systems varies from 29.97 (effectively 30) for NTSC and 25 for PAL, the volume of data that is generated for encoding at FD1 resolution by the two systems is effectively identical ($720 \times 480 \times 30 = 720 \times 576 \times 25 = 10,368,000$). For the sake of mathematical purists, it is understood that 29.97 is not equal to 30, but, from the network design and bandwidth calculations perspective, those numbers are the same, thus making the amount of data produced at FD1 resolutions the same in both NTSC and PAL systems.

Half D1 reduces the number of horizontal pixels by half to 360×480 for NTSC and 360×576 for PAL. In practice, on video capture card specifications, a *cropped D1* is often used to mean an FD1. When an FD1 references resolutions of 704×480 for NTSC and 704×576 for PAL, consider that the cropped D1 might be posing as an FD1. A cropped D1 reduces the number of horizontal pixels from 720 to 704. Cropping, however, also applies to resolutions other than D1.

Given that the encoding bit rate, not the resolution, directly affects the bandwidth usage, understanding resolution standards and the preceding numbers is not as important in the bandwidth calculations as recognizing that the higher the resolution, the better the image quality. When deploying an IP/TV solution, image quality should be a design consideration because different levels of image quality might be applicable for different applications.

Keep in mind, however, the practical coupling that exists between a higher image quality (resulting from a higher resolution) and the encoding bit rate. Higher resolution video transmissions typically use higher encoding bit rates. The implication is that higher bit rates are also associated with better image quality and larger file sizes for stored images, not just higher bandwidth usage. In the final analysis, a designer and an SMB considering IP/TV deployment need to come to grips with the fact that image quality is a subjective matter. However, there are guidelines to help with the subjectivity. For example, an MPEG-2 FD1 stream is of higher quality than an MPEG-1 HD1 stream. Table 9-2 summarizes the combined characteristics of the Broadcast Servers that are available for implementing an IP/TV solution.

Table 9-2 *IP/TV Broadcast Server Characteristics*

Broadcast Server Characteristic Description	Characteristics Values
Model	3425, 3425A, 3426, 3427-C1, 3427-C2, 3427-C3, 3432
Video capture cards	1-port and multiport Winnov, Optibase MovieMaker
Supported codecs	MPEG-1, MPEG-2, MPEG-4, H.261
Supported video resolutions	FD1, HD1, Common Intermediate Format (CIF), Quarter CIF (QCIF)
Supported video inputs	Composite and S-video for both NTSC and PAL systems
Number of possible streams	Up to 8 using IP/TV version 3.5 on higher-end servers
Number of video cards per server	1 to 5

The 3432 model has the IP/TV Server software installed on it but is considered an Archive Server because it comes with a larger storage capacity. The spectrum of the IP/TV solution Broadcast Servers' capabilities, as reflected in Table 9-2, accommodates a wide range of business requirements. The high degree of configuration granularity, which also implies a high degree of scalability, makes the solution viable for SMBs and larger enterprises alike.

After you identify the solution-specific user requirements (live broadcasts, prerecorded scheduled replays, VoD capability, the number of simultaneous streams, image quality), you need to match the requirements with the appropriate server model, ensure that an adequate IP infrastructure is in place, and decide how the content will be produced and managed. Then, of course, you need to address the budget, implementation, and training requirements as part of the overall design process, as discussed in Chapter 1, "Effective Networking Solution Design Process."

The IP/TV Viewer

The IP/TV Viewer allows user workstations to receive video transmissions from the Broadcast Servers. It runs as a standalone application, a browser-activated helper application, or a browser plug-in. IP/TV version 3.5 also allows Apple QuickTime software as a client application. Always check the latest version requirements between different components of a solution, unless it is purchased as a complete turnkey system.

The Viewer receives information from the Content Manager about the scheduled and available on-demand programs. The Viewer allows users to subscribe to the scheduled events or to play an on-demand program at a specified time. The Viewer also allows for browsing among all of the currently running programs. Anyone able to flip through the cable or satellite TV channels should be well prepared for working with the Cisco IP/TV Viewer. The Viewer is supported on Windows-based platforms, including Windows 98, 2000, and XP.

Workforce Optimization Through IP/TV

Consider what the IP/TV application has to offer to an SMB's employees or customers: live broadcasts, scheduled or on-demand viewing of prerecorded events, and synchronized presentations. In addition, you can deploy IP/TV in monitoring or surveillance mode. These offerings readily translate into corporate communications and distance learning that can significantly reduce time-consuming and costly travel requirements. Easy access to educational material and more personalized company communications without having to engage in long-distance travel are factors that can enhance employee morale and optimize productivity. The final result can be an improved bottom line—not just through direct cost savings but also reflected in a more optimal use of employees' time.

The Value of an Intranet in an SMB Environment

One of the fundamental means of communication that should not be overlooked in any SMB environment is the use of an intranet for internal company administration. The intranet can be as simple or as sophisticated as the web designer and business administrators choose to make it, but if it's going to be effective and used by employees, it has to be easy to navigate, understandable, and routinely updated (not once every six months, but more like daily or even several times a day).

In contrast to any external websites an SMB has, the intranet is intended for internal use and consumption only. Provided that proper security measures have been implemented, the intranet can be used for what might be considered confidential information to the outside world. Intranet uses include the following:

- Human resources services and announcements
- IT help desk support

Human Resources Services and Announcements

The human resources (HR) department can take advantage of an intranet in many ways. Any HR form that employees need to fill out could be posted on the intranet in Portable Document Format (PDF) for easy downloading and printing. Posting such forms online would prevent the problem of the HR department running out of printed copies of certain forms—a surprisingly common occurrence—and having to track down those forms someplace on a local hard disk to be printed or perhaps e-mailed later to an employee. In addition, HR is likely to have many announcements that, instead of just being tacked to bulletin boards, could be posted to the intranet. (However, some announcements might have to be put on bulletin boards due to legal requirements.)

Announcements could include company policies, press releases, or job openings that are being made available to employees before being advertised externally. Enrollment into benefits plans or even employee address changes could all be handled through the intranet and possibly even be integrated with internal databases. Similar to HR, any other department or area of an SMB's operations can readily benefit from the effective use of the intranet, provided that an effective mechanism (that is, trained personnel) has been established to keep the intranet regularly updated.

IT Help Desk Support

An intranet-based IT help desk might include an interactive web page that solicits information about problems in a more rigorous manner than if users simply sent a freeform e-mail to a network administrator stating that something on the network is not working. The required answers solicited through an intranet-based input screen are still forwarded to a network administrator via an e-mail message, but the e-mail now contains the specific information that an administrator needs to tackle the problem more effectively.

Network administrators might also choose to post a series of answers to the most frequently asked questions (FAQs) or the most frequent problems that arise in an SMB's IT environment. Because relationships often tend to be strained between the overworked IT support staff and the other employees of an SMB, the IT staff could use the intranet to their advantage to provide updates about upcoming upgrades or changes to the network, to post mini-tutorials on various aspects of applications and/or networking solutions use, and perhaps even to offer an occasional humorous insight into what life is like in the IT department.

Because the key to the effective use of the intranet by IT, HR, or any other department is keeping it updated, resources need to be allocated for that purpose. The good news is that in today's work environments, the level of computer knowledge that most SMB employees (not just IT staff) need to function effectively is quite high. Expanding that knowledge for a select few with the basic skills of web design might prove to be fairly easy and, at the same time, might be a valuable investment for an SMB to enhance its internal operations through the use of the intranet.

Summary

The trend toward unified communications is fueled by the proliferation of communication devices with their own unique interfaces and means of receiving and storing messages. Another force that drives the development of unified communications solutions is the need for people to be productive and effective, regardless of their location and what communication devices are available to them.

A key element of any unified communications solution is a UMS. The Cisco Unity solution represents a UMS that is part of a comprehensive suite of IP communications solutions. Unity offers intelligent voice messaging, allows e-mail, voice mail, and faxes to be viewed from a single inbox, and facilitates distributed administration between the subscribers and the Unity administrator. Unity integrates with numerous phone systems and includes networking options for integration with other voice mail messaging systems as well.

The Cisco IP/TV solution delivers live and prerecorded (scheduled and on-demand) events to the user's desktop. High granularity in IP/TV configuration makes it viable for a wide spectrum of SMBs. Combined with Unity from Cisco, both solutions have a significant potential for enhancing employees' productivity. SMBs should be mindful of the value of the intranet for enhancing business administration.

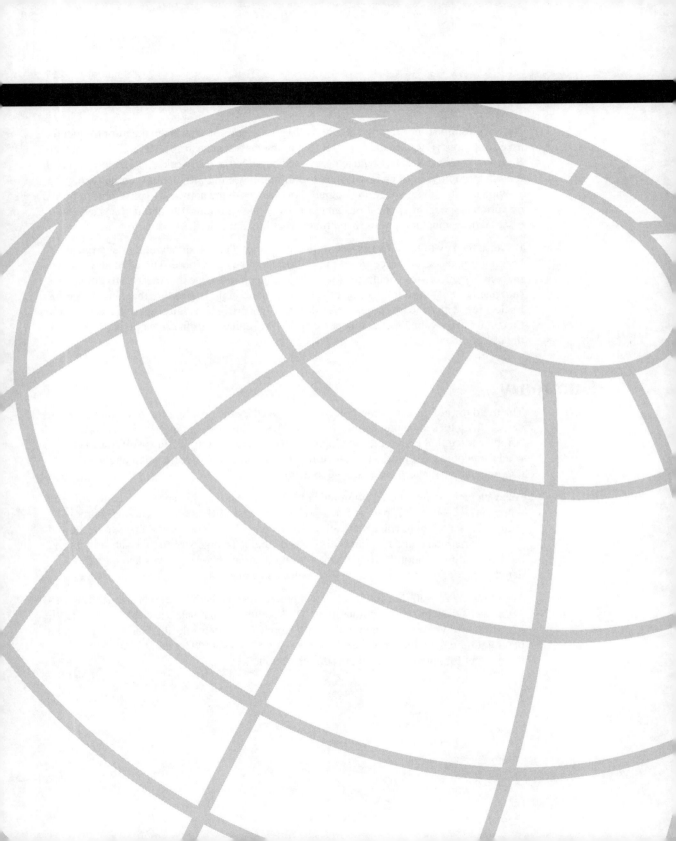

CHAPTER 10

Front and Back Office Integration Solutions

A strategy for the integration of the front and back office applications represents the culmination of the networking solutions discussed in the preceding chapters. The front office applications should allow SMBs to practice better customer relationship management (CRM) after they are integrated effectively with the back office applications that are often viewed as part of the enterprise resource planning (ERP) system. (Remember, CRM is a business strategy and philosophy, not just technology!)

Imagine the routine task of placing an order via a company's website. At some point in the process, a screen pops up and presents additional items that might be of interest to you, based on the item that you ordered. Later, due to your order total exceeding a certain hefty monetary value, another screen offers an automatic promotion: a special discount for an item that is overstocked.

The preceding scenarios represent classic examples of front/back office integration where the typical front/back office applications (order placement and inventory control, respectively) interact in real time to enhance your experience and, in all likelihood, the SMB's bottom line. In the back of your mind, think of all of the underlying networking technologies and solutions, as well as application integration techniques, that have combined to give you that integrated purchasing experience.

The importance that SMBs place on having an integrated applications environment, which can manifest via several techniques, further reinforces the concept of the networking infrastructure as a utility, as discussed in Chapter 3, "Network Infrastructure Requirements for Effective Solutions Implementation." While the network utility becomes more and more robust and transparent to the end users (not unlike electricity or plumbing), it simultaneously facilitates deployment of varied, complex, competitive, highly integrated, and creative applications.

Applications integration has many guises. It occurs as a process via Enterprise Applications Integration (EAI) tools or some old-fashioned programming (coding) if discrete but noncommunicating modules either from a single or multiple vendors already exist and need to be preserved. The latter integration method also applies for SMBs with in-house developed isolated systems. Applications integration could be a design decision to deploy from scratch an integrated suite from a single vendor that combines elements of what traditionally might be a CRM, an ERP, or newer business applications. A single vendor suite deployment might be a reaction to the previous scenarios of homegrown or too many disjointed applications that no longer meet business needs and simply need to be replaced.

Integration can also mean the addition (seamless or not) of new modules to an existing environment that is already based on open standards, protocols, and platforms. Variants and combinations of the preceding integration techniques apply. What SMBs can count on with regard to the applications environment is that the applications will continue to evolve and become more feature rich, while at the same time preserving their core functions that relate to business fundamentals. The implication is that the process of applications integration is continuous.

Business applications evolve as a function of various economic and political forces, including economic downturns and upswings, globalization, and free trade. The results are competitive pressures for greater productivity and innovation as well as the creation of new workforce models (distributed workforce, telecommuting, flexible work hours, flatter organizational structures). These conditions, in turn, demand responsive applications.

In the course of business operations of a typical SMB that is pummeled by forces beyond its control, changes to applications and their subsequent integration and/or reintegration are not necessarily a singular event with a clearly defined beginning and end. Application integration can become a continuous process with periods of greater activity and subsequent lulls between them.

The surges in the integration activity occur when incompatibilities are discovered due to vendors upgrading their software with new features or when new and disruptive economic and political trends emerge in the marketplace to force changes in business operations. The changes could stem from new laws and regulations that SMBs are required to comply with, new enabling technologies that become widespread, or new markets for SMB's products and services.

Yet, having an integrated applications environment can provide a 360-degree view of all the customer interactions and internal business operations, a perspective that facilitates more informed tactical and strategic, real-time business decision making. This all might sound a bit ideal, but you can decide whether it is or not.

Generically, the trend in computing toward integration is real, and the networking solutions discussed thus far clearly reflect that trend. However, applications integration can be difficult, full of pitfalls, and expensive. Also, the technical obstacles to applications integration can easily pale into insignificance when compared to possible employee or management resistance to the cultural and operational changes that must occur within a business for integration projects to work and to create a fast, positive return on investment (ROI).

Getting Past the Jargon

Networking professionals concerned with network topologies, LAN/WAN connectivity options, bandwidth capacities, routing/switching protocols, security, or IP Telephony are painfully aware of a computing frontier that they do not want to explore due to its excruciating diversity and seemingly infinite amount of detail and variation. This vast frontier is the end-user applications and their enabling operating systems, databases, and services.

However, a complete lack of understanding by networking professionals of the applications environment (or by the applications experts of the networking technologies) generally leads to substandard information technology (IT) operations in SMB environments. Integration, by its nature—whether of applications or elements of the network infrastructure, such as routing, switching, and security functions—requires the elimination of boundaries.

Disappearing boundaries force networking professionals to communicate effectively with the applications experts to enable some of the more complex integration deployments to work. Similarly, elimination of boundaries between front and back office requires the understudying of the business processes that go on in both areas. In addition, SMBs should undertake the project of the integration of the front and back office applications with a high degree of commitment, which must span the initial architectural design (business process flow, database structure), the implementation stage, and, finally, the system utilization with any subsequent enhancements or refinements.

Front Office: Concepts and Applications

The concept of *front office* in computing refers to the applications that are facing the customer or that the customer interacts with directly. Setting business strategy and philosophy aside, the front office applications are frequently equated with CRM. The names of front office applications (apps) depend on which software and/or integration vendor is promoting them and are often based on what promoters consider the current age to be. In the e-age, it's eSales, eMarketing, eService, or, generically, eApps. In the age of automation, it's Marketing automation, Customer Service automation, Sales Force automation, or Field Service automation. In the next age, new expressions are bound to emerge.

Front office applications are usually available either as standalone modules for each unique customer contact channel or as integrated suites. The trend toward suites emerged in the 1990s. Although suites are still prevalent, ironically enough, they are giving way to what might be viewed as just the opposite: a trend toward smaller and more specific point applications that are more specialized for different categories of SMBs, even in such generic areas as sales, marketing, or field service. This is an example of the computing environment being subject to cyclic trends!

Collectively, the primary purpose of the front office apps is to enable SMBs to sell their products and services effectively. Marketing might precede the sale, and service will follow it. But without sales, any SMB's days are numbered. At the most fundamental level, the concept of sales equates to taking an order for a product or service. Thus, the classic example of a front office application is order entry.

NOTE	There is not full agreement among applications vendors whether order entry is a front or back office application. For the purpose of the discussion that follows, consider that order entry is an element of the front office, whereas all of the applications supporting the processing of an order through its fulfillment and delivery to the customer are part of the back office.
	You should also note that in some instances, CRM applications are considered part of ERP. In other words, although general classifications like front office, back office, CRM, ERP, or e-business suites are useful, they should not be construed as cast in concrete, and their definitions can vary from one vendor to another. The core issue for designers is to ensure the maximum level of integration between all of the SMB's applications, along with an effective network infrastructure to support them.

An order can be submitted to an SMB for processing via self-service on an e-commerce website, in real time through an interaction with a call center agent, or perhaps even in what might be considered an old-fashioned or a totally novel way, where it arrives via a postal service, courier, fax, e-mail, voice mail, Instant Messenger or a Short Message Service (SMS). Consider these multiple means through which orders can be placed. Websites, call centers, and mailrooms become the interface points between the applications and the customers, whether the customer interacts with the application directly or through an intermediate agent that transfers the customer order information into the application.

At these interface points, the applications solutions facing the customer and the networking solutions providing the necessary and secure infrastructure over which the apps operate must meet and interoperate. These same interface points are where the integration between the front office (effectively a CRM solution, as long as the CRM strategy and philosophy have been adapted) and the back office (elements or all of an ERP solution) also takes place. The ideal model then becomes a fully integrated computing platform (networking, front office, back office) that equips the front office employees with the most effective tools to service the customer base. Better yet, if customers can be satisfied and loyal using self-service, it's another plus for applications integration.

Back Office: Concepts and Applications

Back office refers to the applications that are facing away from the customer, which the customer does not interact with directly. These applications tend to be more numerous than the front office ones and span a spectrum of categories that are related to SMB business types.

Classic back office applications include product design and production, accounting, inventory control (or its more sophisticated successor, the supply chain management [SCM]), human resources, and credit checking. Each SMB sector is bound to have its own unique vertical back office applications pertaining to its line of business.

When all of the back office (and possibly even the front office) applications are integrated to manage the company's resources, the system might end up being referred to as an ERP. However, as alluded to earlier in this chapter, integration seems to be a never-ending process, no matter how integrated the application environment appears at any given point in time. For example, assume that an SMB acquires an integrated mid-range market ERP system that meets 95 percent of the SMB's requirements. This means that some specific and unique applications that are required for the business to function are not included in that particular ERP, thus forcing that SMB into further integration.

NOTE   As *enterprise* denotes in the term *enterprise resource planning (ERP)*, an ERP system is aimed at enterprises. However, the ERP expression is finding its way into the SMB software market as well.

Enterprise Applications Integration Tools

Enterprise Applications Integration (EAI) refers to the planning, methodology, and tools that are used in the process of creating a cohesive applications environment within an enterprise. Think of it as a means toward achieving a unified applications solution, not unlike trends toward unified communications and messaging, as discussed in Chapter 9, "Unified Communications Solutions."

Cohesion or integration could be desirable between new and legacy applications, between applications from different vendors, or between disparate, noncommunicating applications from the same vendor. Generically, the elements of EAI methodology involve the following:

- Development of proprietary resource adapters to establish communication between the applications

- Mapping of data structures, either directly between the applications or to a common model

- Subsequent presentation and/or updating of data and messages throughout the business process or multiple processes that are part of the integration effort

The volume of applications developed over the past several decades is vast and inestimable. They utilize numerous operating systems and varied computing platforms that span mainframes, minicomputers, PCs, and handheld gadgets. These factors have contributed to the development of mostly proprietary solutions in the EAI market.

A proprietary integration solution might be perfectly acceptable in the absence of standards-based approaches. However, the use of a proprietary solution should be a design decision that is accompanied by an understanding of the typical consequences: higher costs and fewer choices in integration vendors. To the benefit of the enterprises and SMBs alike, two standards-based approaches to applications integration have emerged:

- Java 2 Enterprise Edition (J2EE) Connection Architecture (JCA)
- Web Services

J2EE Connection Architecture

J2EE Connection Architecture (JCA) defines a standard architecture that allows J2EE platforms housing Java applications to connect with Enterprise Information Systems (EISes) and, consequently, integrate disparate EISes. In the context of JCA, an EIS represents the information infrastructure for an enterprise, whether it is an ERP system, a legacy database system, or a mainframe transaction processing system. The main architectural components of JCA include resource adapters, system contracts, and the Common Client Interface (CCI).

The resource adapters are software drivers that allow Java applications to connect with an EIS. They are unique to each EIS and plug into the application server. If the Java application server vendors (or in-house developers) support JCA, their products will be able to connect with EISes, provided that the EIS vendors offer an adapter for each of their systems. Effectively, there are one-to-many mappings for EIS and Java application server vendors, which implies lower development costs due to reusability. Naturally, language support for JCA is limited to Java, and a J2EE-compatible application server is required for JCA to operate, which could be viewed as a limitation of the architecture.

Version 1.5 of the JCA specification that was published in late 2003 defines additional system contracts above the connection management, transaction management, and security that were part of original version 1. They include life cycle management, work management, transaction inflow, and message inflow. System contracts are the mechanisms through which the resource adapters interact with a J2EE server. For example, a security contract allows for a secure access to an EIS, whereas a transaction inflow contract allows an imported transaction to be propagated by the resource adapter to the application server.

Conceptually, the purpose of the system contracts is similar to that of CCI. The difference is the vendor target audience. Whereas CCI, which defines a common client application programming interface (API) for accessing EISes, is aimed at larger EIA tools vendors, the resource adapters and system contracts combination is aimed at a wider spectrum of developers.

Web Services

Web Services represents another set of tools for applications integration. The intent behind Web Services is to provide open standards for communication between applications that present context-driven information to their users. Major software vendors are involved in the development of Web Services standards.

A partial definition from the Web Services Architecture Working Group defines a *web service* as "a software system identified by URI whose public interfaces and bindings are described using XML." XML stands for Extensible Markup Language, and Uniform Resource Identifier (URI) is defined in RFC 2396 as "a compact string of characters for identifying an abstract or physical resource." Any Web Services–compliant software system or applications should be able to discover a Web Service interface in another application and subsequently interact with it by exchanging XML messages via the Internet protocols. Sounds simple and promising.

The benefit of Web Services is their platform and programming language independence. The emerging challenge for Web Services, which is causing concern among some developers and industry observers, is the increasing amount of expertise required to use them due to the ever-growing number of standards that fall under the Web Services (WS) umbrella. The standards include WS-Transaction, WS-Security, WS-Trust, WS-Context, WS-Coordination, WS-Federation, and much more. In addition, numerous protocols are included in the XML standard, creating an acronym soup of their own. As the Web Services and XML standards continue to evolve and proliferate, the market will ultimately determine their acceptance and their role in the applications integration arena.

One example of an XML and Web Services–based integration tool is the Universal Applications Network (UAN), developed by Siebel Systems in collaboration with partners and technology vendors. Siebel positions UAN as a standards-based architecture that is used for the development of Business Integration Applications (BIAs) aimed at industry-specific and cross-industry business processes. Cross-industry business processes include Order Management, Customer Lifecycle Management, Sales Management, Partner Relationship Management, and more. Specific industries for which Siebel has developed BIAs include communications, energy, financials, and automotive.

Consider an applications environment in need of integration, either in terms of business processes or a specific industry. Apply to that environment a tool on the order of Siebel's BIAs. The separation between the front and back office aspects of the applications environment tends to disappear because many business processes span both front and back office functions. Thus, clearly understanding the nature of the business operations and being able to define business processes become the first steps in any applications integration effort.

Is Integration for Me?

The answer is "Yes," but I do not expect everyone to agree with it.

The "Yes" is only if SMBs want to have a holistic view of the business that transcends even the concepts of CRMs and ERPs as discrete application categories.

And the "Yes" is only if SMBs understand that they are going to face challenges in the course of any attempt to integrate their applications and, consequently, must have a sufficiently refined business vision and strategy to sustain them through those challenges.

The answer is "Yes" if the SMBs are convinced of the value of benefits resulting from having front and back office applications integrated together.

The reader should be able to readily intuit under what conditions the answer might be "No."

Integration Challenges

The fundamental assumption regarding the applications integration process is that, as was the case with the networking infrastructure, the SMB is not starting from scratch with the option of purchasing a brand-new, fully integrated applications suite that perfectly meets the business requirements. That situation would be ideal but rarely if ever happens. Even when the opportunity exists at the time a business begins its operation, don't expect to find an applications suite installed and ready to roll that addresses all of the aspects of business operations.

I have faced the challenge of working with startups and mature businesses alike where sales and marketing were promising potential and current customers a pie in the sky that could not be delivered technically, and only a verbal communication existed between those areas. Even the technical service area responsible for the delivery of the product lacked integration between aspects of its operation.

The reality of the applications environment is that the need for application integration becomes pronounced only after the business has been in operation for a period of time, with a few management and IT personnel changes in the process. Although you might call it lack of foresight or a reactive approach, it is a fact of life that is well understood by IT consultants in the SMB arena.

Thus, creating and subsequently maintaining an integrated applications environment is going to be challenging. In addition, if an SMB subscribes to the previously stated observation that applications integration is an ongoing process rather than a singular event, the challenge might loom even larger. There must be a benefit to overcoming the challenge; otherwise, why would an SMB want to engage in the process? As is the case when implementing a CRM or an ERP solution, an integrated applications environment needs to be driven by a set of clearly defined goals and be an element of the overall business strategy.

Consider the following factors that can contribute to the challenge of wanting to integrate a disjointed applications environment:

- **Defining the nature of business operations**—Creative entrepreneurs who start a wide range of businesses might develop complex operations that often, and especially in the initial stages of the business, center on themselves or a few of their associates. In effect, these individuals become the business applications and data repositories, compensating for any software shortcomings.

  Before any talk about applications integration (or bringing in new applications) in those kinds of scenarios, business processes need to be clearly understood and, preferably, documented before proceeding. Here's the rub. Clearly defining business processes and unwrapping them from around individuals is a challenging process that might be difficult to achieve if undertaken internally. Time constraints, lack of proper internal expertise, and unwillingness of the key players to participate in the process are key factors. The process might prove expensive if outsourced. Other scenarios where business processes become synonymous with individuals are situations in which employees enjoy extensive tenure in their positions. Any attempt at innovation, greater efficiency, or streamlining is met with heavy-handed tactics due to seniority.

- **The right external expertise or internal resource allocation**—Selection of the appropriate expertise for an integration project is critical. If the project is to be outsourced, you should select vendors based on such factors as previous experience, level of expertise, trust, and cost. If applications integration is undertaken internally, the challenge might be to sustain the internal resources' level of commitment to the project if the project begins to run over the time allotted and if deliverables are lacking—conditions that often occur.

- **Duration**—Determining the duration of an applications integration project is an estimate at best. As such, SMBs need to be prepared for unexpected delays and disruptions to business operations due to glitches and bugs that inevitably creep into any programming effort or merging of various databases. Applications integration for an SMB can be thought of as a miniature version of a business merger integration, where data structures from different systems need to be understood and integrated into a single database.

- **Cost and complexity**—Given the complexity of integration projects, determining their cost is a tricky business. If the project is outsourced at a fixed cost, and the integration company starts running into problems, some of the choices that an SMB faces are to pick up the extra tab, litigate, or end up with an initial bill and an unfinished project. None of these options is pleasant. Reaching some kind of a reasonable compromise with the integrator is probably the best solution.

  If the project is undertaken internally, the developers might not have the discipline to come up with the actual projected cost of the project. This in turn might lead to delays or an eventual abandonment of the project if its impact begins to be felt too much, through the SMB's lack of attention to other aspects of the business operations.

If a networking professional wonders why a prospective SMB is not happy with its overall IT environment, although its networking infrastructure might be operating seamlessly, look no further than the nature of the applications. The applications environment can ultimately make or break an SMB. Applications integration becomes even more challenging in situations in which the SMB relies either on completely in-house developed software or on applications that have been modified to meet the SMB's unique needs. In the case of the latter, the issue becomes what to do if the vendor creates new versions of the software that must have the same changes made to them. In the case of the former, integration might actually necessitate the replacement of all of the applications, meaning that the integration becomes an applications conversion.

The Case for Integration

The case for integration is compelling. Even with all the potential integration challenges, SMBs always need to consider the alternative of doing nothing proactive about their applications environment and addressing their emerging business needs by managing the applications in a haphazard, reactive manner.

The integration challenges might loom large at first, but when understood and placed in the context of the overall business strategy, they should not stand in the way of any SMB looking at maintaining and expanding a successful business. Not understanding the challenges that lie ahead before proceeding with an integration project is probably the major reason for SMBs' discontent with their applications environment and their unrealized expectations from integration projects to improve it. Consider the benefits of applications integration:

- **Enhanced CRM**—When front and back office applications are integrated to support common business processes, the customers and the SMBs benefit. Such advantages might include being able to do a credit check or having shipping details available at the time an order is placed, allowing partners access to leads from the SMB's contacts databases, or offering different interactive sessions via a company's website as a function of a customer type. Whatever the benefits, they create an impression of more personalized and customized service. For SMBs that offer multiple products or services applications, integration might offer a single rather than a segmented view of the customer. For example, if the customer happens to also be a vendor of a diversified, multiservice, multiproduct SMB, that fact might be lost in a nonintegrated applications environment. In turn, interacting with a customer without a complete customer profile detracts from CRM.

- **Complete view of the business**—Business intelligence and/or decision support via analytics tools are at work here. When all of the applications access and update a common database, reporting, detection of trends, and scenario simulation are much more possible than if data is scattered across multiple and incompatible databases.

- **Business process optimization**—Integration can reduce labor costs due to elimination of duplicate data entry, enhance product development cycles by communicating schedule or materials changes to procurement, or keep production going with smaller inventories due to tighter coupling between those processes and responsiveness of inventory to a revved up or a slower production schedule.

- **The bottom line**—Enhanced CRM, better view of the business, and optimized processes should readily translate into an improved bottom line.

The Case Against Integration

The case against integration can also be compelling, especially if the integration process is not understood. The challenges have already been outlined: duration, cost, clearly defining business processes, and selecting the right expertise. All of these require allocation of business resources to the integration process. But consider the implications of having disjointed islands of automation, especially if the business is poised to grow:

- **Lack of scalability**—Increase in the volume of customer transactions or any type of business activity (production, new product design and development, accounting) will strain operations with manual interfaces between business processes. Increase in the volume of duplicate data entry, potentially inconsistent data, and shortages or overstocking of inventory all strain the ability of the business to grow and to service its customers.

- **Increased internal and external miscommunication**—When customers and/or partners must interact with SMB employees who lack the complete picture of a customer or partner, chances for miscommunication and duplicate communication increase drastically. Internal communications between employees are also likely when manual reports, memos, or e-mails have to be used to communicate information that should be available directly from an integrated database. That information might be related to the logistics and scheduling associated with product development, inventory, or promotions.

- **Loss of customer loyalty**—The end result of the lack of scalability and internal and external miscommunications is the loss of customer loyalty, especially given the competitive nature of the global marketplace.

It should not be surprising that a case against integration quickly adds more reasons to engage in the integration process. Engaging in an integration project, even if initially only at the level of defining the requirements, lays the groundwork for any programming, new software, or even the replacement of the entire system by the integrators.

The Integrators

Applications integration represents a large and mature industry. Those engaged in the integration process scale from micro businesses on the order of an individual IT consultant to computer industry giants like IBM, and everything in between.

Software vendors that offer consulting services are probably capable of some degree of applications integration. If not, they work with partners who offer such services. The integrators that are outlined next include a specific firm, a generic profile of an IT consultant with programming skills, and even SMB employees who, through their skills and knowledge, can compensate manually for the lack of integration while at the same time laying the groundwork for eventually bringing automated integration to fruition.

The Synergex Solutions

Synergex is an example of an integration solutions provider for SMBs that has partnered with Cisco at the hardware provider level. The benefit to SMBs from the partnership is via an end-to-end business solution that delivers a scalable network infrastructure and an integrated applications environment.

Synergex also partners with platform and software vendors. OS vendors fall into the category of platform partners. Offerings from the software partners include CRM solutions from SalesLogix and Salesforce.com, analytics tools from VisualSmart, and integration design tools from DataJunction. Through the combination of varying partnerships and its professional services, Synergex delivers integration capabilities to the SMB market in industries such as health care, banking, manufacturing, and distribution.

A key integration offering from Synergex to software vendors and SMB end users alike is the *integration enabling* of applications via tools such as Web Services, integration adapters, and standard APIs. The implication for software vendors from having their applications integration enabled is likely a greater salability of their products. Assuming a scenario in which, over a period of time, an SMB purchases applications that are standards-based integration enabled, the implication for the SMB is the ability to maintain an integrated applications environment, even if the SMB does not purchase an integrated applications suite to begin with. And given the growing appeal of point applications and the need for responsiveness to change in business environments, integration-enabled point apps might become the wave of the future.

IT Consultants with Programming Skills

Individual IT consultants with programming and business management skills who operate on a contract basis could be the perfect answer for smaller SMB integration projects. But the scope of the project needs to be defined before any programming is performed, and it must be considered appropriate for a single individual to undertake it. Otherwise, results might be a long way off.

In the course of defining the integration requirements, a knowledgeable consultant might easily uncover software features and capabilities that are not even being used (although they could be beneficial to the business), standards-based integration options that already exist in the applications but that the SMB is not aware of (the integration project could turn out to be easy!), and, perhaps, the need for a few manual data transfer procedures more than for extensive programming.

When an IT consultant places the needs of the SMB before any preconceived idea of what must be done, the outcome, although it can be beneficial to both parties, is not necessarily actual integration programming. Instead, training, software upgrades or replacement, additional software, or simply change in business procedures could ease or eliminate any perceived lack of applications integration.

In-House Analyst

One type of an integrator that SMBs should not overlook is an employee who creates manual interfaces within business processes where none exist due to lack of applications integration. Such an individual might perform the following functions:

1 Collect data from multiple sources and different structures. (Most applications have a data export function.)

2 Map all of the data to a common format. (Use any editing tools available.)

3 Transfer the data into a single database (preferably relational) that can be queried via numerous standard as well as ad hoc reports.

4 Use his or her analytical skills (human intelligence as opposed to analytics tools) to detect trends and discrepancies.

5 Provide the SMB management with distilled, succinct information about business activities.

Naturally, the type of integration outlined in the preceding steps has its drawbacks in terms of scalability, especially when business operations increase and become more complex. Also, this example deals only with analytics. There is also the cost of keeping this kind of an employee on board. But the issue of cost is relative and needs to be looked at in the context of other alternatives.

From the CRM perspective, this type of integration might appear completely useless. But consider other functions that this kind of an individual could perform. If access to product inventory is simply not available to employees who are facing the customer in service or marketing, a *manual interface* of creating a daily inventory report in the form of a text file that is shared over the network can still be of assistance to the front office folks when dealing with their customers.

Items that are not available and their expected arrival dates could also be reported on in this manner if, for various reasons, some employees who interact with the customers cannot have access to the real-time inventory database. There is room in those kinds of SMB scenarios for additional static reports that might be viewed as useful by different groups of employees within a business. In fact, developing those kinds of procedures could prove invaluable if an SMB later decides to implement a more automated integration solution.

Summary

Integration of the front and back office applications enhances CRM, optimizes business processes, and affords SMBs a more complete view of the business operations and customers. Challenges to integration relate to cost, duration, selection of expertise, and the need to allocate resources to clearly define business operations. Lack of integration causes poor scalability, miscommunication, and loss of customer loyalty.

Application integrators rely on proprietary EIA tools or standards-based JCA and Web Services. Partial integration via manual data transfer procedures is usually better than none. Integrators span the spectrum from individual consultants to companies like IBM. Cisco partners with many of the integration vendors at the hardware or networking technology levels. Networking solutions described in the preceding chapters are foundational to a solid integrated applications environment.

The Future of SMB Networking

The future of SMB networking is bright but challenging. The challenges stem from the growing maturity of networking technologies and the pervasiveness of network installations. Maturing technologies imply that the baggage of their youthful incarnations is often still found at SMB sites and must be dealt with. The spectrum of the networking equipment capabilities, software, and standards versions continues to widen. Compatibility and interoperability challenges follow. Maturing technologies also imply an increasingly crowded and competitive vendor marketplace, while the pervasiveness of network installations implies that widespread changes to the network infrastructure could be very disruptive.

What is the bright side of this challenging equation? SMBs and network designers alike are forced to develop new skill sets, which opens up new jobs and new opportunities. They must learn to navigate judiciously through the ever-larger maze of networking options and choices to come up with the correct and applicable solutions. They must learn to plan upgrades and changes with a new degree of refinement that minimizes disruption to business operations.

They must also recognize that it is their responsibility to spur vendors to new heights of creativity and innovation in the networking field. Vendors, in turn, have opportunities to create increasingly integrated and capable network devices, to continue to simplify the process of network solutions configuration, and to offer their customers upgrade paths that allow their networks to remain responsive and up to date rather than continually becoming outdated.

Do SMBs face any other network-related challenges? Talk to any SMB executives or their IT personnel! Viruses, worms, spam, and spyware surface quickly as thorny network issues. These scourges are still usually addressed at the applications level. Yet it is the networks themselves that allow them to propagate and to create time-consuming and costly distractions for multitudes of users and IT staff. Laws of the lands might try to stem this disruptive tide, but they will not eliminate it.

On the bright side again, networking vendors have an opportunity to push the end-user requirements of nondisruptive and secure desktops to the lower network layers. The slimy, disruptive swarm of viruses, worms, and spam should not even be given a chance to reach the end user. I am looking forward to a truly personal computer that allows me to network with anyone at any time and that clearly informs me about the nature and source of any communication that is coming my way. I daresay that I am speaking on behalf of many SMBs.

BIBLIOGRAPHY

Recommended Further Reading

Bellamy, John C. *Digital Telephony*, 3rd ed. New York: John Wiley & Sons, 2000.

Clark, Kennedy, and Kevin Hamilton. *Cisco LAN Switching*. Indianapolis: Cisco Press, 1999.

Green, James Harry. *The Irwin Handbook of Telecommunications Management*. New York: McGraw-Hill, 2001.

Keagy, Scott. *Integrating Voice and Data Networks*. Indianapolis: Cisco Press, 2000.

TIA/EIA Building Telecommunications Wiring Standards. Englewood, CO: Global Engineering Documents, 1996.

Recommended Websites

Cisco Systems, Inc.: http://www.cisco.com

Hewlett-Packard: http://www.hp.com

Information Sciences Institute, University of Southern California: http://www.isi.edu

Institute of Electrical and Electronic Engineers: http://www.ieee.org

International Telecommunication Union: http://www.itu.int

Internet Engineering Task Force: http://www.ietf.org

Network Appliance, Inc.: http://www.netapp.com

SAP: http://www.sap.com

Siebel Systems: http://www.siebel.com

Synergex: http://www.synergex.com

World Wide Web Consortium: http://www.w3.org

E

CISCO SYSTEMS

Cisco Press

Your **first-step** to networking starts here

Are you new to the world of networking? Whether you are taking your first networking class or simply need a better understanding of a specific technology to choose your next networking class, Cisco Press First-Step books are right for you.

➤ **No experience required**

➤ **Includes clear and easily understood explanations**

➤ **Makes learning easy**

Check out each of these First-Step books that cover key networking topics

- **Computer Networking First-Step**
  ISBN: 1-58720-101-1

- **LAN Switching First-Step**
  ISBN: 1-58720-100-3

- **Network Security First-Step**
  ISBN: 1-58720-099-6

- **Routing First-Step**
  ISBN: 1-58720-122-4
  September 2004

- **TCP/IP First-Step**
  ISBN: 1-58720-108-9
  October 2004

- **Wireless Networks First-Step**
  ISBN: 1-58720-111-9

Visit **www.ciscopress.com/firststep** to learn more.

What's your next step?

Eager to dig deeper into networking technology? Cisco Press has the books that will help you move to the next level. Learn more at **www.ciscopress.com/series**.

ciscopress.com

Learning begins with a first step.

CISCO SYSTEMS

Cisco Press

NETWORK BUSINESS SERIES

JUSTIFY YOUR NETWORK INVESTMENT

Network Business books deliver:

A clear and approachable writing style—no in-depth technical knowledge required

Technology overviews that promote informed decision making

Implementation scenarios that outline various business models

ROI and TCO metrics that assist with complex technology decisions

Interviews with industry leaders that provide real-world insights on technology decisions

Detailed case studies that showcase relevant technologies

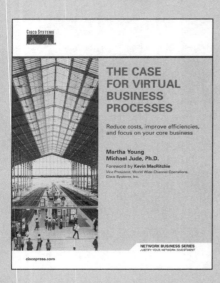

Look for Network Business titles at your favorite bookseller

The Case for Virtual Business Processes
Young / Jude • ISBN: 1-58720-087-2

IP Telephony Unveiled
Brown • ISBN: 1-58720-075-9

Planet Broadband
Yassini • ISBN: 1-58720-090-2

Power Up Your Small-Medium Business
Aber • ISBN: 1-58705-135-4

The Road to IP Telephony
Carhee • ISBN: 1-58720-088-0

Taking Charge of Your VoIP Project
Walker / Hicks • ISBN: 1-58720-092-9

The Business Case for E-Learning
Kelly / Nanjiani • ISBN: 1-58720-086-4 • Coming Soon

Network Business Series. **Justify Your Network Investment.**

Visit **www.ciscopress.com/series** for details about the Network Business series and a complete list of titles.

Cisco Press

FUNDAMENTALS SERIES
ESSENTIAL EXPLANATIONS AND SOLUTIONS

When you need an authoritative introduction to a key networking topic, **reach for a Cisco Press Fundamentals book**. Learn about network topologies, deployment concepts, protocols, and management techniques and **master essential networking concepts and solutions**.

Look for Fundamentals titles at your favorite bookseller

802.11 Wireless LAN Fundamentals
ISBN: 1-58705-077-3

**Cisco CallManager Fundamentals:
A Cisco AVVID Solution**
ISBN: 1-58705-008-0

Data Center Fundamentals
ISBN: 1-58705-023-4

IP Addressing Fundamentals
ISBN: 1-58705-067-6

IP Routing Fundamentals
ISBN: 1-57870-071-X

Voice over IP Fundamentals
ISBN: 1-57870-168-6

Visit **www.ciscopress.com/series** for details about the Fundamentals series and a complete list of titles.

Learning is serious business.
Invest wisely.

CISCO SYSTEMS

Cisco Press

CISCO CERTIFICATION SELF-STUDY
#1 BEST-SELLING TITLES FROM CCNA® TO CCIE®

Look for Cisco Press Certification Self-Study resources at your favorite bookseller

Learn the test topics with **Self-Study Guides**

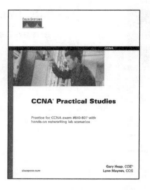

Gain hands-on experience with **Practical Studies** books

Prepare for the exam with **Exam Certification Guides**

Practice testing skills and build confidence with **Flash Cards and Exam Practice Packs**

Visit **www.ciscopress.com/series** to learn more about the Certification Self-Study product family and associated series.

Learning is serious business.
Invest wisely.

CISCO SYSTEMS

Cisco Press

CCIE PROFESSIONAL DEVELOPMENT
RESOURCES FROM EXPERTS IN THE FIELD

CCIE Professional Development books are the **ultimate resource for advanced networking professionals**, providing practical insights for effective network design, deployment, and management. **Expert perspectives, in-depth technology discussions, and real-world implementation advice** also make these titles essential for anyone preparing for a CCIE® exam.

CISCO SYSTEMS

CCIE® Professional Development
Routing TCP/IP
Volume I

A detailed examination of interior routing protocols

ciscopress.com   Jeff Doyle, CCIE No. 1919

Look for CCIE Professional Development titles at your favorite bookseller

Cisco BGP-4 Command and Configuration Handbook
ISBN: 1-58705-017-X

Cisco LAN Switching
ISBN: 1-57870-094-9

Cisco OSPF Command and Configuration Handbook
ISBN: 1-58705-071-4

Inside Cisco IOS Software Architecture
ISBN: 1-57870-181-3

Network Security Principles and Practices
ISBN: 1-58705-025-0

Routing TCP/IP, Volume I
ISBN: 1-57870-041-8

Routing TCP/IP, Volume II
ISBN: 1-57870-089-2

Troubleshooting IP Routing Protocols
ISBN: 1-58705-019-6

Troubleshooting Remote Access Networks
ISBN: 1-58705-076-5

Visit **www.ciscopress.com/series** for details about the CCIE Professional Development series and a complete list of titles.

Learning is serious business.
Invest wisely.

SEARCH THOUSANDS OF BOOKS FROM LEADING PUBLISHERS

Safari® Bookshelf is a searchable electronic reference library for IT professionals that features more than 2,000 titles from technical publishers, including Cisco Press.

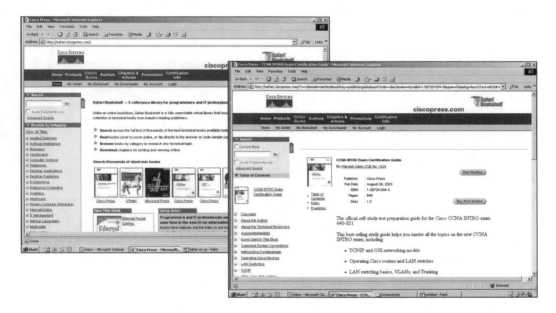

With Safari Bookshelf you can

- **Search** the full text of thousands of technical books, including more than 70 Cisco Press titles from authors such as Wendell Odom, Jeff Doyle, Bill Parkhurst, Sam Halabi, and Karl Solie.

- **Read** the books on My Bookshelf from cover to cover, or just flip to the information you need.

- **Browse** books by category to research any technical topic.

- **Download** chapters for printing and viewing offline.

With a customized library, you'll have access to your books when and where you need them—and all you need is a user name and password.

CISCO SYSTEMS

Cisco Press

3 STEPS TO LEARNING

STEP 1   **STEP 2**   **STEP 3**

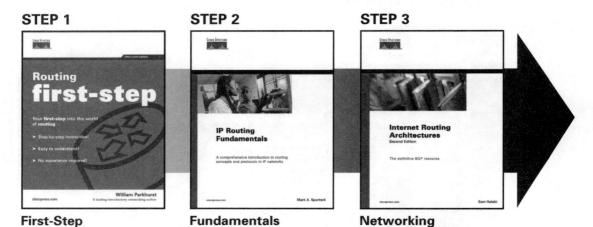

First-Step   Fundamentals   Networking
                                    Technology Guides

STEP 1   **First-Step**—Benefit from easy-to-grasp explanations.
             No experience required!

STEP 2   **Fundamentals**—Understand the purpose, application,
             and management of technology.

STEP 3   **Networking Technology Guides**—Gain the knowledge
             to master the challenge of the network.

NETWORK BUSINESS SERIES

The Network Business series helps professionals tackle the
business issues surrounding the network. Whether you are a
seasoned IT professional or a business manager with minimal
technical expertise, this series will help you understand the
business case for technologies.

Justify Your Network Investment.

Look for Cisco Press titles at your favorite bookseller today.

Visit **www.ciscopress.com/series** for details on each of these book series.

DISCUSS
NETWORKING PRODUCTS AND TECHNOLOGIES WITH CISCO EXPERTS AND NETWORKING PROFESSIONALS WORLDWIDE

VISIT NETWORKING PROFESSIONALS
A CISCO ONLINE COMMUNITY
WWW.CISCO.COM/GO/DISCUSS

CISCO SYSTEMS

THIS IS THE POWER OF THE NETWORK. now.